Avenues

Program Guide and Assessment Handbook

LEVEL E

HAMPTON-BROWN

Contents

Writing Assessments

Unit Writing Tests

Unit 1

Unit 2

Unit 3

Unit 4

Unit 5

Unit 6

Unit 7

Unit 8

Reading Fluency Measures

Student Profile: Year-End Summary

Effective Education for English Language Learners

by Eugene E. García, Ph.D.

English Language Learners Today

As we look at the students in our classrooms, we see a picture much different from the classrooms of our childhoods. According to the 2000 U.S. census, approximately one in three schoolchildren is from an ethnic or racial minority group, one in six speaks a language other than English at home, and one in ten is born outside the U.S. The linguistic and cultural diversity of the U.S. school population has increased dramatically during the past decade and will continue to increase. The concept of "minority group" will soon become obsolete, with no one group being a majority.

Educating children from immigrant and ethnic-minority families is a major concern in school systems across the country. Administrators, teachers, parents, and policymakers urge each other to do something different—change teaching methods, adopt new curricula, allocate more funding. Such actions might be needed, but they will not be meaningful until we think differently about English language learners.

A New View of English Language Learners

We are acutely aware that many English language learners come from families that are poor and non-English speaking. Too often, we have viewed these students only from the perspective of what they need to learn and from what they don't have. We need to move from this needs, or deficit, approach to an asset-inventory approach. That is, we need to perceive students' native language and culture as resources, or assets, instead of as problems. Students acquire language, culture, and accompanying values in the home and community environment and bring these assets with them to school.

In the past, when we have focused solely on the teaching of the English language, students received instruction to improve their English with the false understanding that learning English was all they needed. English language learners are capable and deserve the same access to the content standards as mainstream students.

These students do, however, need specialized instructional strategies that will ensure both their access to the standards and their success in achieving those standards. Specialized strategies for English language learners include:

- an interactive environment in which students constantly communicate for authentic purposes

- frequent opportunities to share and connect their prior knowledge and experiences to their peers' knowledge and to the academic content being studied

- multi-level activities and sheltering techniques to allow students at every level of English proficiency access to grade-level concepts and vocabulary

- assessment that tests students in the way they have been taught. That is, teachers assess student progress at benchmark proficiency levels—Beginning, Intermediate, and Advanced—in order to see progress on academic standards even as students move through the stages of language acquisition.

This new view has profound implications for the education of linguistically diverse students. It argues for the respect and integration of students' languages, values, beliefs, histories, and experiences. It argues for increased rigor and higher expectations—all supported by specialized instructional strategies. And it recognizes the active role that students must play in their own learning process.

Effective Education, continued

The New View in Practice

My wife, Erminda García, put this new view into practice in her third-grade classroom at Alianza Elementary School in Watsonville, California. At the beginning of the year, she asked students to consider this thematic study: "Three R's: Resourcefulness, Responsibility, and Respect." Students considered how they could become resourceful, responsible, and respectful in relationship to each other and to what they had to accomplish in the classroom.

Students' languages were immediately identified as resources. Students then articulated the ways in which other resources (parents, family, books, computers, etc.) could be used to enhance their academic pursuits.

For example, Rigoberto came to Erminda's classroom in September, after having arrived from Mexico in the last two months of the preceding academic year. A note in his file indicated a set of academic weaknesses. Erminda's first set of inquiries addressed what Rigoberto brought as resources. She asked him to talk about himself, his family, his community, and his educational experiences orally with her and in an interactive journal using his languages.

This asset inventory allowed her to place Rigoberto in the best academic circumstances, so that he could serve as a resource to others, and to maximize the classroom resources that could be made available to him. That made him an immediate participant in his own and his peers' education.

Knowing Rigoberto's resource portfolio allowed Erminda to modify instruction in ways that would support his learning. She began moving him from his native language in his journal into comfortable and skilled writing in English. Knowing what he could do in one language gave her a set of possible instructional "avenues" that she could use to develop English expertise.

Erminda also structures her classroom for interactive learning. She organizes desks in ways that promote the sharing of students' language resources: children sit in groups of four, with desks facing each other. Even in whole-group instruction, children are paired for interactive response. During instruction, students select from resource materials in English and native languages, often using each other for assistance in selecting those materials. Examples of learning are always put on display in whatever language the learning was accomplished, whether those resources are published works, brainstorm charts, or actual student products.

Finally, Erminda and all of her school colleagues established content benchmarks for each grade level and then assessed student work on a regular basis. The teachers used these ongoing assessments to identify both strengths and weaknesses; then, they could use specific instructional links to increase student learning. In this classroom, like other effective classrooms we have studied, there is always a concern for instruction focused on the articulated standards and ongoing assessments of student learning.

Guiding Principles for Curriculum, Assessment, and Instruction

The theory, research, and practices described above can be summarized in a set of North Star principles that can guide the work of educators serving English language learners. The North Star does not tell a traveler the precise way to travel. It does, however, provide an unwavering and ever-present indicator of the traveler's location in relation to the journey. The following guidelines are meant to inform your classroom journey toward academic success for your English language learners.

✪ *The languages and experiences of the student and her or his family and community are recognized and respected.*

Curriculum and assessment sometimes ignore students' primary languages, even when primary language instruction is a major aspect of the program. And too often instruction based on a mainstream curriculum suffers from a mainstream approach. For example, English language learners are sometimes asked to write about vacations or travel; many students—especially those in urban or poor schools—cannot meaningfully participate in such an activity. Teachers need to choose reading material and instructional activities that are more intrinsically interesting, relevant, and motivating for English language learners.

✪ *High standards are the basis for curriculum, instruction, and assessment.*

Most school districts and states have articulated English language arts standards. Standards make clear the expectations for students' skill level at each grade. Therefore, curriculum, assessment, and instruction for English language learners must reflect and be aligned with the standards; specialized instructional strategies, delivered by quality materials with built-in supports, must provide these students access to those high standards.

Effective Education, continued

⭐ *Assessment is on-going and makes progress visible even as students move through the stages of language acquisition.*

Standardized tests given to students in the spring are not intended to inform instruction, since results of such tests are not distributed or discussed until the fall. Standardized tests have their place in an accountability system, but they are not and should never be understood as the best way to assess specific student needs or to indicate instructional changes required to address the needs.

Instruction needs to provide feedback that informs instruction; therefore, it is imperative that such assessments occur at regular and strategic times during the year and that teachers test what they are teaching and in ways that reflect that teaching. Since most classrooms have students at varying levels of language proficiency and since teachers must use specialized strategies to teach those students, it follows that assessing student learning must be a multi-level activity. Teachers then have access to rich information regarding students' learning on a continuous basis.

Moreover, instruction can be modified to target specific student needs, which have been made visible by the multi-level assessment. Of significance, too, is the development and growth information that becomes available. Theoretically and empirically, we have come to understand that language and literacy development is not linear, that it can be unique to each student. Regular assessment allows us to maximize instructional opportunities.

⭐ *Teachers are able to use assessment results to inform, adapt, and maximize language and literacy instruction.*

Assessment that is "usable" provides information about performance on specific standards in language and literacy. It provides multiple products—authentic products as well as numerical scores—that allow teachers to verify students' language and literacy engagement. Usable assessment also makes progress visible and lets the teacher see and explore trends for an individual student, as well as for groups of students. And finally, usable assessment identifies specific instructional strategies for reteaching, which helps individual students develop in specific areas.

✪ *Students are actively involved in the development and implementation of the instructional process.*

The older and more mature the student gets, the more that student is able to be a partner in the teaching and learning process. Students can meaningfully participate in their own education by:

- contributing their prior knowledge to the study of new topics

- examining their own work and sharing their reflections

- reviewing and even expanding on their mastery of the local and state standards. Teachers should always consider it important to let students know the expectations and to provide them with numerous examples of student work.

In this manner, students become part of the process and assume a role in assessing their own learning.

Conclusion

These guiding principles, much like the North Star directs a night traveler, can give important insights into curriculum design, instruction, and assessment. Following these principles is beneficial to all learners, but imperative in the delivery of high-quality, standards-based instruction to our linguistically and culturally diverse students.

You will find that the curriculum design and instruction in Avenues reflects these North Star principles, and the *Avenues* **Assessment Handbook** provides assessment tools that yield usable results, across the many domains of literacy. Use these tools to monitor student progress across the year and use the results to inform your teaching.

ABOUT THE AUTHOR OF THIS ARTICLE

Dr. Eugene García is Vice President for University-School Partnerships and Dean of the College of Education at Arizona State University. He has received numerous academic and public honors and has published extensively in the area of language teaching and bilingual development. He holds leadership positions in numerous professional organizations and regularly serves as a panel reviewer for federal and state agencies. He served as a Senior Officer and Director of the Office of Bilingual Education from 1993–1995 and continues to conduct research in the areas of effective schooling for linguistically and culturally diverse student populations.

Program Goals

The goal of *Avenues* is to move English learners through the stages of language acquisition, while providing comprehensive, standards-based instruction at each student's level of language proficiency. The chart below summarizes the skills in *Avenues*.

Avenues Scope and Sequence Strands

Program Level	A	B	C	D	E	F
Language Development and Communication	•	•	•	•	•	•
Language Functions	•	•	•	•	•	•
Language Patterns and Structures	•	•	•	•	•	•
Concepts and Vocabulary	•	•	•	•	•	•
Reading	•	•	•	•	•	•
Learning to Read: concepts of print, phonemic awareness, phonics, decoding, and word recognition	•	•	•	•	•	•
Reading Strategies	•	•	•	•	•	•
Comprehension	•	•	•	•	•	•
Fluency		•	•	•	•	•
Literary Analysis and Appreciation	•	•	•	•	•	•
Listening, Speaking, Viewing, and Representing	•	•	•	•	•	•
Cognitive Academic Skills	•	•	•	•	•	•
Learning Strategies	•	•	•	•	•	•
Critical Thinking	•	•	•	•	•	•
Research Skills	•	•	•	•	•	•
Strategies for Taking Tests		•	•	•	•	•
Writing	•	•	•	•	•	•
Handwriting	•	•	•	•	•	•
Writing Purposes, Modes, and Forms	•	•	•	•	•	•
Writing Process		•	•	•	•	•
Writer's Craft		•	•	•	•	•
Grammar, Usage, Mechanics, Spelling	•	•	•	•	•	•
Technology and Media	•	•	•	•	•	•
Cultural Perspectives	•	•	•	•	•	•

Multi-level progress tests allow you to assess students' mastery of individual skills and standards at three benchmark proficiency levels:

BEGINNING   **I**NTERMEDIATE   **A**DVANCED

This assessment design makes visible students' progress on the standards, even as they move through the stages of language acquisition.

Linking Instruction to Assessment

English learners come from a variety of backgrounds and academic experiences. Some may be literate in their home language, while others may have few formal literacy skills. In order to plan appropriate instruction, it is important to know each student's starting profile, including:

- English proficiency level
- Repertoire of skills
- Reading level

State- and district-administered tests as well as the *Avenues* assessment tools can help you develop the picture of where students are when they enter the program:

❶ Determining English Proficiency Level

Standardized instruments such as the *Reading Proficiency Tests in English* (RPTE), *California English Language Development Test* (CELDT), or the *Language Assessment Scales* (LAS) identify a student's level of language proficiency. *Avenues* also offers a Language and Literacy Pretest at each grade to determine if the student is at the Beginning, Intermediate, or Advanced level of English proficiency. Use this information to select the appropriate strategy— Beginning, Intermediate, or Advanced—from the Multi-Level Strategies that appear throughout the Teacher's Edition.

❷ Determining Skills Profile

The *Avenues* Language and Literacy Pretest also provides information about performance in three skill areas: Vocabulary, Grammar, and Comprehension / Critical Thinking so that you have a starting profile of strengths and weaknesses.

❸ Determining Reading Level

The Reading Fluency measures in *Avenues*, or other district tests that report reading level, can help you place students into reading groups, choose from the Reading Options provided for each selection in the Teacher's Edition, and select appropriate Leveled Books.

Use these assessment tools to help students get started right in *Avenues*. The Unit Progress Tests and other progress monitoring tools described later in this Overview will help you track student performance throughout the year and deliver effective, differentiated instruction all year long.

Assessment Tools to Inform Instruction

Avenues provides a comprehensive array of assessment tools that allow you to diagnose, monitor progress in language and literacy, and sum up yearly progress for each student. See the **Language and Literacy Tests Teacher's Guide** for more information on the Pretest and Posttest (available fall 2004). The other assessment tools in the chart below are described in this Assessment Handbook.

Assessment Tool	Description	Diagnosis	Progress Monitoring	Summative
Language and Literacy Tests • **Pretest** • **Posttest**	These tests contain multiple-choice items for vocabulary, grammar, and comprehension skills and optional performance assessments for listening, speaking, and writing. Use the **Pretest** results to determine each student's initial proficiency level and to inform instruction. Compare the **Pretest** and **Posttest** results to determine each student's yearly progress through the stages of language acquisition.	✓		✓
Multi-Level Unit Progress Tests B I A	Use these multi-level progress tests to assess students' mastery of standards in vocabulary, grammar, and comprehension / critical thinking at three benchmarks: Beginning, Intermediate, and Advanced.		✓	
Student Self- and Peer-Assessments	These tools help students reflect on their learning and performance.		✓	
Language Assessments	These performance assessments measure students' facility with oral grammar and the functions of language.		✓	
Good Writing Traits Rubric	Use this holistic tool to evaluate all kinds of student writing.	✓	✓	✓
Writing Progress Form	Use this form to see student progress in each writing trait over time.		✓	
Writing Self-Assessment	This form helps students reflect on their writing and target areas to work on.		✓	
Writing Conference Form	Use this form when you meet with a student or family members to discuss the student's writing and set new learning goals.		✓	
Writing Checklists	Students use these checklists to make sure that their work contains the key features of the writing form.		✓	
Unit Writing Test (for Advanced Students)	Multiple-choice items test written conventions such as spelling, usage, and sentence fluency. Students also plan and draft a written composition.		✓	
Reading Fluency Benchmark Passages (for Advanced Students)	Three timed benchmark passages—administered three times per year—help you see gains in reading fluency.	✓	✓	✓

Avenues offers lessons in the *Reading Basics* for a complete scope and sequence of phonics skills—from letters and sounds to multisyllabic words. Assessment tools in the *Reading Basics* **Teacher's Guide** allow you to place students into the phonics scope and sequence and evaluate mastery of phonics and decoding skills.

Assessment Tool	Description	Diagnosis	Progress Monitoring	Summative
Reading Basics **Placement Test**	Use the test to place students into the phonics lessons.	✓		
Concepts of Print Assessment	This test measures basic book and print concepts. Use with newcomers and preliterate students.	✓	✓	✓
Phonological and Phonemic Awareness Assessment	Also for use with newcomers and preliterate students, this test measures a student's ability to identify rhyme, segment syllables, and isolate, blend, and manipulate sounds.	✓	✓	✓
Decoding Word Lists	Each list contains words with targeted letter-sound correspondences to give a quick check on decoding ability.		✓	
Progress Checks	Seven multiple-choice tests measure decoding skills and knowledge of high frequency words.		✓	✓

Unit Progress Tests

Purpose and Description

Avenues is designed for multi-level instruction and multi-level assessment. The Unit Progress Tests use standardized test formats to measure student performance in three domains:

1 Vocabulary Tests students' understanding of the Key Words in each selection as well as other important vocabulary skills such as using context clues and word parts.

2 Grammar Assesses students' mastery of the focus grammar skills in each unit.

3 Comprehension / Critical Thinking Evaluates students' mastery of unit comprehension, literary analysis, and critical thinking skills.

You can test the way you teach because each Unit Progress Test is available at three benchmarks—Beginning, Intermediate, and Advanced. For example, if you are using the Beginning strategies with a student, the student will take the Beginning test form.

Standard: New Vocabulary Words

BEGINNING	INTERMEDIATE	ADVANCED
Use Visuals Prompt students to use the photos and illustrations on pages 64–69 to identify Key Words. Say: **Point to a seed. Show me something special. Point to a beautiful thing.**	**Create a Story** Have small groups make up a story based on the words. Students take turns adding sentences that include the Key Words. Provide a story starter such as: *Once there was a beautiful garden...*	**Relate Words** Have students use three or more Key Words in one sentence: *A flower garden is a special place. The stem of the vegetable plant has a flower. Ugly seeds grow into beautiful flowers.*

Multi-Level Instruction

Multi-Level Assessment

B — Unit Progress Tests

I — Unit Progress Tests

A — Unit Progress Tests

The Unit Progress Tests have been adapted to each student's proficiency level by means of the item formats, language level, and text density. In addition, for the Beginning Progress Tests, all the items are read aloud.

To see these leveling techniques, compare these vocabulary items across the three test forms.

Vocabulary Item Formats

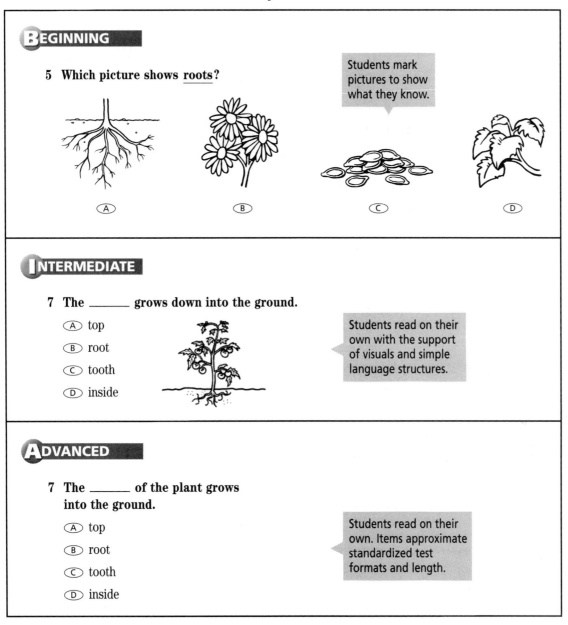

BEGINNING

5 Which picture shows <u>roots</u>?

Ⓐ   Ⓑ   Ⓒ   Ⓓ

Students mark pictures to show what they know.

INTERMEDIATE

7 The _____ grows down into the ground.

Ⓐ top
Ⓑ root
Ⓒ tooth
Ⓓ inside

Students read on their own with the support of visuals and simple language structures.

ADVANCED

7 The _____ of the plant grows into the ground.

Ⓐ top
Ⓑ root
Ⓒ tooth
Ⓓ inside

Students read on their own. Items approximate standardized test formats and length.

As the year progresses, students will make progress on the standards and in their language proficiency. Monitor their performance on the Unit Progress Tests. When a student scores 85% or higher on two consecutive Unit Progress Tests, begin to use the instructional strategies for the next higher proficiency level and assign the corresponding test form. Initially, students may receive lower scores when they begin to take the more difficult test form.

Unit Progress Tests, continued

Administering the Tests

The Unit Progress Test can be assigned after students have read the selections in the unit and completed the unit activities. You can give the Intermediate and Advanced tests in one group administration because the directions and sample items match. The Beginning test is designed to be read aloud and should be administered separately.

Make a copy of the test for each student, or use the consumable test booklets available separately from Hampton-Brown. Follow the directions for each test that appear before the test pages in this Handbook. The directions include complete scripting for working through sample items.

Give students as much time as they need to complete the items in a subtest and mark their answers.

Scoring the Tests and Reporting Results

Tests can be scored by hand or machine. For hand-scoring and reporting, follow these steps:

1. Record results on the Student Profile. Make sure that the Profile is for the corresponding **B**, **I**, or **A** Progress Test. Write the student's name and test date at the top.

2. Use the Answer Key to score the test.

3. Circle the item number of each correct answer. Compare the number of correct answers to the number given for Mastery. If the number correct matches or exceeds the Mastery number, circle the plus sign (+). If not, circle the minus sign (–).

4. Then multiply the number correct by the points per item to calculate the score for each subtest.

5. Finally, add together the scores for all of the subtests to calculate the total test score.

For machine-scoring and reporting:

1. Use machine-scorable answer cards compatible with either Scantron™ or NCS scanners. Have students fill in their answers on the test pages or record them directly on the machine-scorable answer cards. If students record their answers on the test pages, the answers can be transferred onto the answer cards for machine-scoring.

2. Use the Unit Progress Tests CD-Rom to import scanned data and produce an item analysis report for each student by each domain: Vocabulary, Grammar, and Comprehension / Critical Thinking. The CD-Rom will also produce a completed Class Profile so that you can see skills that are problematic for groups of students and plan reteaching.

Student Profile, Level D Unit 2 Progress Test

Unit 2 • Student Profile for Intermediate Progress Test

DIRECTIONS Record the student's name and test date. Use the **Answer Key** on page 21a to score the student's test. Then, in the Student Profile, circle the item number of each correct answer and circle the plus or minus sign to indicate mastery. Calculate the subtest scores and then the total test score. To help you group students for reteaching, transfer the minus sign for any unmastered skill to the **Class Profile** (page 12f).

Student Name _Stella Jones_   Date _Nov. 6_

Subtest	Tested Skills	ITEM ANALYSIS		TEST SCORES		
		Item Numbers	Mastery	No. Correct	Points	Score
VOCABULARY	Key Words	①②③④⑤ ⑥⑦⑧⑨ 10	8 out of 10 ⊕ –	9	× 4	36/40
GRAMMAR	Verbs (be, have)	⑪ ⑫ ⑬ ⑭	3 out of 4 ⊕ –	8	× 3	14/24
	Questions	15 16 17 18	3 out of 4 ⊕ –			
COMPREHENSION / CRITICAL THINKING	Make Comparisons	㉑ ㉒ ㉓ ㉔ 25	4 out of 5 ⊕ –	6	× 4	14/36
	Relate Main Idea and Supporting Details	19 20 ㉖ ㉗	3 out of 4 + ⊖			
			TOTAL UNIT 2 PROGRESS TEST			84/100

USEFUL INFORMATION

The Item Analysis gives you information about the mastery of specific skills. Each skill is tested with a minimum of 4 items.

MASTERY

Stella met the Mastery criterion for Key Words. She answered 9 out of 10 questions correctly.

She did not meet the criterion for Main Idea, so the minus sign is circled.

SUBTEST SCORES

The subtest score equals the number of items correct multiplied by the number of points per item. Stella's score for the Vocabulary subtest is 36/40.

Unit Progress Tests, continued

Using the Test Results

The Progress Tests are designed to give you specific information about each student's progress so that you can make informed instructional decisions. The Class Profile will help you see at a glance how to group students for reteaching. To complete and use the form:

1. Write each student's name in the first column and fill in the bubble for the test form taken.

2. Then refer to the individual Student Profiles to identify any skill not yet mastered. Transfer only the minus (–) signs to the Class Profile. (The Tested Skills listed down the column on the Student Profile match those listed across the top of the Class Profile.)

3. Look down the columns of the Class Profile to locate the minus signs and quickly see which students need work on the same skills.

The last two rows of the Class Profile show the reteaching resources and practice exercises for each skill.

- **Vocabulary** Ideas for reteaching Key Vocabulary appear on pages T38–T39 of this Assessment Handbook. Use the *Leveled Books Teacher's Guide* and *English at Your Command!* to reteach other vocabulary-related skills. Additional practice exercises appear in the *Avenues* Practice Book.

- **Grammar** Use *English at Your Command!* to reteach grammar skills to Intermediate and Advanced students. For Beginning students, see the grammar reteaching ideas on pages T40–T41 of this Assessment Handbook. Additional practice exercises appear in the *Avenues* Practice Book.

- **Comprehension** The *Leveled Books Teacher's Guide* contains reteaching lessons for each tested comprehension skill. These lessons are appropriate for students at any proficiency level. Additional practice exercises appear in the *Avenues* Practice Book.

Class Profile, Level C Unit 2 Progress Test

GROUPING

By recording only the minuses, it is easy to look down a column and see which students need reteaching in the same skill.

RETEACHING RESOURCES

Use this section to see tools for reteaching. The key at the bottom of the page identifies each component.

Unit 2 • Class Profile

Date __Nov. 7__

DIRECTIONS Use the **Unit 2 Student Profiles** to complete this chart. In each row, write the student's name, fill in the bubble for the test form taken, and mark a minus sign (–) for any skill not yet mastered. Then group students and use the reteaching ideas and practice exercises to help students reach mastery.

Student Name	Test Form	TESTED SKILLS — High Frequency Words	Key Words	Verbs	Relate Problem and Solution	Relate Main Idea and Details
Aguayo, Lupe	Ⓑ ● Ⓐ			–	–	
Blackfoot, Charlie	Ⓑ Ⓘ ●		–	–		
García, Mindy	● Ⓘ Ⓐ			–		–
Hayashi, Gina	● Ⓘ Ⓐ				–	
Jones, Stella	Ⓑ ● Ⓐ					–
Kim, Jinhee	Ⓑ Ⓘ ●					
Kumar, Amir	● Ⓘ Ⓐ					
Lee, Ho-Young	Ⓑ Ⓘ ●				–	
Lee, Ming	Ⓑ ● Ⓐ					
López, Don	Ⓑ Ⓘ ●					–
Lu, Francine	Ⓑ Ⓘ ●					
Márquez, Manuel	● Ⓘ Ⓐ					
Méndez, Claudio	Ⓑ ● Ⓐ				–	
Ortiz, Hector	Ⓑ ● Ⓐ					
Park, Anna	● Ⓘ Ⓐ			–		
Pérez, Luke	Ⓑ Ⓘ ●		–	–		
Putin, Irena	● Ⓘ Ⓐ	–				
Reese, Maya	Ⓑ Ⓘ ●					–
Reyes, Katie	Ⓑ ● Ⓐ	–	–			
Ríos, Juan Carlos	Ⓑ ● Ⓐ			–		–
Singri, Barbie	Ⓑ Ⓘ ●				–	
Yee, Robert	● Ⓘ Ⓐ			–		
RETEACHING RESOURCES		Ⓘ Ⓐ AH T38	Ⓘ Ⓑ Ⓐ AH T39–T40	Ⓑ AH T41 Ⓘ Ⓐ EAYC 268–272	Ⓑ Ⓘ Ⓐ LB TG	Ⓑ Ⓘ Ⓐ LB TG
PRACTICE EXERCISES		PB 27, 30, 40	PB 29, 39	EAYC 333–335	PB 35	PB 36–37, 44

Unit 2 | Seed to Sandwich

KEY: **AH:** Assessment Handbook   **EAYC:** English at Your Command!   **LB TG:** Leveled Books Teacher's Guide   **PB:** Practice Book

12f

RETEACHING GRAMMAR

Anna Park took the B test form, so you should select from the reteaching ideas on pages T41–T42 of this Handbook.

Luke Pérez took the A test form, so you will find an appropriate reteaching lesson on pages 268–272 of *English at Your Command!*

Self-Assessment Form

Purpose and Description

The Self-Assessment Form helps students reflect on their work. Simple prompts lead them to evaluate their progress in speaking and reading in English. To fill out the form:

1. Have students work with a partner to do Number 1, following the prompts to use the unit language functions and patterns orally. They can then assess whether or not they have learned these skills.

2. For the My New Words section, ask students to list new words they learned. Encourage them to list any words they find interesting—words with unusual sounds or spellings, words with special meanings, or even unusually long words.

3. Students can work alone or with partners to complete Numbers 2 and 3, which focus on their progress in reading and their mastery of important comprehension skills. For the What I've Read section, have them check off the selections they read in the Avenues Student Book and list the titles of other texts they read during the unit.

You can review the Self-Assessment Forms when you meet with students and their families in periodic conferences.

Self-Assessment Form, Level D Unit 2

Peer-Assessment Form

Purpose and Description

The Peer-Assessment Form gives students a chance to provide personalized feedback to their classmates. The form can be used to evaluate a variety of work, including speaking, writing, drawing, and role-play. First, students write the date and check off the type of work being evaluated. Then they identify things their partners did well. Beginning students can dictate their ideas to you or a more proficient classmate.

Students are also asked to identify areas that need improvement and to make specific suggestions for their partners to try next time. You may want to discuss and post examples of constructive feedback the first few times that students evaluate each other's work. See *English at Your Command!* for suggestions that students can use in Peer Conferences.

Peer-Assessment Form, Level D

Language Assessments

Purpose and Description

Avenues is designed for integrated instruction and assessment. Each unit contains numerous opportunities for students to use language as they participate in authentic communicative activities. You can observe students during these activities to assess their progress in moving through the stages of language acquisition. The Language Assessments facilitate the evaluation process because they

- identify speaking activities in which students will engage in the language functions targeted for the unit

- identify selection visuals that can be used to prompt language production

- provide scoring rubrics with sample responses that will help you relate what you observe to specific language proficiency levels.

Conducting the Performance Assessment

Each unit offers 3 performance assessment opportunities. These opportunities are clearly identified on the unit's Language Assessment form. During these performance assessments, work with pairs and small groups of students so that the assessment process is manageable. Observing a student 5–6 times a year will allow you to assess movement through the stages of language acquisition. Thus, it is not necessary to test every student at every testing point. For example, if you test 4–5 students at each of the 3 testing points per unit, you can obtain 5–6 evaluations per student per year.

Interpreting the Results

After working through a number of units in *Avenues*, you will have accumulated several Language Assessments for each student. As you review the ratings over time, you should begin to see a pattern emerge. For example, for students who are clearly at the beginning stage of English language development, you will find that the Beginning box is usually checked for most of the assessments. This will enable you to tailor instruction to students' individual levels of language proficiency using the Multi-Level Strategies in the Teacher's Edition.

As a student makes progress in language development, you will begin to note that you are checking off the Intermediate or Advanced boxes more frequently. Once the assessments begin to indicate increased proficiency, begin using teaching ideas from the Multi-Level Strategies that reflect the student's higher proficiency. Once a student consistently demonstrates characteristics of the Advanced proficiency level, you may wish to consider evaluating that student against the criteria designated by your school or district for exit from the ESL program.

Language Assessment Form, Level D Unit 2

LANGUAGE FUNCTIONS

Provide time for students to prepare before they begin each activity. Then observe pairs or small groups.

Name Anna Park

Unit 2 • Language Assessment

THE UGLY VEGETABLES
Date Oct. 8

PERFORMANCE ASSESSMENT 1
Testing Point: Design a Shoebox Garden, page T98b
• **Language Function:**
Ask and Answer Questions
• **DIRECTIONS** Listen as the student asks and answers questions about the plants. Check the box in the Rubric that most closely matches your observation.

Rubric

☑ **BEGINNING** Uses fragments (this is? tulips) or short questions and statements with errors (What are plants? Plants are tulips.)

☐ **INTERMEDIATE** Forms short questions and statements (What are these plants? They are tulips.) or more detailed sentences with errors (Are many flowers in your garden? Yes, are many in a garden.)

☐ **ADVANCED** Forms detailed questions and statements (What kind of flowers are in your garden? There are tulips and roses in my garden.)

HOW A PLANT GROWS
Date Oct. 22

PERFORMANCE ASSESSMENT 2
Testing Point: Guess the Plant, page T118a
• **Language Function:**
Ask and Answer Questions
• **DIRECTIONS** Listen as the student asks and answers questions about the objects. Check the box in the Rubric that most closely matches your observation.

Rubric

☐ **BEGINNING** Uses fragments (food? rice) or simple questions and statements with errors (Is that food? Yes, it food.)

☑ **INTERMEDIATE** Forms short questions and statements (How does it grow? It grows in water.)

☐ **ADVANCED** Forms detailed questions and statements (Why do you eat it? It tastes good with other food.)

UNIT WRAP-UP
Date Nov. 4

PERFORMANCE ASSESSMENT 3
Testing Point: End of Unit
• **Grammar: Questions**
• **Visual Prompt:** Student Book pages 68–69
• **DIRECTIONS** The student pretends to be a reporter, and you pretend to be the girl. Say: Ask me if I am a gardener and if my garden is big. Now ask if the garden has flowers. Continue, eliciting other questions.

The student correctly uses questions with:
☑ is	☐ who	☑ where
☐ are	☑ what	☐ how
☑ does	☐ when	☑ why

• **Grammar: Verbs** (forms of be and have)
• **Visual Prompt:** Student Book pages 68–69
• **DIRECTIONS** Now the student pretends to be the girl. Ask: How old are you? Do you have a big family? Point to a carrot. Ask: What is this? Point to the tomatoes. Ask: What are these? Point to the man wearing a hat and ask: What does he have?

The student correctly uses the verbs:
☑ am	☑ are	☐ have
☑ is	☐ has	

Unit 2 | Bloom and Grow   90

USING THE RUBRICS

On October 8, the Beginning box is checked because Anna used only fragments as she asked and answered questions about the Shoebox Gardens. She asked: *What this?* and said: *This flower.*

On October 22, Anna was able to form short questions and statements. She asked: *Is it paper?* and said: *It comes from trees.* That is why the Intermediate box is checked.

GRAMMAR

At the end of each unit, use the suggested visuals in the Student Book to prompt production of the targeted grammar skills. Check off the structures the student uses.

Here, Anna used five different question words during the role-play: *is, does, what, where,* and *why.* You can continue to prompt the student to see if she will ask questions with the other words listed in the box.

Writing Assessments

Kinds of Writing in *Avenues*

In *Avenues* students have daily opportunities to develop as writers.

- Informal Daily Writing activities encourage them to record, discover, and refine their ideas.
- Literature Journals help them respond to reading and express their opinions.
- Writing in response to literature leads students to make connections across the curriculum.
- Writing Projects allow students to learn and use the traits of good writing.

Tools for Writing Assessment

Avenues also offers an array of writing assessment tools to evaluate writing on a regular basis, to plan writing instruction, and to conference with students and their families about writing progress. The following pages describe these assessment tools:

- Writing Checklists
- Good Writing Traits Rubric
- Good Writing Traits Class Profile
- Writing Progress Form
- Unit Writing Tests
- Writing Self-Assessment Form
- Writing Conference Form

Writing Checklists

These checklists identify for both students and teachers the key features of most writing forms that students create in the Writing Content Connections. Students can use the checklist to plan their work before they write. You and students can then review the checklist to evaluate the writing once it is completed.

Writing Checklist, Level D Unit 2

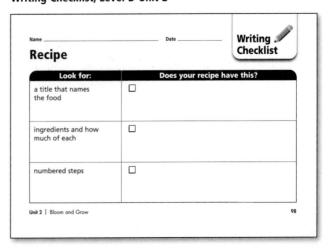

Good Writing Traits Rubric

The **Good Writing Traits Rubric** is a holistic tool for evaluating any written composition on the five traits of good writing. Use the rubric throughout the year to monitor a student's progress in all the traits, but target one trait for instruction over a sustained period of time. Follow these steps to complete the rubric

1. At the top of the form, write the student's name, the date, and the writing assignment.

2. Read the descriptions under each trait. Check off those that most closely match your assessment of the student's work.

3. See where the check marks cluster and assign an overall scale score.

Good Writing Traits Rubic, Levels C–F

Name: Don López   Date: Oct. 28

Assignment: Writing Project: Information Article

Overall Scale Score: **3**

Good Writing Traits Rubric

Scale	Focus and Coherence	Organization	Development of Ideas	Voice	Written Conventions
4	**Related Ideas** ❑ Paragraphs and the writing as a whole are focused. **Completeness** ❑ The writing feels complete. It has a beginning, relevant details, and a conclusion.	**Structure** ☑ The organizing strategy is well-suited to the writer's purpose. **Progression of Ideas** ☑ Ideas flow logically and smoothly, with meaningful transitions.	**Content Quality** ❑ The writer takes a risk and treats the topic in an interesting way, with insight and thoughtfulness. **Elaboration** ❑ Ideas are developed in depth.	**Individuality** ❑ The writing sounds genuine and unique. **Word Choice** ❑ Words and phrases are interesting and appropriate to the writer's purpose and audience.	**Grammar, Usage, Mechanics, and Spelling** ❑ There are only a few errors. **Sentence Fluency** ❑ Sentences are varied and effective.
3	**Related Ideas** ☑ Paragraphs and the writing as a whole are mostly focused, but there are a few sudden shifts. **Completeness** ☑ The writing feels complete. It has a beginning, mostly relevant details, and a conclusion.	**Structure** ❑ The organizing strategy is generally suited to the writer's purpose. **Progression of Ideas** ❑ Most ideas flow logically and smoothly, but there are a few gaps.	**Content Quality** ☑ The writer does not take much of a risk, but does treat the topic in a thoughtful way. **Elaboration** ☑ Ideas are somewhat developed.	**Individuality** ❑ For the most part, the writing sounds genuine and unique. **Word Choice** ❑ Words and phrases are mostly interesting and appropriate to the writer's purpose and audience.	**Grammar, Usage, Mechanics, and Spelling** ☑ Errors are minor and/or infrequent. **Sentence Fluency** ☑ There is some sentence variety. Sentences are generally effective.
2	**Related Ideas** ❑ There are a number of sudden shifts between ideas. **Completeness** ❑ The writing feels somewhat incomplete. It is missing a beginning and/or an ending. Important details seem to be missing.	**Structure** ❑ There is an organizing strategy, but it does not suit the writer's purpose. **Progression of Ideas** ❑ There are breaks in logic and very few transitions.	**Content Quality** ❑ The topic is covered, but in an uninteresting way. **Elaboration** ❑ Ideas are listed or mentioned superficially.	**Individuality** ☑ A few passages sound genuine and unique. **Word Choice** ☑ Words and phrases are somewhat interesting and appropriate to the writer's purpose and audience.	**Grammar, Usage, Mechanics, and Spelling** ❑ Errors are frequent, but the meaning is clear. **Sentence Fluency** ❑ Sentences are somewhat awkward and have missing words.
1	**Related Ideas** ❑ The writing is not focused. **Completeness** ❑ There is no sense of completeness.	**Structure** ❑ No organizing strategy is evident. **Progression of Ideas** ❑ Writing is illogical, wordy, and/or repetitious.	**Content Quality** ❑ The writing is uninteresting. **Elaboration** ❑ There is little or no development of ideas.	**Individuality** ❑ There is little or no sense of the writer. **Word Choice** ❑ Words and phrases are not appropriate to the writer's purpose or audience.	**Grammar, Usage, Mechanics, and Spelling** ❑ Errors are severe and/or frequent and are a barrier to understanding. **Sentence Fluency** ❑ Sentences are awkward and have missing words.

Good Writing Traits
Class Profile

This form will help you plan instruction. It allows you to see at a glance the writing trait(s) that the majority of your students need to work on. Follow these steps to fill out the form:

1. At the top of the form, record the writing assignment and the date.

2. Review each student's **Good Writing Traits Rubric**. Find the scale score for each trait and transfer the student's initials to that cell. Each student's initials will appear in five cells—one for each trait.

3. After all of the initials have been transferred, for each writing trait, find where most students are clustered and draw a dot. Then you can connect the dots to show where the class needs practice (the lowest point) and where the class is showing the strongest work (the highest point).

Once you identify the area of greatest need, provide opportunities for students to focus on that particular writing trait. See the Practice Activities on pages T42–T45 of this Handbook. Work on each trait for several weeks. You can then compare Class Profiles for subsequent writing assignments to see changes in class performance over time.

INDIVIDUAL SCORES

Don's scores range from a 2 for Voice to a 4 for Organization and Development of Ideas. His performance on each trait is indicated by the initials *DL*.

Good Writing Traits Class Profile, Levels D–F

Good Writing Traits Class Profile

Assignment _Writing Project: Information Article_   Date _Oct. 29_

DIRECTIONS Use the **Good Writing Traits Rubric** on page 97 to score students' work. Then plot the scores on the Rubric below by writing each student's initials in the appropriate cell. Identify the trait(s) with which the most students need practice. Then use the practice activities in this Handbook to strengthen students' abilities in that trait(s).

Scale	Focus and Coherence	Organization	Development of Ideas	Voice	Written Conventions
4	MG JK CB	MM CB (DL)	AK BS	MG	BS JK
3	MM AK IP ML (DL) SJ	IP FL JR RM GH AK SJ ML CM	(DL) CM MR CB	JK FL JR MM CB	FL CM (DL)
2	GH FL JR BS CM LA HL MR	AP BS MG HL	GH IP FL JR LP ML SJ HL MG JK MM	BS HL IP (DL) AK ML	GH MG SJ JR AK ML HL IP CB
1	AP KR LP RY HO	MR HO LA KR RY LP	AP KR HO RY LA	GH KR SJ LP HO RY AP MR CM LA	AP KR HO LP MM LA RY
Practice Activities	Assessment Handbook page T42	Assessment Handbook page T42	Assessment Handbook page T42	Assessment Handbook page T42	Assessment Handbook page T42

GROUP PERFORMANCE

The dot is drawn here because 9 out of 21 students earned a scale score of 3 on Organization. This is the highest point on the line graph, indicating the class's greatest strength.

MAKING INSTRUCTIONAL DECISIONS

This is the lowest point of the line graph, indicating the area of greatest need. Students will benefit from several weeks of practice activities that focus on this trait.

Writing Progress Form

Use the Writing Progress Form to monitor students' progress as writers over time. Periodically complete the form; for example, at the end of grading periods, or to share with students and their families in writing conferences. (See pages T32–T33 for more information about writing conferences.) Follow these steps to complete the form:

1. Write the student's name at the top of the form.

2. Select several writing samples. In the first column, record the information about each writing sample: the title of the writing form, the purpose of the writing, and the date it was completed.

3. Review the completed rubric for each sample. Transfer the score for each trait from the rubric to the rows on the chart.

4. Note the student's strengths and needs. Highlight the samples that represent the student's best work in a given trait and collect the samples in the student's writing portfolio.

Writing Progress Form, Levels D–F

Name _Don López_

Writing Progress Form

DIRECTIONS Review the completed Rubric for each writing sample. Record the score for each trait in the chart to see the student's strengths as well as the traits that need development. Then highlight the writing samples that exemplify the student's best work by trait and collect them in the student's writing portfolio.

	Focus and Coherence	Organization	Development of Ideas	Voice	Written Conventions
Writing Form: _Information Article_ Purpose: _Give Information_ Date: _10/28_	3	4	3	2	3
Writing Form: _Dream Statement_ Purpose: _Express Ideas_ Date: _11/30_	3	3	4	3	3
Writing Form: _Folk Tale_ Purpose: _Entertain_ Date: _12/18_	4	3	3	2	3
Writing Form: _____ Purpose: _____ Date: _____					
Writing Form: _____ Purpose: _____ Date: _____					
Writing Form: _____ Purpose: _____ Date: _____					

Unit Writing Tests

The **Unit Writing Tests** provide an additional way for you to evaluate students' writing skills. They are designed for Advanced students.

Revising and Editing Subtest

In the Revising and Editing section of the test, students read a brief passage and then answer multiple-choice items that measure their mastery of the conventions of written English: grammar, usage, mechanics, spelling, and sentence fluency.

Unit Writing Test, Level D Unit 2
(Revising and Editing Subtest)

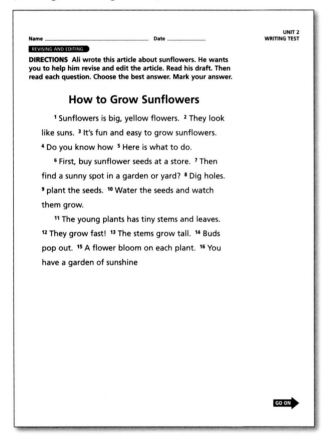

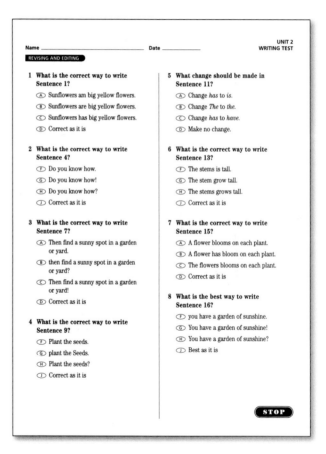

Unit Writing Tests, continued

Written Composition Subtest

The second section of the test presents a theme-based, open-ended writing prompt. Below the prompt is a box with a list of things that students should keep in mind as they plan and draft their compositions. This part of the test gives students a chance to put their writing skills to use and acquaints them with the kinds of writing prompts they may encounter on standardized tests.

Unit Writing Test, Level D Unit 2
(Written Composition Subtest)

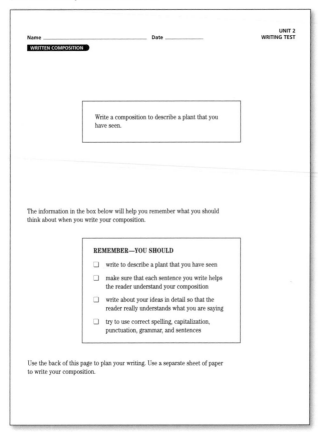

Name _____ Date _____

UNIT 2
WRITING TEST

WRITTEN COMPOSITION

Write a composition to describe a plant that you have seen.

The information in the box below will help you remember what you should think about when you write your composition.

REMEMBER—YOU SHOULD

☐ write to describe a plant that you have seen

☐ make sure that each sentence you write helps the reader understand your composition

☐ write about your ideas in detail so that the reader really understands what you are saying

☐ try to use correct spelling, capitalization, punctuation, grammar, and sentences

Use the back of this page to plan your writing. Use a separate sheet of paper to write your composition.

Administering the Tests

The Unit Writing Test can be assigned to Advanced students after they have completed the unit. Make a copy of the test for each student. Follow the directions for each test that appear before the test pages in this Assessment Handbook. Provide a separate piece of paper for students to write their composition.

Scoring the Tests

Use the **Writing Test Student Profile** to record the test results:

- Use the **Answer Key** to score the Revising and Editing section. Circle the item number of each correct answer. Compare the number of correct answers to the number given for Mastery. If the number correct matches or exceeds the Mastery number, circle the plus sign (+). If not, circle the minus sign (–).

- Multiply the number correct by the points per item to calculate the score for each subtest.

- Use the **Good Writing Traits Rubric** to evaluate the composition on each writing trait. Then assign an overall score. Multiply that score by the number of points indicated.

- Finally, add together the scores for all of the subtests to calculate the total test score.

Writing Test Student Profile, Level D Unit 2

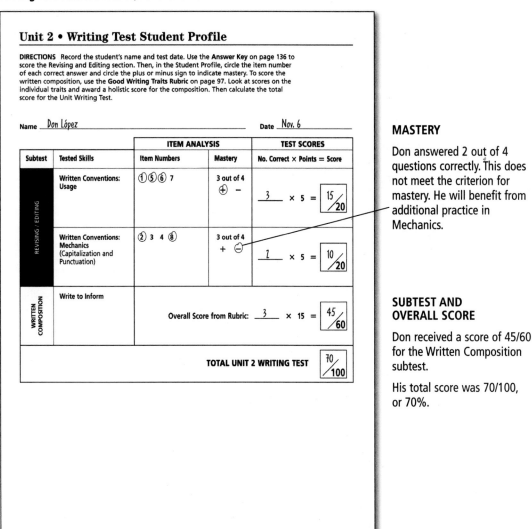

MASTERY

Don answered 2 out of 4 questions correctly. This does not meet the criterion for mastery. He will benefit from additional practice in Mechanics.

SUBTEST AND OVERALL SCORE

Don received a score of 45/60 for the Written Composition subtest.

His total score was 70/100, or 70%.

Conferencing with Students and Their Families

Writing Conferences are an excellent way to involve students in thinking critically about their writing and setting their own learning goals. How often you plan the conferences depends on what you find most useful for each student. For some students, you may want to plan three or four conferences over the course of the school year. In this way, you will have a body of representative work to review and respond to. There are three forms that will help you conduct a useful, engaging writing conference:

- **Writing Progress Form** (see page T28)
- **Writing Self-Assessment Form**
- **Writing Conference Form**

Writing Self-Assessment Form

After students complete each Writing Project, have them fill out the Writing Self-Assessment Form and keep it in the writing portfolio. This form uses simple prompts and graphics to help students review the steps of the writing process and to reflect on things they did well. The last prompt asks students to list something they want to work on in their future writing.

Writing Self-Assessment Form, Levels D–F

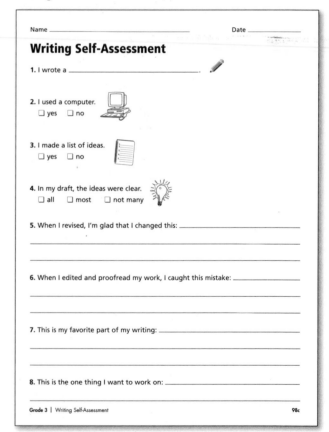

Writing Conference Form

Use this form to guide a dialogue between yourself and the student. Make a copy. Then gather three representative examples of the student's written work and a completed **Writing Progress Form**. (See page T28.)

Review each writing sample together. First ask the student:

- *What do you like best about your writing?*
- *What did you learn from writing this?*

Listen to the student's responses and record them in the section called **Writer's Ideas**. Then share your thoughts about the writing sample and record them in the section called **Teacher's Ideas**. Continue to review each of the samples together in this way.

Next, discuss the questions at the bottom of the form. Record the student's responses. You may both want to sign the form and agree on one important learning goal.

Writing Conference Form, Levels C–F

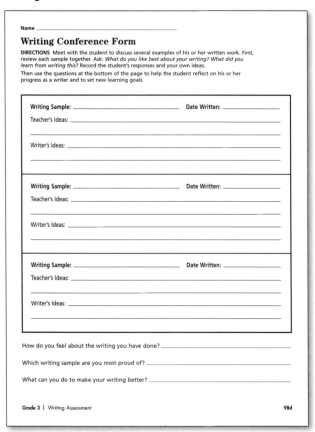

Reading Fluency Measures

Purpose and Description

Oral reading fluency is strongly correlated to reading comprehension. Whether text is being read silently or aloud, much of its meaning comes from the way it sounds. *Avenues* offers three benchmark passages to measure a student's oral reading fluency. You can administer these passages three times: at the beginning of the year, in winter, and in spring to monitor the student's progress.

Administering and Scoring the Fluency Passages

You will need: a stopwatch for one-minute timed readings, the Teacher Copy and the Student Copy of the three passages. To obtain the fluency measure:

1 **Administer All Three Passages**

Give the student the unnumbered copy of the passage. Place your copy so that the student cannot see what you record. Ask the student to do his or her best reading and set the timer. Mark a slash (/) through any word that is skipped or mispronounced. (Tell the student to skip a word after 3 seconds.) Stop the student at exactly one minute and put a bracket after the last word.

2 **Score the Readings**

Use the word counts on the right side of your copy to count the number of words attempted. Subtract the total number of errors to calculate the number of words read correctly per minute, or wcpm.

3 **Record the Results**

Use the **Fluency Progress Report** to record the results. Place a dot to indicate the words read correctly per minute for each of the three readings. Then write the median (middle) score in the box at the bottom of the page. Compare the median score to the grade-level norm for that season. The norms shown are 2002-2003 data.

Fluency Progress Report, Level D

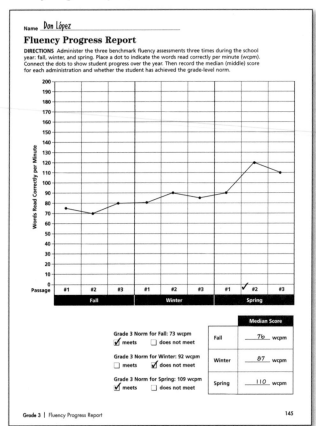

Teacher Copy, Benchmark Fluency Passage #1, Level D

MARKING THE PASSAGE

Slashes indicate words that the student skips or mispronounces.

Name Don López   **Date** Nov. 6

It rained all day long. The wind and rain knocked the	11
remaining leaves to the ground where they were swept into the	22
street. Today was a typical fall day.	29
Just two days ago, the sun was out and the temperatures	40
were very pleasant. Raking leaves into large playful piles was very	51
relaxing.	52
The family worked together gathering the maple leaves into	61
piles. Kids will be kids, and they loved jumping and hiding in the	74
leaves. Even their dog liked to romp around in the leaves. It was	87
fun for everyone.	90
The next day, the weather changed slightly. Clouds began	99
to roll into the area and darken the sky. It did not rain then, but	114
it was clear that winter was near. The family thought that the	126
ground would be covered in no time. Winter was approaching fast.	137
They awoke to the rain hitting the roof of their home. It was	150
a light rain, so they figured it would rain all day. They were right.	164
Now the kids would not be able to play in the leaves. The leaves	178
were all wet and brown. They were no longer dry and colorful.	190
The winds picked up speed and sent the piles of leaves	201
blowing across the yard and into the street. The kids thought they	213
were pretty lucky to have been able to play in the leaves yesterday.	226
Later in the day, the street sweeper came into their	236
neighborhood and, with its mighty vacuum, gobbled up the leaves	246
that had found their way into the street. The leaves were gone.	258
That night the kids were tucked into bed for the evening. As	270
they slept, the rain turned to snow.	277
The kids dreamed of sledding and snowmen. The next morning	287
their dreams came true. Snow!	292

TIMING THE READING

A bracket indicates where the student stopped at the one-minute mark.

SCORE	$\dfrac{81}{\text{words attempted in one minute}}$	−	$\dfrac{5}{\text{number of errors}}$	=	$\dfrac{76}{\substack{\text{words correct per} \\ \text{minute (wcpm)}}}$

Grade 3 | TEACHER COPY: Benchmark Fluency Passage #1   140

CALCULATING WCPM

76 wcpm = 81 words attempted minus 5 errors

Student Profile: Year-End Summary

Purpose and Description

The **Student Profile: Year-End Summary** is where all of the assessment in *Avenues* comes together. The form provides you with a snapshot of each student's cumulative performance in Vocabulary, Grammar, Comprehension and Critical Thinking, Language, and Writing.

To fill out the form, review the collection of test results and performance assessments from the year.

1 **Unit Progress Tests Student Profiles**

For each unit, fill in the bubble for the test form taken. Then transfer the score on each subtest and the total test score. (Note that the number of items in a subtest may vary across units or forms, so you should use only the total score to make comparisons.)

2 **Language Assessments**

Review results on the Language Assessments (see pages T22–T23) and summarize the student's language growth. Comment on progress through the levels of English proficiency and command of an increasing number of more complex language patterns and structures.

3 **Writing Progress Form and the Writing Test Profiles**

Review these forms (see pages T28 and T31). Record the student's best score on each writing trait. Add your observations about the student's strengths as a writer and the areas that need further practice.

Determining Adequate Yearly Progress

As a final step, complete the **Yearly Progress** box to indicate growth in proficiency level across the year.

- Record the starting date and the initial proficiency level based on the results of the *Avenues* Language and Literacy Pretest or your state- or district-approved proficiency instrument.

- Then look at performance on the **Unit Progress Tests**, noting especially if the student successfully moved to taking a form for a higher proficiency level. Also consider growth in proficiency level indicated by performance on the **Language Assessments**. The *Avenues* Language and Literacy Posttest can be administered to provide a formal measure of growth.

- Consider all the information you have to determine the ending proficiency, then circle the appropriate level and date the form.

INTEGRATING INSTRUCTION AND ASSESSMENT

Stella scored over 85 on the Unit 5 and Unit 6 tests. The teacher then began using Advanced strategies and tests with Stella.

Student-Profile: Year End Summary, Level D

Teacher ___Mrs. Colón___   Student Name ___Stella Jones___   Date ___May 20, 2004___

Student Profile: Year-End Summary

UNIT PROGRESS TESTS

DIRECTIONS Fill in the bubble of the test form taken. Then refer to each **Progress Test Student Profile** to record the score on each subtest. Because the number of items in a subtest varies across units, use only the total to make comparisons.

	UNIT 1 SCORE			UNIT 2 SCORE			UNIT 3 SCORE			UNIT 4 SCORE			UNIT 5 SCORE			UNIT 6 SCORE			UNIT 7 SCORE			UNIT 8 SCORE		
	Ⓑ	●	Ⓐ	Ⓑ	●	Ⓐ	Ⓑ	●	Ⓐ	Ⓑ	●	Ⓐ	Ⓑ	●	Ⓐ	Ⓑ	●	Ⓐ	Ⓑ	Ⓘ	●	Ⓑ	Ⓘ	●
VOCABULARY		30			36			34			32			40			50				32				28
GRAMMAR		20			14			16			24			26			20				24				26
COMPREHENSION / CRITICAL THINKING		16			24			20			22			20			20				12				16
POSSIBLE TOTAL	100	100	100	100	100	100	100	100	100	100	100	100	100	100	100	100	100	100	100	100	100	100	100	100
STUDENT TOTAL		66			84			70			78			86			90				68				70

AUTHENTIC ASSESSMENTS

Language Assessment

DIRECTIONS Review the completed performance assessments and look for:

• progress through the levels of language proficiency
• command of an increasing number of more complex language patterns and structures.

Your observations:

Stella made a lot of progress this year, but she still needs to work on verb tense.

Writing Assessment

DIRECTIONS Review the completed **Writing Progress Form** and the **Student Writing Profiles** and note the student's best score on each trait.

Focus and Coherence	Organization	Development of Ideas	Voice	Written Conventions
3	4	3	2	3

Your observations:

Stella usually writes in a very organized way. As her vocabulary continues to grow, she can improve her voice, especially word choice.

YEARLY PROGRESS

DIRECTIONS Review the *Avenues* Pretest or standardized test results and circle the student's initial proficiency level. Then review the **Unit Progress Tests** and **Language Assessments**, or the *Avenues* Posttest, and circle the student's current level.

Started ___Aug. 30___ as Ⓑ Ⓘ Ⓐ
(date)

Ended ___May 20___ as Ⓑ Ⓘ Ⓐ
(date)

CONTINUING SUPPORT

The Year-End Summary can travel in the student's cumulative folder. These comments will help Stella's next teacher know which skills to focus on.

ADEQUATE YEARLY PROGRESS

One form sums up yearly progress at a glance.

Reteaching Vocabulary

Reteaching Routine

Group students who did not master the Key Vocabulary. Use the following routine, along with the **Picture Dictionary** at the end of the Student Book to reteach each Key Word. Then select from the Practice Options to reinforce learning. Match the practice to the student's proficiency level.

1 Find and Say the Word

Display the Picture Dictionary and say the word. Have students locate the word in their books and repeat it after you.

2 Teach the Meaning

Read aloud the definition and the context sentence. Then use the picture and labels to elaborate by restating the meaning and giving additional examples. For example, for the word *root*, you might say: *The root is a part of the plant that you can't see. Some roots grow deep into the ground, or dirt. Have you ever tried to pull a carrot out of the ground? It's hard to do!*

3 Make Connections

Discuss with students when they might hear or use the word. For example, they might hear *roots* in science class or use the word when they work in a garden.

4 Write and Remember

Have students record the word in a notebook. Ask them what they notice about its sounds and spelling. Then help them think of a way to remember the word. It may be a drawing, a sentence with the word, or a translation in their home language.

Practice Options

Listen and Sing

Materials *Language Songs* Big Book, Song CD

Have students listen as you play the song or chant several times. Invite students to join in. Then have them find each Key Word on the page and read the sentence. Intermediate and Advanced students can then use the word in a new sentence.

Tell a Story

Materials index cards

Write each Key Word on a separate card and distribute the cards. Use a silly or scary story-starter to begin telling a story. Then call on each student to add a sentence to the story that uses her or his Key Word. Advanced students can record the story as it is being told and then read it back to the group when it is finished.

Follow My Command

Use each Key Word in a command for students to act out. For example, you can tell them to: *Show me what it is like to walk up a* <u>hill</u>. *Now hold up your arms like tree* <u>branches</u>.

Pick the Picture

Materials Picture Dictionary

Direct students to a page in the dictionary. Then say a sentence that relates to one of the entries. For example, for the Key Word *cloud*, say: *This is something you can see in the sky. It is white and moves.* Ask students to point to the picture and tell you the Key Word.

Explain Your Drawing

Materials paper, pencils, crayons, markers

List the Key Words on the board. Have each student choose a word and draw a picture to go with it. Then invite students to explain how the picture goes with the word.

Word Search

Materials graph paper with 1/4-inch squares, pencils, Picture Dictionary

Students choose a few Key Words to write in different directions on graph paper placing one letter in each box. Then they fill in each remaining box with a letter of the alphabet. Below the grid, they copy the corresponding definitions from the Picture Dictionary. Students exchange pages with a partner and try to find all of the hidden words.

Sentence Scramble

Materials oak tag, Picture Dictionary

Copy the definition for each Key Word on a strip of paper. Then cut the definition apart into several short phrases and put the pieces in an envelope. Distribute the envelope to pairs of students and challenge them to reconstruct the sentence, find the Key Word, and use it in a sentence.

Make a Match

Materials index cards, pencils

Have students write each Key Word on a separate card. Then pair students and have them arrange the cards face down. Students take turns turning over two cards. If the words are the same, the player uses the word in a sentence and keeps the cards. The player with the most cards wins.

Create a Riddle

Materials paper, pencils

Pairs of students can write a riddle for a Key Word. For example, *I am here and I am there. Where am I? (everywhere)* Each pair reads the riddle aloud and challenges classmates to guess the word.

Sort the Words

Materials index cards, pencils

Think of several categories for the Key Words that relate to meaning. List the categories on the board. Then have students work in pairs to write each Key Word on an index card and sort the words into the appropriate category.

Relate the Words

Materials index cards, pencils

Partners write each Key Word on an index card and place the cards face down. Students then choose two cards at a time and tell how they might go together. For example, <u>Sunlight</u> makes the <u>frost</u> melt.

Making News

Materials newspapers, paper, scissors, glue, markers

Invite students to bring in several newspaper headlines and advertisements. Have them substitute some of the words for the Key Words. Then discuss how the meaning changes. Students can illustrate the new headlines and ads.

Reteaching Grammar to Beginners

Reteaching Routine

Beginners will benefit from the hands-on, interactive reteaching routine described here. Learn the three steps of the routine, then refer to the skill you are targeting to find specific ideas.

1 Make it Concrete

Use role-play, Picture Cards, or real objects to set a context for using the skill. Model the skill orally. Then have students practice it as you provide positive feedback and correction.

2 Make it Interactive

Have students work in pairs or small groups to gather examples of the grammar skill and use the examples orally or in writing.

3 Make it Memorable

Involve students in an appropriate song or chant from the *Language Songs* **Big Book** (see below), taking advantage of the music and rhythm to help them store memory of the structure. Once students can recite the song or chant easily, place self-stick notes over words that reflect the target structure. Then have one group recite, pausing for another group to supply the missing words. Or, have groups substitute new words that are the same part of speech or add new lines to recite an innovation. Use these songs and chants:

Structure	*Language Songs* Big Book	Page	Structure	*Language Songs* Big Book	Page
Sentence Types	Communicate!	5	Verb Tense	The Contest (past)	26
Nouns	Many Pennies	29		Texas (past)	28
	Homes (plural)	12		Fair Exchange (present, future)	30
Verbs	Wanda Jane	16	Helping Verbs (*modals*)	The Contest	26
	Risi e Bisi	24	Helping Verbs (*is, are*)	Going Into Town	32
Adjectives	In the Ocean	17	Complete Sentences	Every Author	8
Pronouns	Risi e Bisi	24	Adverbs	Fair Exchange (Substitute *happily* with other adverbs.)	30

Practice Options

Sentence Types Unit 1 Progress Test

Materials index cards, each with a question starter or an exclamation mark; Picture Cards

Step 1 Pairs act out a favorite activity. Model asking questions and using other sentence types: *Who likes to skate? You are a great dancer!*

Step 2 Students ask a question or make an exclamation about each picture.

Nouns Unit 2 Progress Test

Materials magazines with large color pictures

Step 1 Display a magazine page and ask students to point to as many people, places, and things as they can. Then name each one and have students echo the noun.

Step 2 Distribute new pages and have students name and list the singular and plural nouns.

Action Verbs; Subject-Verb Agreement
Unit 3 Progress Test

Materials Picture Cards, magazines

Step 1 Display pictures of one or more animals. Make statements about their actions.
Step 2 Role-play a trip to the zoo. Say: *I see one alligator. I see three flamingos.* Ask students what the animal does or the animals do.

Adjectives Unit 4 Progress Test

Materials objects such as pencils, erasers

Step 1 Display the objects and use color, shape, size, and number words to describe them.
Step 2 Pairs think of more ways to describe an object and classmates guess what it is.

Nouns and Pronouns Unit 5 Progress Test

Materials butcher paper, self-stick notes

Step 1 Have students say some sentences about themselves and their classmates. Record the sentences. Point to each noun and name it. Then cover it with a self-stick note and model substituting a pronoun. Have students echo the new sentences.
Step 2 Pairs say sentences about themselves and their families. Partners repeat the sentences, substituting pronouns.

Verb Tense (present, past, future)
Unit 6 Progress Test

Materials action figures and tabletop toys

Step 1 Tell a story emphasizing the verbs as you move the action figures. Retell the story moving the figures and pausing for students to supply the verbs.
Step 2 A student acts out a story, while a partner describes the action. Then the actor tells what he or she did and will do.

Helping Verbs (*modals*) Unit 6 Progress Test

Materials rulers, erasers, and other objects

Step 1 Role-play being a salesperson trying to convince students to buy classroom objects: *I can help you do well in school. You must buy this ruler.*
Step 2 Switch roles.

Helping Verbs (*is, are*) Unit 7 Progress Test

Step 1 Play Simon Says with two students at a time. As each one follows your prompt, describe what is happening. For example, *Ana is jumping. They are smiling.*
Step 2 Repeat the game. Supply the subject and have the class provide the progressive verb.

Complete Sentences Unit 7 Progress Test

Materials Picture Cards, oaktag strips

Step 1 Make a sentence strip for each picture. Have students echo the subject, the predicate, and the entire sentence.
Step 2 Cut the strips between the subject and predicate. Distribute them and display the pictures. Have students circulate to connect the parts and then match the sentence to the correct picture.

Adverbs Unit 8 Progress Test

Materials Picture Cards or magazine pictures showing actions

Step 1 Display a picture and describe the action, emphasizing the adverb. Then ask questions such as *How does she run? When do they sleep?*
Step 2 Partners write labels that describe the actions shown in the pictures.

Practicing the Traits of Good Writing

Use the **Class Writing Profile** to assess which writing trait to target for further practice. Then select from the activities below to develop students' abilities to distinguish the trait in published writing and develop the trait in their own writing.

☑ Focus and Coherence

A composition that is focused and coherent feels complete. Each paragraph is focused, too. The writing has an interesting beginning, relevant details, and a satisfying conclusion.

Listen for the Trait

Read aloud selections that exemplify focused, complete writing. Start with one or more of these selections in the Level E Student Book:

- "My Rows and Piles of Coins," pages 380–399, for completeness
- "Money," pages 408–423, for related ideas

Good Beginning Scavenger Hunt

Have students review familiar books to find two beginning sentences that grab their attention. Then have students write alternative, boring beginning sentences. Each student then introduces the book to the group and reads the first few paragraphs aloud—once with the boring beginning, and again with the author's beginning. Encourage the group to discuss what makes a good beginning (use this activity to study satisfying conclusions).

English at Your Command!

Teach or review these Handbook pages to help students build complete stories and paragraphs:

- Story Maps, pages 79–83
- Paragraphs, pages 145–150
- Parts of a Story, page 164
- Parts of a Report, pages 304–305

☑ Organization

Organization encompasses the overall structure of a composition. In a well-organized piece, the writer's organizing strategy suits his or her purpose. Ideas flow logically, with meaningful transitions.

Listen for the Trait

Whenever you read aloud a story or article, have students think and talk about how the author organized his or her writing. Have students draw or use **Kidspiration** software to make a graphic organizer of the selection. Ask: *How did the author organize the writing? Does it make sense?* Or have students retell the story. Ask: *Was this story easy or hard to retell? Why?*

Main Idea Mix-Up

Choose a nonfiction selection with which students are familiar. Type the selection one sentence per line and cut apart the sentences. Have students work with a partner to order the sentences into paragraphs and then into a paragraph order that makes sense.

English at Your Command!

Teach or review the use of graphic organizers in Chapter 2 ("Picture It!") of the Handbook as tools for organizing ideas during prewriting. You might also teach outlining as a way of organizing research notes:

- Make an Outline, pages 300–301

☑ Development of Ideas

A composition with well-developed ideas has details that help the reader understand the topic or characters very well. The writer develops the topic in an interesting, creative, and in-depth way.

Listen for the Trait

Read aloud books that are good examples of interesting or creative ways to develop a topic or story. These selections in the Level E Student Book are particularly creative:

- "Twister," pages 134–167, for the way the author builds suspense
- "Hello, Fish!," pages 240–257, for the interest the verses of the poem add to the nonfiction presentation
- "The Tree That Would Not Die," pages 340–363, for the way history is presented from the perspective of a tree
- "Call Me Ahnighito," pages 438–453, for the way the author tells the story from the point of view of the meteorite

Five Ways to Use a _____

Have students list five unusual ways to use something quite ordinary, such as a pencil, a pocket, or a toothbrush. Then invite students to share their ideas. Ask students to discuss which ideas appeal to them the most and why.

A New View Brainstorming

Have students select a story they think is "just OK" and brainstorm all the different ways it could be told to make it more interesting. For example, the writer could:

- have the character write letters to tell what is happening
- turn a nonfiction article into a story by giving information from the perspective of a rock, animal, tree, mountain, etc.

On and On and On

One of the best ways to encourage elaboration is to have students spend a lot of time during the prewriting stage brainstorming alone and with others. Encourage students to:

- do a quickwrite or a freewrite in order to capture as many ideas as they can in five minutes
- brainstorm with a group a never-ending sentence about a story character or story plot
- make webs to capture and relate ideas

Dialogue Role-Play

To help students develop more realistic, elaborated dialogue, encourage partners to role-play story scenes. Have the actors use a tape recorder, or have one pair of students role-play while another pair takes notes on the dialogue.

Show-Not-Tell Word Wall

Give each student a packet of small self-stick notes to use during reading time. Encourage students to write words that show what someone is like or what is happening (e.g., students might write vivid adjectives, descriptive adverbs, and alternatives to the word *said*, such as *groaned* or *sighed*). Students should write one word per note. Each day, have students add the words to a display in the Writing Center, under the appropriate headings.

English at Your Command!

Teach or review these pages in the Handbook to help students collect and develop ideas in depth:

- Clusters, pages 70–71
- How to Collect Ideas, pages 172–173
- Add Details, page 186
- Show, Don't Tell, page 187

Practicing the Traits of Good Writing, continued

Voice

A composition with an identifiable voice sounds genuine and unique—unlike anyone else's. Words and phrases are interesting and appropriate to the writer's purpose and audience.

Listen for the Trait

Read aloud books in which the words convey a sense of the writer—that is, they sound as if a real person is speaking and cares about his or her message. These selections in the Level E Student Book have a particularly strong voice:

- "In Gary Soto's Shoes," pages 48–61
- "The Lotus Seed," pages 272–283
- "The Tree That Would Not Die," pages 340–363

Act It Out

Display the word *walking*. Have pairs act out and then list different ways a person can walk. Create a class list, encouraging students to add adverbs or use more specific verbs to describe the action. Repeat with other overused or uninteresting action words, like *said* or *sat down*.

Guess the Purpose

Have students gather a variety of published works—trade books, textbooks, pamphlets, ads, magazines, Web pages, etc. Then have partners work together to guess the author's purpose and audience: *Why did the writer write this? Whom did the writer write it for?* Partners should then put a self-stick note on the back of the published work, exchange works with another pair, and then repeat the activity, discussing any differences among themselves.

Make Comparisons

Choose brief selections from two distinctly different authors—for example, Dr. Seuss and Eve Bunting—or two selections written for different ages (e.g., a picture book and a young-adult novel). Read a bit from each book. Ask: *What is different? How can you tell?* Encourage students to notice differences in word choice, topics, and types of sentences used by the author.

Give Voice to Voice

One of the best ways to help students develop a genuine voice is to have students read their drafts aloud often—to themselves and to others—during the drafting and revising steps.

English at Your Command!

Teach or review these pages in the Handbook to focus on aspects of the writer's craft:

- Synonyms and Antonyms, pages 35–41
- How to Write for a Purpose, pages 174–176
- How to Write for a Specific Audience, page 177
- How to Make Your Writing Better, pages 178–188

☑ Written Conventions: Sentence Fluency

When sentence fluency is present in a written composition, the words, phrases, and sentences flow in a way that communicates the writer's ideas.

Listen for Sentence Variety

Read aloud books with a variety of sentence types. These selections in the Level E Student Book are a good place to start:

- "If the Shoe Fits," pages 18–39
- "Twister," pages 134–167
- "The Secret Footprints," pages 208–231
- "My Rows and Piles of Coins," pages 380–399

Sentence Puzzles

Write simple sentences on separate slips of paper.

- The man crossed the street.
- The girl waits at the corner.
- The cars go slowly.
- The truck turns left.

Have partners cut at least two sentence strips apart between the subject and the predicate. Then have partners exchange their "puzzle pieces" with another pair, put them back together, and read aloud the reassembled sentences for sense.

Endless Sentence

Create an endless sentence and have partners work together to break it up into manageable sentences.

English at Your Command!

Teach or review these grammar skills in the Handbook, depending on the needs of your students:

- Improve Your Sentences, pages 182–183
- Sentences, pages 232–238
- Grammar Practice for Sentences, pages 381–383

☑ Written Conventions: Grammar, Usage, Mechanics, and Spelling

A written piece is most effective when the conventions of written English help express, not hinder, the writer's ideas.

Runaway Sentence

Copy a paragraph from a book you are currently reading onto a very long sentence strip. Omit the end punctuation marks and don't capitalize the first word of any sentence. Have a group work together to cut the sentences apart in the right places, add the correct punctuation marks, and capitalize the first words. Then have the group read the sentences aloud to check their punctuation and capitalization.

Read Aloud for...*Mechanics?* Yes!

Read aloud the picture book *Yo! Yes?* by Chris Raschka for a quick and fun way to study the importance and impact of end punctuation.

English at Your Command!

Teach or review these pages in the Handbook:

- Handwriting and Spelling Guide, pages 210–229
- Using Nouns in Writing, page 245
- Using Pronouns in Writing, page 251
- Using Adjectives in Writing, page 257
- Using Verbs in Writing, page 268
- Using Adverbs in Writing, page 271
- Using Prepositions in Writing, page 273
- Capital Letters, pages 276–281
- Punctuation Marks, pages 282–287

Unit Progress Tests

▶ **Directions**

▶ **Student Profiles**

▶ **Class Profiles**

▶ **Beginning, Intermediate, and Advanced Tests**

▶ **Self-Assessment Forms**

▶ **Peer-Assessment Form**

Unit 1 • Directions for ⓑ Progress Test

Distribute the test pages. Before students begin each subtest, read aloud the directions and use the script to work through each sample item.

VOCABULARY

Read aloud the directions on page 1. Then work through the sample item. Say:

Sample

Look at the pictures in the box. Which picture shows a jacket? Point to the picture. **(Pause.)** *The second bubble is filled in because the second picture shows a jacket.*

Items 1–6

Read each question aloud. Provide time for students to mark their answers.

GRAMMAR

Read aloud the directions on page 3. Then work through the sample item. Say:

Sample

Look at the picture in the box. Read each group of words. Which question is correct? The last bubble is filled in because that question is written correctly.

Items 7–10

Read each item aloud. Provide time for students to mark their answers.

Read aloud the directions on page 4. Then work through the sample item. Say:

Sample

Look at the picture in the box. The sentence says: Felipe's run wins the game. *Which mark goes at the end of the sentence? Look at the three choices. The third bubble is filled in because an exclamation mark goes at the end of this sentence.*

Items 11–13

Read each item aloud. Provide time for students to mark their answers.

COMPREHENSION / CRITICAL THINKING

Selection 1 and Items 14–17

Read aloud the directions on page 5. Say: *Now listen to the selection. The title is:*

A Funny Phone Call

Look at Picture 1.   Jin answers the phone. He says, "Hello. . . Dad? I am so happy to hear from you!"

Look at Picture 2.   Jin hears a strange noise. He worries.

Look at Picture 3.   Dad asks, "Jin, did you call me just now?" Jin says, "No, you just called me!"

Look at Picture 4.   Dad says, "I know what happened. My phone was in my pocket. I bumped a button. Then the phone called you!" Jin laughs.

Then read each question aloud. Provide time for students to mark their answers.

Selection 2 and Items 18–21

Read aloud the directions on page 7. Say: *Now listen to the selection. The title is:*

Meet Margaret Mahy

Look at the first picture.   Margaret Mahy's father read stories to her. Margaret loved the sounds of the words! That is why she started to write her own stories.

Look at the next picture.   Margaret grew up and got a job in a library. Then, she stopped her work at the library. She needed more time to write.

Look at the next picture.   Now Margaret Mahy lives by the sea with her cats and her dog. She writes books for children. She writes about lions and other animals.

Look at the last picture.   Many children love Margaret's books. They write letters to her. Margaret writes letters back to the children.

Then read each question aloud. Provide time for students to mark their answers.

Unit 1 • Directions for ⓘ and ⒶProgress Tests

Distribute the test pages. Before students begin each subtest, read aloud the directions and use the script to work through each sample item.

VOCABULARY

Read aloud the directions on page 1. Then work through the sample item. Say:

Sample
Read the sentence in the box. (Pause.) *Which word goes in the blank? Let's try each one:*

> *Carlo wears his new* car *to school.*
> *Carlo wears his new* book *to school.*
> *Carlo wears his new* jacket *to school.*
> *Carlo wears his new* building *to school.*

The third bubble is filled in because jacket *is the best answer.*

Items 1–6
Tell students to complete the remaining items in the same way. Provide time for students to mark their answers.

Read aloud the directions on page 2. Then work through the sample item. Say:

Sample
Read the sentence in the box. (Pause.) *What does the underlined word* enormous *mean?*

> huge
> weak
> pretty
> broken

The first bubble is filled in because enormous *means* huge.

Items 7–10
Tell students to complete the remaining items in the same way. Provide time for them to mark their answers.

GRAMMAR

Read aloud the directions on page 3. Then work through the sample item. Say:

Sample
Read each group of words in the box. (Pause.) *Which is a complete sentence?*

> The man with the hat.
> Jenny has a new coat.
> Walks around the room.
> Eats beans and rice for lunch.

The second bubble is filled in because Jenny has a new coat *is a complete sentence.*

Items 11–14
Tell students to complete the remaining items in the same way. Provide time for them to mark their answers.

Read aloud the directions on page 4. Then work through the sample item. Say:

Sample
Read the underlined sentence. (Pause.) *What is the best way to write it? Look at the four choices. The third bubble is filled in because* Does your family have a pet? *is the best way to write the sentence.*

Items 15–18
Tell students to complete the remaining items in the same way. Provide time for them to mark their answers.

COMPREHENSION / CRITICAL THINKING

Selections and Items 19–27
Read aloud the directions for each selection. Provide time for students to read the selection and mark their answers.

DIRECTIONS Record the student's name and test date. Use the **Answer Key** on page 10a to score the student's test. Then, in the Student Profile, circle the item number of each correct answer and circle the plus or minus sign to indicate mastery. Calculate the subtest scores and then the total test score. To help you group students for reteaching, transfer the minus sign for any unmastered skill to the **Class Profile** (page 1f).

Student Name _____ Date _____

Subtest	Tested Skills	ITEM ANALYSIS		TEST SCORES
		Item Numbers	Mastery	No. Correct × Points = Score
VOCABULARY	Key Words	1　2　3　4　5　6	5 out of 6 　+　−	_____ × 4 = ⬚/24
GRAMMAR	Sentence Types	7　8　9　10　11　12　13	6 out of 7 　+　−	_____ × 4 = ⬚/28
COMPREHENSION / CRITICAL THINKING	Analyze Story Elements (characters)	14　15　16　17　18　19　20　21	6 out of 8 　+　−	_____ × 6 = ⬚/48
			TOTAL UNIT 1 PROGRESS TEST	⬚/100

Unit 1 • Student Profile for Intermediate Progress Test

DIRECTIONS Record the student's name and test date. Use the **Answer Key** on page 10a to score the student's test. Then, in the Student Profile, circle the item number of each correct answer and circle the plus or minus sign to indicate mastery. Calculate the subtest scores and then the total test score. To help you group students for reteaching, transfer the minus sign for any unmastered skill to the **Class Profile** (page 1f).

Student Name _____ Date _____

Subtest	Tested Skills	ITEM ANALYSIS		TEST SCORES
		Item Numbers	Mastery	No. Correct × Points = Score
VOCABULARY	Key Words	1 2 3 4 5 6	5 out of 6 + −	_____ × 4 = ☐ /40
	Context Clues	7 8 9 10	3 out of 4 + −	
GRAMMAR	Complete Sentences	11 12 13 14	3 out of 4 + −	_____ × 3 = ☐ /24
	Sentence Types	15 16 17 18	3 out of 4 + −	
COMPREHENSION / CRITICAL THINKING	Analyze Story Elements (characters)	19 20 21 22 27	4 out of 5 + −	_____ × 4 = ☐ /36
	Distinguish Fact and Opinion	23 24 25 26	3 out of 4 + −	
			TOTAL UNIT 1 PROGRESS TEST	☐ /100

Unit 1 • Student Profile for Advanced Progress Test

DIRECTIONS Record the student's name and test date. Use the **Answer Key** on page 10a to score the student's test. Then, in the Student Profile, circle the item number of each correct answer and circle the plus or minus sign to indicate mastery. Calculate the subtest scores and then the total test score. To help you group students for reteaching, transfer the minus sign for any unmastered skill to the **Class Profile** (page 1f).

Student Name _____   **Date** _____

Subtest	Tested Skills	ITEM ANALYSIS		TEST SCORES
		Item Numbers	Mastery	No. Correct × Points = Score
VOCABULARY	Key Words	1 2 3 4 5 6	5 out of 6 + −	____ × 4 = ☐ /40
	Context Clues	7 8 9 10	3 out of 4 + −	
GRAMMAR	Complete Sentences	11 12 13 14	3 out of 4 + −	____ × 3 = ☐ /24
	Sentence Types	15 16 17 18	3 out of 4 + −	
COMPREHENSION / CRITICAL THINKING	Analyze Story Elements (characters)	19 20 21 22 27	4 out of 5 + −	____ × 4 = ☐ /36
	Distinguish Fact and Opinion	23 24 25 26	3 out of 4 + −	
			TOTAL UNIT 1 PROGRESS TEST	☐ /100

© Hampton-Brown

Unit 1 • Class Profile

Date _____

DIRECTIONS Use the **Unit 1 Student Profiles** to complete this chart. In each row, write the student's name, fill in the bubble for the test form taken, and mark a minus sign (–) for any skill not yet mastered. Then group students and use the reteaching ideas and practice exercises to help students reach mastery.

Student Name	Test Form	TESTED SKILLS					
		Key Words	Context Clues	Complete Sentences	Sentence Types	Analyze Story Elements (character)	Distinguish Fact and Opinion
	Ⓑ Ⓘ Ⓐ						
	Ⓑ Ⓘ Ⓐ						
	Ⓑ Ⓘ Ⓐ						
	Ⓑ Ⓘ Ⓐ						
	Ⓑ Ⓘ Ⓐ						
	Ⓑ Ⓘ Ⓐ						
	Ⓑ Ⓘ Ⓐ						
	Ⓑ Ⓘ Ⓐ						
	Ⓑ Ⓘ Ⓐ						
	Ⓑ Ⓘ Ⓐ						
	Ⓑ Ⓘ Ⓐ						
	Ⓑ Ⓘ Ⓐ						
	Ⓑ Ⓘ Ⓐ						
	Ⓑ Ⓘ Ⓐ						
	Ⓑ Ⓘ Ⓐ						
	Ⓑ Ⓘ Ⓐ						
	Ⓑ Ⓘ Ⓐ						
	Ⓑ Ⓘ Ⓐ						
	Ⓑ Ⓘ Ⓐ						
	Ⓑ Ⓘ Ⓐ						
	Ⓑ Ⓘ Ⓐ						
	Ⓑ Ⓘ Ⓐ						
	Ⓑ Ⓘ Ⓐ						
RETEACHING RESOURCES		Ⓑ Ⓘ Ⓐ AH T38	Ⓘ Ⓐ LB TG	Ⓘ Ⓐ EAYC 232, 236–237	Ⓑ AH T40 Ⓘ Ⓐ EAYC 232–234	Ⓑ LB TG Ⓘ Ⓐ LB TG	Ⓘ Ⓐ LB TG
PRACTICE EXERCISES		PB 5, 13	PB 10–11	EAYC 382	EAYC 381, 382	PB 9	PB 18

KEY: **AH:** Assessment Handbook   **EAYC:** English at Your Command!
LB TG: Leveled Books Teacher's Guide   **PB:** Practice Book

Unit 1 • Online with Gary Soto

DIRECTIONS Listen to each question. Then choose the correct picture.
Mark your answer. *(4 points each)*

⭐**Sample**

Which picture shows a <u>jacket</u>?

1 Which picture shows <u>brand-new</u> shoes?

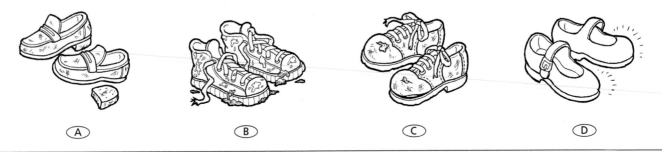

2 Which girl has <u>outgrown</u> her jacket?

3 Which picture shows a way to <u>communicate</u>?

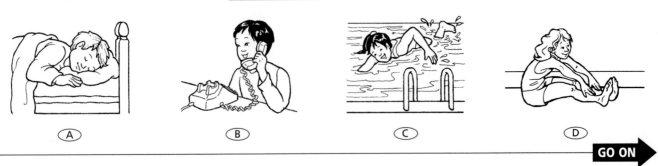

GO ON ➡️

VOCABULARY

4 Which girl <u>refuses</u> something?

F   G   H   J

5 Which boy gets a <u>hand-me-down</u> shirt?

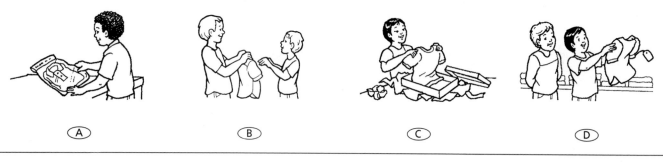

A   B   C   D

6 Which boy acts <u>proudly</u>?

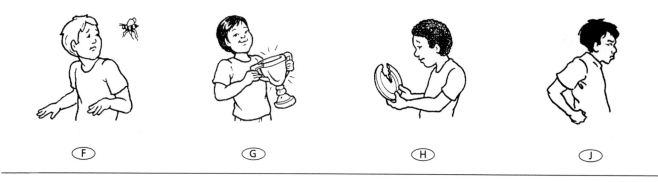

F   G   H   J

STOP

© Hampton-Brown

GRAMMAR

DIRECTIONS Look at the picture. Read each group of words. Choose the correct question. Mark your answer. *(4 points each)*

⭐ **Sample**

Ⓐ that is his dog.

Ⓑ Dog is that his?

🅒 Is that his dog?

9

Ⓐ he does laugh?

Ⓑ Does he laugh?

Ⓒ He laugh does.

7

Ⓐ New are the shirts.

Ⓑ Are the shirts new?

Ⓒ The shirts new are?

10

Ⓕ Apples do they have?

Ⓖ Do they have apples.

Ⓗ Do they have apples?

8

Ⓕ Is Kira home?

Ⓖ home Kira is.

Ⓗ Home is Kira?

STOP

GRAMMAR

DIRECTIONS Look at the picture. Listen to the sentence. What mark goes at the end? Mark your answer. *(4 points each)*

⭐**Sample**

Felipe's run wins the game

- (A) .
- (B) ?
- (C) !

11 It is time for dinner

- (A) .
- (B) ?
- (C) !

12 Please help me

- (F) .
- (G) ?
- (H) !

13 Does the bird talk

- (A) .
- (B) ?
- (C) !

STOP

COMPREHENSION / CRITICAL THINKING

DIRECTIONS Listen to the selection. Then listen to each question. Choose the best answer. Mark your answer. *(6 points each)*

A Funny Phone Call

Jin answers the phone. He says, "Hello...Dad? I am so happy to hear from you!"

Jin hears a strange noise. He worries.

Dad asks, "Jin, did you call me just now?"
Jin says, "No, you just called me!"

Dad says, "I know what happened. My phone was in my pocket. I bumped a button. Then the phone called you!"
Jin laughs.

GO ON ➡

© Hampton-Brown

COMPREHENSION / CRITICAL THINKING

14 The phone rings. What does Jin do?

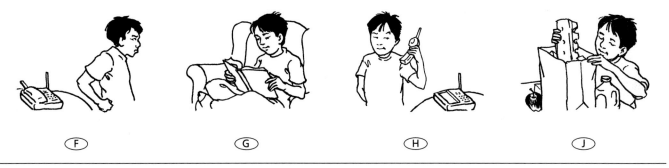

Ⓕ   Ⓖ   Ⓗ   Ⓙ

15 Jin thinks Dad is on the phone. How does Jin feel?

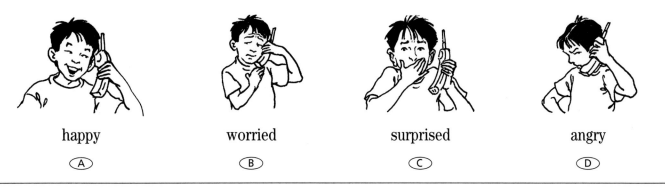

happy	worried	surprised	angry
Ⓐ	Ⓑ	Ⓒ	Ⓓ

16 Jin hears a strange noise. How does Jin feel?

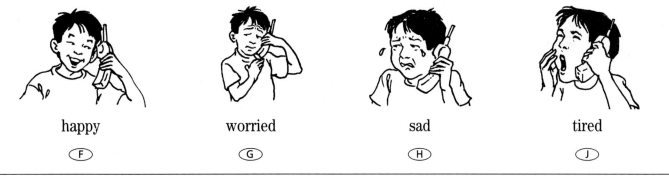

happy	worried	sad	tired
Ⓕ	Ⓖ	Ⓗ	Ⓙ

17 Jin finds out what happened. What does he do next?

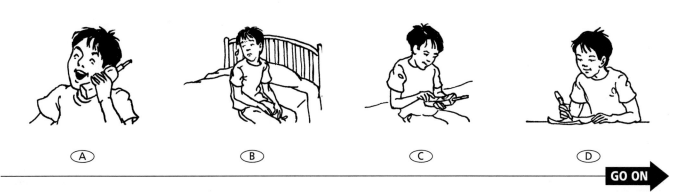

Ⓐ   Ⓑ   Ⓒ   Ⓓ

GO ON ➡

COMPREHENSION / CRITICAL THINKING

DIRECTIONS Listen to the selection. Then listen to each question.
Choose the best answer. Mark your answer. *(6 points each)*

Meet Margaret Mahy

Margaret Mahy's father read stories to her. Margaret loved the sounds of the words! That is why she started to write her own stories.

Margaret grew up and got a job in a library. Then, she stopped her work at the library. She needed more time to write.

Now Margaret Mahy lives by the sea with her cats and her dog. She writes books for children. She writes about lions and other animals.

Many children love Margaret's books. They write letters to her. Margaret writes letters back to the children.

© Hampton-Brown

GO ON

COMPREHENSION / CRITICAL THINKING

18 Margaret's father read stories to her. How did this make her feel?

sleepy   angry   happy   surprised
Ⓕ   Ⓖ   Ⓗ   Ⓙ

19 Why did Margaret stop her work at the library?

to swim   to write   to sell books   to draw pictures
Ⓐ   Ⓑ   Ⓒ   Ⓓ

20 Margaret writes books for children. How does this make her feel?

angry   happy   sad   worried
Ⓕ   Ⓖ   Ⓗ   Ⓙ

21 Children write letters to Margaret. What does she do?

Ⓐ   Ⓑ   Ⓒ   Ⓓ

STOP

© Hampton-Brown

Unit 1 • Online with Gary Soto

VOCABULARY

DIRECTIONS Read each item. Choose the word that goes in the blank.
Mark your answer. *(4 points each)*

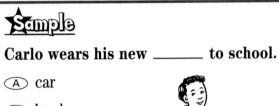

Sample

Carlo wears his new _____ to school.

Ⓐ car

Ⓑ book

● jacket

Ⓓ building

1 **Shana has _____ her sweater.**

Ⓐ lost

Ⓑ torn

Ⓒ folded

Ⓓ outgrown

2 **Juan buys _____ shoes at the store.**

Ⓕ dirty

Ⓖ tired

Ⓗ brand-new

Ⓙ hand-me-down

3 **He writes a postcard to _____ with a friend.**

Ⓐ hide

Ⓑ shop

Ⓒ laugh

Ⓓ communicate

4 **Sara buys some clothes. She likes her new _____.**

Ⓕ dog

Ⓖ style

Ⓗ coins

Ⓙ friend

5 **Did you _____ the rip in my shirt? I just saw it.**

Ⓐ finish

Ⓑ return

Ⓒ notice

Ⓓ change

6 **Phuong takes her award _____.**

Ⓕ sadly

Ⓖ softly

Ⓗ loudly

Ⓙ proudly

STOP

© Hampton-Brown

VOCABULARY

DIRECTIONS Read each sentence. Choose the meaning of the underlined word. Mark your answer. *(4 points each)*

⭐**Sample**

Three children fit in the enormous chair.

Ⓐ huge
Ⓑ weak
Ⓒ pretty
Ⓓ broken

7 Tina wore pants made of <u>denim</u>.

Ⓐ a small toy
Ⓑ a kind of cloth
Ⓒ a type of flower
Ⓓ something to eat

8 My shoes are covered with mud. They are <u>filthy</u>!

Ⓕ tight
Ⓖ shiny
Ⓗ too big
Ⓙ very dirty

9 I was <u>exhausted</u> after the long walk.

Ⓐ too busy
Ⓑ surprised
Ⓒ very tired
Ⓓ dangerous

10 The story was very sad. I <u>wept</u> when I read it.

Ⓕ cried
Ⓖ slept
Ⓗ yelled
Ⓙ smiled

STOP

GRAMMAR

DIRECTIONS Read each group of words. Choose the complete sentence. Mark your answer. *(3 points each)*

⭐**Sample**

Ⓐ The man with the hat.

Ⓑ Jenny has a new coat.

Ⓒ Walks around the room.

Ⓓ Eats beans and rice for lunch.

11 Ⓐ Julia and her dog.

Ⓑ Paco and the boys.

Ⓒ The girls run home.

Ⓓ Rides the school bus.

12 Ⓕ Has four uncles.

Ⓖ Raúl likes to read.

Ⓗ Sings and dances all day.

Ⓙ Children from many lands.

13 Ⓐ That funny little cat.

Ⓑ Likes blue shoes best.

Ⓒ A tree with red leaves.

Ⓓ Luz rides her bike to school.

14 Ⓕ Colin and his uncle.

Ⓖ Kate washes the car.

Ⓗ The cars on the street.

Ⓙ Makes pancakes for lunch.

© Hampton-Brown

STOP

GRAMMAR

DIRECTIONS Read the sentences. Choose the best way to write each underlined sentence, or choose "Correct as it is." Mark your answer.
(3 points each)

Sample

Does family your have a pet?

Ⓐ Your family does have a pet

Ⓑ Does have your family a pet?

Ⓒ Does your family have a pet?

Ⓓ Correct as it is

15 A dog is that?

Ⓐ Is that a dog.

Ⓑ Is that a dog?

Ⓒ That a dog is?

Ⓓ Correct as it is

16 A cat you do have?

Ⓕ A cat do you have.

Ⓖ Do you have a cat.

Ⓗ Do you have a cat?

Ⓙ Correct as it is

17 You need Pet Fresh today!

Ⓐ you need Pet Fresh today!

Ⓑ You need Pet Fresh today

Ⓒ You need Pet Fresh today?

Ⓓ Correct as it is

18 Go the to pet store and get it?

Ⓕ go to the pet store and get it.

Ⓖ Go to the pet store and get it

Ⓗ Go to the pet store and get it.

Ⓙ Correct as it is

STOP

COMPREHENSION / CRITICAL THINKING

DIRECTIONS Read the selection. Then read each item. Choose the best answer. Mark your answer. *(4 points each)*

The Game

Uncle Geraldo buys three tickets to a soccer game. The U.S. team and the team from Mexico are playing.

"Who wants to go to the game?" asks Uncle Geraldo.

"I want to go!" says Toya. She is excited. She likes the team from Mexico.

"I want to go, too!" says Yago. He likes the U.S. team.

Before the game, Uncle Geraldo buys a Mexican hat for Toya. He buys a U.S. hat for Yago. Then the game starts. The Mexican team makes a goal. Toya cheers for them. Next, the U.S. team makes a goal. Toya frowns. Yago yells for the U.S. team.

Soon the game ends. Each team has one point! Toya smiles. Yago smiles, too. Uncle Geraldo laughs.

"That was a great game!" says Uncle Geraldo.

© Hampton-Brown

GO ON ➡

COMPREHENSION / CRITICAL THINKING

19 Look at the chart. Which of these goes in the blank?

    Ⓐ Toya goes home.

    Ⓑ Toya eats popcorn.

    Ⓒ Toya claps for the U.S. team.

    Ⓓ Toya cheers for the Mexican team.

Character Chart

Events →	Toya's Feelings →	Toya's Actions
Uncle Geraldo buys tickets to a soccer game.	Toya is excited.	Toya goes to the game.
The Mexican team makes a goal.	Toya feels glad.	_____?_____

20 The U.S. team makes a goal. How does Toya feel?

    Ⓕ sad

    Ⓖ tired

    Ⓗ lucky

    Ⓙ happy

21 Yago yells because —

    Ⓐ he is sad about the game

    Ⓑ the U.S. team makes a goal

    Ⓒ Uncle Geraldo brings popcorn

    Ⓓ the Mexican team makes a goal

22 Why do Toya and Yago smile at the end of the game?

    Ⓕ The Mexican team wins.

    Ⓖ Each team scores one goal.

    Ⓗ Uncle Geraldo starts to cheer.

    Ⓙ They cheer for the wrong team.

23 Read each sentence. Which is an opinion?

    Ⓐ The game was great!

    Ⓑ Uncle Geraldo laughs.

    Ⓒ Who wants to go to the game?

    Ⓓ Uncle Geraldo buys three tickets.

© Hampton-Brown

GO ON ➡

COMPREHENSION / CRITICAL THINKING

DIRECTIONS Read the selection. Then read each item. Choose the best answer. Mark your answer. *(4 points each)*

Meet Margaret Mahy

Margaret Mahy lives by the sea in New Zealand. New Zealand is a beautiful place. Margaret Mahy usually wakes up early. She thinks of funny stories and writes down her ideas. When the sun comes up, she takes a walk and eats breakfast. Then she sits at her desk.

Margaret Mahy writes many wonderful books. She writes about lions, kings, and strange things. She writes many letters to children, too. Children write letters to Margaret about her books. Margaret often writes back.

Margaret Mahy is a great author of children's books. She wins many prizes.

About the Author

① **Where was she born?**
Whakatane, New Zealand

② **When was she born?**
March 21, 1936

③ **What was her first book?**
A Lion in the Meadow (1969)

④ **What is her family like?**
She has two daughters.

© Hampton-Brown

GO ON ➡

COMPREHENSION / CRITICAL THINKING

24 **Which of these sentences is a fact?**

   Ⓕ Breakfast is the best time of day.

   Ⓖ New Zealand is a beautiful place.

   Ⓗ Margaret Mahy has two daughters.

   Ⓙ Margaret Mahy's ideas are strange.

25 **Which of these sentences is an opinion?**

   Ⓐ Margaret Mahy was born in 1936.

   Ⓑ Margaret Mahy wins many prizes.

   Ⓒ Margaret Mahy writes about lions.

   Ⓓ Margaret Mahy's books are wonderful.

26 **Which of these sentences is a fact?**

   Ⓕ Margaret Mahy is a great author.

   Ⓖ Margaret Mahy lives in New Zealand.

   Ⓗ Margaret Mahy's house is very pretty.

   Ⓙ Margaret Mahy's lion pictures are funny.

27 **Margaret often writes back to children. This shows that she —**

   Ⓐ misses her daughters

   Ⓑ needs more funny ideas

   Ⓒ cares about the children's pets

   Ⓓ likes to get letters from children

STOP

Unit 1 • Online with Gary Soto

VOCABULARY

DIRECTIONS Read each item. Choose the word that goes in the blank.
Mark your answer. *(4 points each)*

Sample

Carlo wears his new _____ to school.

Ⓐ car

Ⓑ book

Ⓒ jacket

Ⓓ building

1 Shana's sweater is too small.
She has _____ it.

Ⓐ torn

Ⓑ folded

Ⓒ outgrown

Ⓓ published

2 Juan buys _____ shoes at the store.

Ⓕ dirty

Ⓖ tired

Ⓗ brand-new

Ⓙ hand-me-down

3 Sam writes letters to _____ with his
friends far away.

Ⓐ sing

Ⓑ travel

Ⓒ compare

Ⓓ communicate

4 Sara's clothes always look good.
She has a great _____!

Ⓕ dog

Ⓖ style

Ⓗ laugh

Ⓙ friend

5 Did you _____ the rip in my shirt?
I just saw it.

Ⓐ finish

Ⓑ return

Ⓒ notice

Ⓓ change

6 Phuong used her _____ to write
a story.

Ⓕ digestion

Ⓖ invitation

Ⓗ protection

Ⓙ imagination

STOP

VOCABULARY

DIRECTIONS Read each sentence. Choose the meaning of the underlined word. Mark your answer. *(4 points each)*

⭐**Sample**

Three children fit in the **enormous** chair.

- Ⓐ huge
- Ⓑ weak
- Ⓒ pretty
- Ⓓ broken

---

7 Tina wore pants made of **denim**.

- Ⓐ a small toy
- Ⓑ a kind of cloth
- Ⓒ a type of flower
- Ⓓ something to eat

8 When we walked in the mud, our shoes got **filthy**.

- Ⓕ shiny
- Ⓖ too big
- Ⓗ smaller
- Ⓙ very dirty

9 I was **exhausted** after the long walk.

- Ⓐ too busy
- Ⓑ surprised
- Ⓒ very tired
- Ⓓ dangerous

10 The story was very sad. I **wept** when I read it.

- Ⓕ slept
- Ⓖ cried
- Ⓗ yelled
- Ⓙ smiled

STOP

GRAMMAR

DIRECTIONS Read each group of words. Choose the complete sentence. Mark your answer. *(3 points each)*

⭐ **Sample**

Ⓐ The man with the hat.

🅑 Jenny has a new coat.

Ⓒ Walks around the room.

Ⓓ Eats beans and rice for lunch.

11 Ⓐ Paco and the other boys.

Ⓑ Julia and her funny little dog.

Ⓒ The girls ran all the way home.

Ⓓ Do not like to ride the school bus.

12 Ⓕ Raúl likes to read.

Ⓖ Sings and dances all day.

Ⓗ Has four uncles and six aunts.

Ⓙ Children from many different lands.

13 Ⓐ That funny little cat.

Ⓑ Likes blue shoes best.

Ⓒ Luz rides her bike to school.

Ⓓ A beautiful tree with red leaves.

14 Ⓕ Colin and his uncle.

Ⓖ Kate washed the car.

Ⓗ Made pancakes for lunch.

Ⓙ The cars and trucks on the street.

STOP

GRAMMAR

DIRECTIONS Read the sentences. Choose the best way to write each underlined sentence, or choose "Correct as it is." Mark your answer.

(3 points each)

Does family your have a pet? A dog is there at your house?   Do you

<u>Sample</u>   **15**

have a bird? <u>You have do a cat?</u> If you said "yes," you need Pet Fresh!

16

<u>It makes all your rugs smell good!</u> Now you can enjoy your house and your

17

pet, too. What are you waiting for? <u>Go to the pet store?</u> Buy some Pet

18

Fresh today.

⭐Sample

- Ⓐ Your family does have a pet
- Ⓑ Does have your family a pet?
- Ⓒ Does your family have a pet?
- Ⓓ Correct as it is

---

15 Ⓐ Is there a dog at your house.

Ⓑ Is there a dog at your house?

Ⓒ There a dog is at your house?

Ⓓ Correct as it is

16 Ⓕ A cat do you have.

Ⓖ Do you have a cat.

Ⓗ Do you have a cat?

Ⓙ Correct as it is

17 Ⓐ It makes all your rugs smell good

Ⓑ it makes all your rugs smell good!

Ⓒ It makes all your rugs smell good?

Ⓓ Correct as it is

18 Ⓕ go to the pet store.

Ⓖ Go to the pet store

Ⓗ Go to the pet store.

Ⓙ Correct as it is

STOP

DIRECTIONS Read the selection. Then read each item. Choose the best answer. Mark your answer. *(4 points each)*

A Family Name

I hate the first day of school. Every year, the teacher reads our names out loud. When she gets to my name, everyone laughs.

"Wilbur Isaac Newton the Third."

"Call me Win," I always say. Every year I hope the kids will forget my real name. I like Win much better. It's short and easy to say. Besides, there is only one Win.

There are just too many Wilbur Isaac Newtons in my family. My father's name is Wilbur Isaac Newton the Second. My grandfather's name is Wilbur Isaac Newton, too. He's the First, I guess. It is a dumb family tradition. Who wants a hand-me-down name? I wish I could be just Joe Smith or Frank López.

GO ON ➡

COMPREHENSION / CRITICAL THINKING

A Family Name, continued

This year started just like every other year. After my teacher called all the names, she assigned homework. We had to report about a family tradition. Someone yelled, "Win, find out why you have such a funny name!" I thought it was a great idea, and it would not take much research.

When I got home, I asked my grandfather about the history of our name.

"We are named after my two grandfathers," he told me. "One was John Wilbur. He was a quiet man, but he was a hero. He helped rescue six people from a burning factory.

"My other grandfather was a famous explorer, Frederick Newton. He climbed mountains and explored rivers. There is a lake near my hometown named in his honor. Our middle name comes from Isaac Newton, the great mathematician and scientist."

"Wow!" I thought proudly. "I was named after some amazing people! Maybe the name Wilbur Isaac Newton the Third isn't so bad."

When I got off the phone, Dad found some old photos of my great-grandfathers. I couldn't wait to show the pictures to my class.

I did have one more question, though. "Dad, why do you call me Win?"

He laughed, "That's easy. The *W* is for *Wilbur*, the *I* is for *Isaac*, and the *N* is for *Newton*. Put them all together and they spell *Win*!"

© Hampton-Brown

GO ON ➤

COMPREHENSION / CRITICAL THINKING

19 Look at the chart. What <u>action</u> goes on the line for number 19?

  Ⓐ Win writes a report.

  Ⓑ Win says, "Call me Win."

  Ⓒ Win calls his grandfather.

  Ⓓ Win goes to a different class.

20 Look at the chart. What <u>feeling</u> goes on the line for number 20?

  Ⓕ Win feels sad.

  Ⓖ Win feels angry.

  Ⓗ Win feels proud.

  Ⓙ Win feels interested.

Character Chart

Events →	Win's Feelings →	Win's Actions
The teacher calls Win's real name.	Win feels embarrassed.	19
Someone yells, "Win, find out why you have such a funny name!"	20	Win asks his grandfather about their name.

21 Why does Win ask his grandfather about their name?

  Ⓐ He wants to laugh at him.

  Ⓑ He wants to learn about his name.

  Ⓒ He wants to make his father happy.

  Ⓓ He wants to explore lakes and rivers.

22 After Win talks to his grandfather, Win feels —

  Ⓕ angry at his teacher

  Ⓖ proud of his family name

  Ⓗ embarrassed by his father

  Ⓙ interested in his friends' names

23 Which sentence is an opinion?

  Ⓐ It is a dumb family tradition.

  Ⓑ We are named after my two grandfathers.

  Ⓒ He climbed mountains and explored rivers.

  Ⓓ My father's name is Wilbur Isaac Newton the Second.

© Hampton-Brown

GO ON ➡

COMPREHENSION / CRITICAL THINKING

DIRECTIONS Read the selection. Then read each item. Choose the best answer. Mark your answer. *(4 points each)*

Famous Singer Visits Wilson School

Last Friday, students enjoyed a special concert at Wilson School. Cecilia Sánchez played the guitar and sang for almost an hour. The students clapped and cheered when the concert ended.

"She is the best singer in the world!" said Rubén Garza. Many other students agreed.

"She writes wonderful songs!" said Jane Yokoi.

After the concert, Ms. Sánchez visited a fourth-grade class. The students asked many questions. Here are some of her answers.

GO ON ➡

COMPREHENSION / CRITICAL THINKING

Famous Singer Visits Wilson School, continued

Question: When did you learn to play the guitar?

Answer: I learned to play when I was very young. My family lived in a small village in Mexico. My father played the guitar almost every night. Friends and relatives often came to our house to sing and play the guitar. I was very eager to join them! I started to play as soon as my hands were big enough to hold a guitar.

Question: What songs do you like best?

Answer: My favorite songs are the old ones from Mexico. They are very beautiful and communicate deep feelings that people share, like sadness, joy, and love. I like many other kinds of music, too, including songs from all over the world.

Question: Do you still live in Mexico?

Answer: No, I moved to California ten years ago. California is a terrific place for a singer like me. Every day I meet people from all over the world. Every day I learn new songs.

GO ON ➡

24 Which of these sentences is an opinion about Cecilia Sánchez?

Ⓕ She plays the guitar and sings.

Ⓖ She is the best singer in the world.

Ⓗ Students asked her many questions.

Ⓙ She lived in Mexico when she was young.

25 Which of these sentences states a fact?

Ⓐ California is a terrific place.

Ⓑ Old songs are the best songs.

Ⓒ Mexican songs are very beautiful.

Ⓓ Cecilia Sánchez moved to California.

26 Which of these sentences is an opinion?

Ⓕ She writes wonderful songs.

Ⓖ Cecilia Sánchez plays the guitar.

Ⓗ The concert happened on Friday.

Ⓙ The students clapped after the concert.

27 Ms. Sánchez sings to —

Ⓐ show people how to dance

Ⓑ explain how people make money

Ⓒ describe interesting places where people live

Ⓓ communicate deep feelings that people share

STOP

Unit 1 • Answer Key

ⓑ Beginning Progress Test

VOCABULARY
(4 points each)

1 Ⓓ   4 Ⓕ
2 Ⓗ   5 Ⓑ
3 Ⓑ   6 Ⓖ

GRAMMAR
(4 points each)

7 Ⓑ   11 Ⓐ
8 Ⓕ   12 Ⓗ
9 Ⓑ   13 Ⓑ
10 Ⓗ

**COMPREHENSION /
CRITICAL THINKING**
(6 points each)

14 Ⓗ   18 Ⓗ
15 Ⓐ   19 Ⓑ
16 Ⓖ   20 Ⓖ
17 Ⓐ   21 Ⓐ

ⓘ Intermediate Progress Test

VOCABULARY
(4 points each)

1 Ⓓ   6 Ⓙ
2 Ⓗ   7 Ⓑ
3 Ⓓ   8 Ⓙ
4 Ⓖ   9 Ⓒ
5 Ⓒ   10 Ⓕ

GRAMMAR
(3 points each)

11 Ⓒ   15 Ⓑ
12 Ⓖ   16 Ⓗ
13 Ⓓ   17 Ⓓ
14 Ⓖ   18 Ⓗ

**COMPREHENSION /
CRITICAL THINKING**
(4 points each)

19 Ⓓ   24 Ⓗ
20 Ⓕ   25 Ⓓ
21 Ⓑ   26 Ⓖ
22 Ⓖ   27 Ⓓ
23 Ⓐ

ⓐ Advanced Progress Test

VOCABULARY
(4 points each)

1 Ⓒ   6 Ⓙ
2 Ⓗ   7 Ⓑ
3 Ⓓ   8 Ⓙ
4 Ⓖ   9 Ⓒ
5 Ⓒ   10 Ⓖ

GRAMMAR
(3 points each)

11 Ⓒ   15 Ⓑ
12 Ⓕ   16 Ⓗ
13 Ⓒ   17 Ⓓ
14 Ⓖ   18 Ⓗ

**COMPREHENSION /
CRITICAL THINKING**
(4 points each)

19 Ⓑ   24 Ⓖ
20 Ⓙ   25 Ⓓ
21 Ⓑ   26 Ⓕ
22 Ⓖ   27 Ⓓ
23 Ⓐ

Unit 1 • Self-Assessment

I Can Speak English!

1. I learned to tell how I feel.

When I read "If the Shoe Fits,"

I felt _____.

2. I learned to tell what I need.

I need _____.

3. I can ask and answer questions.

Question: _____ is your favorite

character?

Answer: My favorite character

is _____.

I Can Read in English!

4. As I read, I think about why people do things.

☐ yes   ☐ not yet

5. I can tell how a character feels and how that character acts because of those feelings.

Event	→	Rigo's Feelings	→	Rigo's Actions
In "If the Shoe Fits," Angel says Rigo's shoes are stupid.		Rigo feels ____.		Rigo ____.

My New Words

_____

_____

_____

_____

_____

_____

_____

What I've Read

☐ If the Shoe Fits

☐ In Gary Soto's Shoes

☐ _____

☐ _____

© Hampton-Brown

Distribute the test pages. Before students begin each subtest, read aloud the directions and use the script to work through each sample item.

VOCABULARY

Read aloud the directions on page 12. Then work through the sample item. Say:

Sample

Look at the pictures in the box. Which picture shows a jacket? Point to the picture. (Pause.) *The second bubble is filled in because the second picture shows a jacket.*

Items 1–6

Read each question aloud. Provide time for students to mark their answers.

GRAMMAR

Read aloud the directions on page 14. Then work through the sample item. Say:

Sample

Look at the picture in the box. Now read the sentence. (Pause.) *Which word goes in the blank? Let's try each one:*

> This for *is called Little Turtle.*
> This boy *is called Little Turtle.*
> This fast *is called Little Turtle.*
> This take *is called Little Turtle.*

The second bubble is filled in because boy *is the best answer.*

Items 7–13

Read aloud each sentence and its answer choices. Provide time for students to mark their answers.

COMPREHENSION / CRITICAL THINKING

Selection 1 and Items 14–17

Read aloud the directions on page 16. Say: *Now listen to the selection.*

Look at Picture 1.   Long ago, the sun was far away. The animals lived in the dark. Every day was dark.

COMPREHENSION / CRITICAL THINKING   continued

Look at Picture 2.   Squirrel found the sun far away. She took a piece of the sun and put it in her tail. The sun burned her tail. So Squirrel dropped the piece of sun.

Look at Picture 3.   Then Grandmother Spider went to the sun. She took a piece of the sun and put it in her web. The sun did not burn the web!

Look at Picture 4.   Grandmother Spider took the sun to the animals. Now the days are light, and the animals are happy.

Then read each question aloud. Provide time for students to mark their answers.

Selection 2 and Items 18–21

Read aloud the directions on page 18. Say: *Now listen to the selection. The title is:*

Cliff Houses

Look at the first picture.   Long ago, some Native peoples built houses on cliffs. A cliff is a flat place on the side of a mountain.

Look at the next picture.   Life in cliff houses was hard. People climbed up and down the mountain to get home. They carried all their food and water up and down ladders, too.

Look at the next picture.   A cliff house was very different from a temporary house like a tipi. It was made of rocks and mud. People could not move it to a new place.

Look at the last picture.   Cliff houses are still on some cliffs. You can visit these old homes. You can see some old walls and ladders. Native peoples made them long ago.

Then read each question aloud. Provide time for students to mark their answers.

Unit 2 • Directions for ❶ and Ⓐ Progress Tests

Distribute the test pages. Before students begin each subtest, read aloud the directions and use the script to work through each sample item.

VOCABULARY

Read aloud the directions on page 12. Then work through the sample item. Say:

Sample

Read the sentence in the box. (Pause.) *Which word goes in the blank? Let's try each one:*

> Carlo wears his new car *to school.*
> Carlo wears his new book *to school.*
> Carlo wears his new jacket *to school.*
> Carlo wears his new building *to school.*

The third bubble is filled in because jacket *is the best answer.*

Items 1–10

Tell students to complete the remaining items in the same way. Provide time for students to mark their answers.

GRAMMAR

Read aloud the directions on page 14. Then work through the sample item. Say:

Sample

Read the sentence. (Pause.) *Which word goes in the blank? Let's try each one:*

> Once there was a for *named Little Turtle.*
> Once there was a boy *named Little Turtle.*
> Once there was a fast *named Little Turtle.*
> Once there was a take *named Little Turtle.*

The second bubble is filled in because boy *is the best answer.*

Items 11–14

Tell students to complete the remaining items in the same way. Provide time for them to mark their answers.

GRAMMAR continued

Read aloud the directions on page 15. Then work through the sample item. Say:

Sample

Read the sentence. (Pause.) *What is the best way to write the underlined part? Look at the four choices. The third answer shows the correct way to write the words. That is why the third bubble is filled in.*

Items 15–18

Tell students to complete the remaining items in the same way. Provide time for them to mark their answers.

COMPREHENSION / CRITICAL THINKING

Selections and Items 19–30

Read aloud the directions for each selection. Provide time for students to read the selections and mark their answers.

Unit 2 • Student Profile for Beginning Progress Test

DIRECTIONS Record the student's name and test date. Use the **Answer Key** on page 21a to score the student's test. Then, in the Student Profile, circle the item number of each correct answer and circle the plus or minus sign to indicate mastery. Calculate the subtest scores and then the total test score. To help you group students for reteaching, transfer the minus sign for any unmastered skill to the **Class Profile** (page 12f).

Student Name _____ **Date** _____

Subtest	Tested Skills	ITEM ANALYSIS		TEST SCORES
		Item Numbers	**Mastery**	**No. Correct × Points = Score**
VOCABULARY	Key Words	1 2 3 4 5 6	5 out of 6 + −	_____ × 4 = ⧄24
GRAMMAR	Nouns	7 8 9 10 11 12 13	6 out of 7 + −	_____ × 4 = ⧄28
COMPREHENSION / CRITICAL THINKING	Make Comparisons	14 15 16 21	3 out of 4 + −	_____ × 6 = ⧄48
	Relate Main Idea and Details	17 18 19 20	3 out of 4 + −	
			TOTAL UNIT 2 PROGRESS TEST	⧄100

Unit 2 • Student Profile for Intermediate Progress Test

DIRECTIONS Record the student's name and test date. Use the **Answer Key** on page 21a to score the student's test. Then, in the Student Profile, circle the item number of each correct answer and circle the plus or minus sign to indicate mastery. Calculate the subtest scores and then the total test score. To help you group students for reteaching, transfer the minus sign for any unmastered skill to the **Class Profile** (page 12f).

Student Name _____ **Date** _____

Subtest	Tested Skills	ITEM ANALYSIS		TEST SCORES
		Item Numbers	Mastery	No. Correct × Points = Score
VOCABULARY	Key Words	1 2 3 4 5 6 7 8 9 10	8 out of 10 + −	_____ × 4 = ⬚/40
GRAMMAR	Nouns	11 12 13 14 15 16 17 18	6 out of 8 + −	_____ × 3 = ⬚/24
COMPREHENSION / CRITICAL THINKING	Make Comparisons	24 25 26 27	3 out of 4 + −	_____ × 3 = ⬚/36
	Relate Main Idea and Details	23 28 29 30	3 out of 4 + −	
	Relate Problem and Solution	19 20 21 22	3 out of 4 + −	
			TOTAL UNIT 2 PROGRESS TEST	⬚/100

DIRECTIONS Record the student's name and test date. Use the **Answer Key** on page 21a to score the student's test. Then, in the Student Profile, circle the item number of each correct answer and circle the plus or minus sign to indicate mastery. Calculate the subtest scores and then the total test score. To help you group students for reteaching, transfer the minus sign for any unmastered skill to the **Class Profile** (page 12f).

Student Name _____ Date _____

Subtest	Tested Skills	ITEM ANALYSIS		TEST SCORES
		Item Numbers	Mastery	No. Correct × Points = Score
VOCABULARY	Key Words	1 2 3 4 5 6 7 8 9 10	8 out of 10 + −	_____ × 4 = /40
GRAMMAR	Nouns	11 12 13 14 15 16 17 18	6 out of 8 + −	_____ × 3 = /24
COMPREHENSION / CRITICAL THINKING	Make Comparisons	24 25 26 29	3 out of 4 + −	_____ × 3 = /36
	Relate Main Idea and Details	23 27 28 30	3 out of 4 + −	
	Relate Problem and Solution	19 20 21 22	3 out of 4 + −	
			TOTAL UNIT 2 PROGRESS TEST	/100

Unit 2 • Class Profile

Date _____

DIRECTIONS Use the **Unit 2 Student Profiles** to complete this chart. In each row, write the student's name, fill in the bubble for the test form taken, and mark a minus sign (–) for any skill not yet mastered. Then group students and use the reteaching ideas and practice exercises to help students reach mastery.

Student Name	Test Form	TESTED SKILLS				
		Key Words	Nouns	Make Comparisons	Relate Main Idea and Details	Relate Problem and Solution
	Ⓑ Ⓘ Ⓐ					
	Ⓑ Ⓘ Ⓐ					
	Ⓑ Ⓘ Ⓐ					
	Ⓑ Ⓘ Ⓐ					
	Ⓑ Ⓘ Ⓐ					
	Ⓑ Ⓘ Ⓐ					
	Ⓑ Ⓘ Ⓐ					
	Ⓑ Ⓘ Ⓐ					
	Ⓑ Ⓘ Ⓐ					
	Ⓑ Ⓘ Ⓐ					
	Ⓑ Ⓘ Ⓐ					
	Ⓑ Ⓘ Ⓐ					
	Ⓑ Ⓘ Ⓐ					
	Ⓑ Ⓘ Ⓐ					
	Ⓑ Ⓘ Ⓐ					
	Ⓑ Ⓘ Ⓐ					
	Ⓑ Ⓘ Ⓐ					
	Ⓑ Ⓘ Ⓐ					
	Ⓑ Ⓘ Ⓐ					
	Ⓑ Ⓘ Ⓐ					
	Ⓑ Ⓘ Ⓐ					
	Ⓑ Ⓘ Ⓐ					
RETEACHING RESOURCES		Ⓑ Ⓘ Ⓐ AH T38	Ⓑ AH T40 Ⓘ Ⓐ EAYC 239–245	Ⓑ Ⓘ Ⓐ LB TG	Ⓑ Ⓘ Ⓐ LB TG	Ⓘ Ⓐ LB TG
PRACTICE EXERCISES		PB 19, 25	EAYC 383–386	PB 31	PB 22–23	PB 21

KEY: **AH:** Assessment Handbook   **EAYC:** English at Your Command!
LB TG: Leveled Books Teacher's Guide   **PB:** Practice Book

Unit 2 • Native Land

VOCABULARY

DIRECTIONS Listen to each question. Then choose the correct picture.
Mark your answer. *(4 points each)*

⭐**Sample**

Which picture shows a <u>jacket</u>?

Ⓐ   **B**   Ⓒ   Ⓓ

1   Which picture shows a <u>chief</u>?

Ⓐ   Ⓑ   Ⓒ   Ⓓ

2   Which picture shows a <u>village</u>?

Ⓕ   Ⓖ   Ⓗ   Ⓙ

3   Which picture shows a <u>frame</u>?

Ⓐ   Ⓑ   Ⓒ   Ⓓ

GO ON ➡️

VOCABULARY

4 Which home is <u>permanent</u>?

     Ⓕ   Ⓖ   Ⓗ   Ⓙ

5 Find the arrow in each picture. Which arrow points to a <u>pole</u>?

     Ⓐ   Ⓑ   Ⓒ   Ⓓ

6 Find the arrow in each picture. Which arrow points to a <u>region</u>?

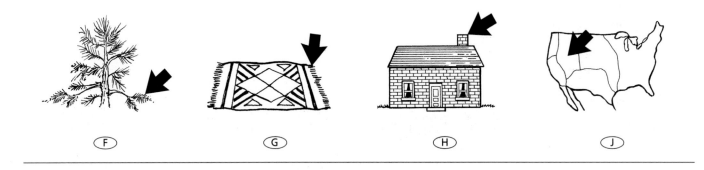

     Ⓕ   Ⓖ   Ⓗ   Ⓙ

STOP

© Hampton-Brown

GRAMMAR

DIRECTIONS Look at the picture. Listen to the sentence with each answer. Choose the word or words that complete the sentence correctly. **Mark your answer.** *(4 points each)*

Sample

This _____ is called Little Turtle.

- Ⓐ for
- Ⓑ boy
- Ⓒ fast
- Ⓓ take

7 Little Turtle lives in a part of the _____.

- Ⓐ united states
- Ⓑ united States
- Ⓒ United states
- Ⓓ United States

8 His likes to swim in the _____.

- Ⓕ wabash river
- Ⓖ Wabash river
- Ⓗ wabash River
- Ⓙ Wabash River

9 His dad uses a _____ on the lake.

- Ⓐ on
- Ⓑ hunt
- Ⓒ boat
- Ⓓ some

10 Dad catches a _____ for dinner.

- Ⓕ eat
- Ⓖ tall
- Ⓗ fish
- Ⓙ over

© Hampton-Brown

GO ON ➡

GRAMMAR

11 People in his village make beautiful _____.

- Ⓐ basket
- Ⓑ baskets
- Ⓒ basketes
- Ⓓ basketies

12 Sometimes the children ride _____.

- Ⓕ pony
- Ⓖ ponys
- Ⓗ ponies
- Ⓙ ponyes

13 Little Turtle sleeps in a _____.

- Ⓐ tipi
- Ⓑ high
- Ⓒ many
- Ⓓ under

STOP

COMPREHENSION / CRITICAL THINKING

DIRECTIONS Listen to the selection. Then listen to each question.
Choose the best answer. Mark your answer *(6 points each)*

1

Long ago, the sun was far away. The animals lived in the dark. Every day was dark.

2

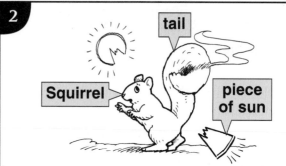

Squirrel found the sun far away. She took a piece of the sun and put it in her tail. The sun burned her tail. So squirrel dropped the piece of sun.

3

Then Grandmother Spider went to the sun. She took a piece of the sun and put it in her web. The sun did not burn the web!

4

Grandmother Spider took the sun to the animals. Now the days are light, and the animals are happy.

© Hampton-Brown

GO ON ➡

COMPREHENSION / CRITICAL THINKING

14 Squirrel and Grandmother Spider are alike.
They try to get a piece of the —

Ⓕ   Ⓖ   Ⓗ   Ⓙ

15 Who tries to bring the sun home?

Squirrel only   Grandmother Spider only   both Squirrel and Grandmother Spider

Ⓐ   Ⓑ   Ⓒ

16 Who brings the sun home?

Squirrel only   Grandmother Spider only   both Squirrel and Grandmother Spider

Ⓕ   Ⓖ   Ⓗ

17 What is a good title for this selection?

How the
Animals Got Light

Why Squirrel
Dropped the Sun

Why Spiders
Live in the Dark

Ⓐ   Ⓑ   Ⓒ

GO ON ➡

DIRECTIONS Listen to the selection. Then listen to each question.
Choose the best answer. Mark your answer. *(6 points each)*

Cliff Houses

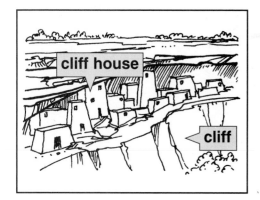

Long ago, some Native peoples built houses on cliffs. A cliff is a flat place on the side of a mountain.

Life in cliff houses was hard. People climbed up and down the mountain to get home. They carried all their food and water up and down ladders, too.

A cliff house was very different from a temporary house like a tipi. It was made of rocks and mud. People could not move it to a new place.

Cliff houses are still on some cliffs. You can visit these old homes. You can see some old walls and ladders. Native peoples made them long ago.

© Hampton-Brown

GO ON

COMPREHENSION / CRITICAL THINKING

18 What is the selection mostly about?

Ⓕ   Ⓖ   Ⓗ   Ⓙ

19 Look at the web. What word goes on the line?

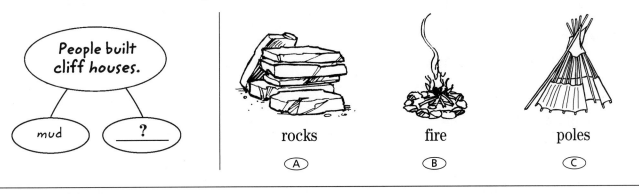

People built cliff houses.

mud   ?

rocks   fire   poles

Ⓐ   Ⓑ   Ⓒ

20 Look at the web. Which of these goes on the line?

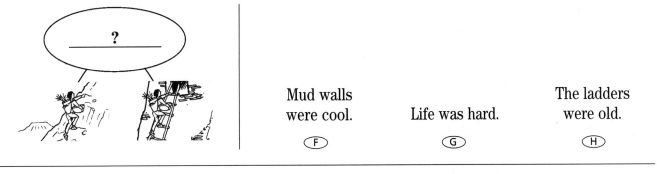

?

Mud walls were cool.   Life was hard.   The ladders were old.

Ⓕ   Ⓖ   Ⓗ

21 Which of these is easy to move?

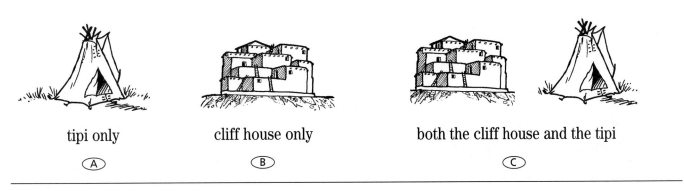

tipi only   cliff house only   both the cliff house and the tipi

Ⓐ   Ⓑ   Ⓒ

STOP

Unit 2 • Native Land

DIRECTIONS Read the sentence. Choose the word or words that go in the blank. Mark your answer. *(4 points each)*

⭐ **Sample**

Carlo wears his new _____ to school.

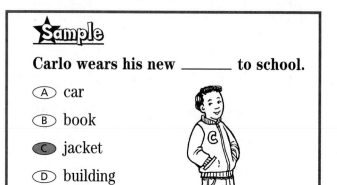

- Ⓐ car
- Ⓑ book
- 🅒 jacket
- Ⓓ building

---

1 They listen to their wise _____.

- Ⓐ play
- Ⓑ path
- Ⓒ chief
- Ⓓ track

2 Long _____ hold up a tipi.

- Ⓕ fires
- Ⓖ poles
- Ⓗ arrows
- Ⓙ flowers

3 The house has a wooden _____.

- Ⓐ idea
- Ⓑ cloth
- Ⓒ frame
- Ⓓ straw

4 There are five homes in our _____.

- Ⓕ cloud
- Ⓖ sheet
- Ⓗ village
- Ⓙ mixture

5 Everyone says "yes" to the idea. They are _____.

- Ⓐ agreed
- Ⓑ covered
- Ⓒ different
- Ⓓ outgrown

Yes	No
卌 卌	
卌 ‖	
17	0

GO ON ➡️

VOCABULARY

6 I had to _____ the basket because it was falling.

- Ⓕ get into
- Ⓖ open up
- Ⓗ push up
- Ⓙ bring out

7 Our new house was made out of strong _____.

- Ⓐ legs
- Ⓑ hope
- Ⓒ order
- Ⓓ material

8 People in the Intermountain _____ make beautiful baskets.

- Ⓕ craft
- Ⓖ region
- Ⓗ branch
- Ⓙ blanket

9 He gave us a _____ to stop.

- Ⓐ plant
- Ⓑ signal
- Ⓒ buffalo
- Ⓓ tradition

10 A _____ home can be moved easily.

- Ⓕ mud
- Ⓖ stone
- Ⓗ colorful
- Ⓙ temporary

STOP

GRAMMAR

DIRECTIONS Read the sentences. Choose the word or words that go in each blank. Mark your answer. *(3 points each)*

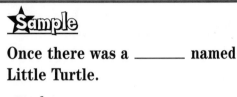

Once there was a _____ named Little Turtle.

ⓐ for

● boy

ⓒ fast

ⓓ take

11 Little Turtle lived in a _____ near a river.

ⓐ tipi

ⓑ high

ⓒ many

ⓓ under

12 The river was called the _____.

ⓕ wabash river

ⓖ Wabash river

ⓗ wabash River

ⓙ Wabash River

13 The children in _____ village played by the river.

ⓐ Little Turtle

ⓑ Little Turtles

ⓒ Little Turtle's

ⓓ Little Turtlies

14 They also rode their _____ beside the river.

ⓕ pony

ⓖ ponys

ⓗ pony's

ⓙ ponies

STOP

GRAMMAR

DIRECTIONS Read the sentences. Choose the best way to write each underlined part, or choose "Correct as it is." Mark your answer.
(3 points each)

 Sample

Miki Schwartz traveled to america from germany.

  Ⓐ america from Germany

  Ⓑ America from germany

  🅲 America from Germany

  Ⓓ Correct as it is

15 Her family lived on a farm near **Omaha, Nebraska**.

  Ⓐ omaha, nebraska

  Ⓑ omaha, Nebraska

  Ⓒ Omaha, nebraska

  Ⓓ Correct as it is

16 Some Sioux people lived near her **familys** farm.

  Ⓕ family's

  Ⓖ familys'

  Ⓗ families

  Ⓙ Correct as it is

17 **Miki** family did not know the Sioux language.

  Ⓐ Mikis

  Ⓑ Miki's

  Ⓒ Mikies

  Ⓓ Correct as it is

18 The children used their **handes** to talk to each other.

  Ⓕ hand

  Ⓖ hands

  Ⓗ hand's

  Ⓙ Correct as it is

© Hampton-Brown

STOP

DIRECTIONS Read the two selections. Then read each item.
Choose the best answer. Mark your answer. *(3 points each)*

Grandmother Spider

Long ago, many animals lived in darkness. Squirrel tried to get them some sun. She hid a piece of it in her tail, but the sun burned her tail. Squirrel dropped the sun.

Then Grandmother Spider tried. She put a piece of sun in her web. The sun did not burn the web. Grandmother Spider brought the sun home and made the animals happy.

web

Squirrel

**Grandmother
Spider**

Rabbit's Tale

Long ago, a part of the world was dark. Brave Rabbit wanted to bring sunshine to all the animals. So, she went to the sun. She tied an arrow to a rope and shot it at the sun. The sun burned up the arrow. Rabbit sat and cried.

Rabbit's tears wet the other arrows, but she did not give up. She shot a wet arrow at the sun. The sun did not burn it! Rabbit pulled the sun to the animals.

arrow

Rabbit

© Hampton-Brown

GO ON ➤

19 **What is the problem in both selections?**

Ⓐ The animals need to rest.

Ⓑ The sun burns the arrows.

Ⓒ The animals live in darkness.

Ⓓ The sun does not like the animals.

20 **How does Squirrel try to help?**

Ⓕ Squirrel tells the sun to shine.

Ⓖ Squirrel pulls the sun to the animals.

Ⓗ Squirrel hides a piece of the sun in her tail.

Ⓙ Squirrel asks Grandmother Spider to bring the sun.

21 **To help the animals, Grandmother Spider —**

Ⓐ hides the sun

Ⓑ puts a piece of the sun in a web

Ⓒ moves the sun to the top of a mountain

Ⓓ tells Rabbit to break off a piece of the sun

22 **How does Rabbit try to get the sun to the animals?**

Ⓕ She shoots arrows at the sun.

Ⓖ She cuts off a piece of the sun.

Ⓗ She ties a rope around the sun.

Ⓙ She asks the sun to visit the animals.

23 **What lesson does Rabbit teach the animals?**

Ⓐ Keep running.

Ⓑ Never give up.

Ⓒ Make strong webs.

Ⓓ Stay away from the sun.

24 **Both Grandmother Spider and Rabbit are —**

Ⓕ sad and alone

Ⓖ angry and tired

Ⓗ smart and brave

Ⓙ beautiful and funny

GO ON ➡

COMPREHENSION / CRITICAL THINKING

DIRECTIONS Read the selection. Then read each item. Choose the best answer. Mark your answer. *(3 points each)*

Sarah Winnemucca

1   Sarah Winnemucca was born in 1844. She was a Native American. Her people were called the Northern Paiute. She lived in a desert we now call Nevada. Only a few plants and animals lived there. The Paiute people ate pine nuts from the trees. They hunted deer and rabbits.

Nevada before the English settlers came

2   Then life changed for the Paiute people. English settlers came to live nearby. They cut down trees and built fences to keep their cattle together. The trees, deer, and rabbits were gone. The Paiute people were hungry.

3   Some Paiute people wanted to fight with the settlers. Sarah's grandfather was different. He wanted to be friends with them. He sent Sarah to live with a new family. Sarah learned English from them.

4   Sarah grew up. She tried to help everyone understand each other and be friends. She spoke to the English leaders to share the Paiute people's ideas. Many people called her "the voice of her people."

Nevada after the English settlers came

© Hampton-Brown

GO ON ➡

COMPREHENSION / CRITICAL THINKING

25 **Look at the chart. How were the Paiute people and the settlers the same?**

(A) Both raised cattle.

(B) Both ate pine nuts.

(C) Both spoke English.

(D) Both lived in the desert.

Comparison Chart

	Land	Food	Language
Paiute People	desert pine trees	pine nuts deer rabbits	Paiute
Settlers	desert fences ranches	cattle	English

26 **How was the land different after the settlers came?**

(F) All the rivers dried up.

(G) The trees disappeared.

(H) The desert became too wet.

(J) A new forest started to grow.

27 **Both Sarah and her grandfather —**

(A) spoke English

(B) spoke for the Paiute people

(C) wanted the settlers to go away

(D) wanted the people to understand each other

28 **What is paragraph 2 mostly about?**

(F) Cattle lived on the land.

(G) The settlers built fences.

(H) The Paiute people were hungry.

(J) Life changed for the Paiute people.

29 **What is the selection mostly about?**

(A) cattle

(B) Nevada

(C) Sarah Winnemucca

(D) Sarah's grandfather

30 **Read this main idea.**

> Sarah Winnemucca had special skills.

Which of these details tells more about this main idea?

(F) Sarah grew up.

(G) Sarah was born in 1844.

(H) Sarah ate rabbits and deer.

(J) Sarah spoke two languages.

STOP

Unit 2 • Native Land

DIRECTIONS Read the sentence. Choose the word or words that go in the blank. Mark your answer. *(4 points each)*

Sample

Carlo wears his new _____ to school.

Ⓐ car

Ⓑ book

● jacket

Ⓓ building

1 Everyone listened to their wise _____ .

Ⓐ play

Ⓑ path

Ⓒ chief

Ⓓ track

2 Long _____ hold up a tipi.

Ⓕ fires

Ⓖ poles

Ⓗ arrows

Ⓙ flowers

3 The house has a wooden _____ .

Ⓐ idea

Ⓑ cloth

Ⓒ straw

Ⓓ frame

4 All the people in the _____ cooked food for the feast.

Ⓕ cloud

Ⓖ sheet

Ⓗ village

Ⓙ mixture

5 Everyone says "yes" to the idea. They are _____ .

Ⓐ agreed

Ⓑ covered

Ⓒ different

Ⓓ outgrown

GO ON ➡

6 All the members of my _____ have the same ancestors.

- Ⓕ club
- Ⓖ style
- Ⓗ tribe
- Ⓙ class

7 The new house was made out of strong _____.

- Ⓐ history
- Ⓑ material
- Ⓒ experience
- Ⓓ imagination

8 People in the Intermountain _____ make beautiful baskets.

- Ⓕ craft
- Ⓖ region
- Ⓗ branch
- Ⓙ blanket

9 The leader gave a _____ to tell the people what to do.

- Ⓐ signal
- Ⓑ forest
- Ⓒ problem
- Ⓓ longhouse

10 We built a _____ house so we can move it easily.

- Ⓕ large
- Ⓖ stone
- Ⓗ colorful
- Ⓙ temporary

STOP

GRAMMAR

DIRECTIONS Read the sentences. Choose the word or words that go in each blank. Mark your answer. *(3 points each)*

Once there was a ___Sample___ named Little Turtle. He lived in a ___11___

near a gentle river. The river was called the ___12___. Little Turtle loved his

home, but he had one wish. He wanted a pony.

A rich man named Strong Wind lived in ___13___ village. Strong Wind

had many ___14___. "If you win the race tomorrow," Strong Wind told

Little Turtle,. "You will receive a pony." Now Little Turtle had a chance

to make his wish come true!

Sample

Ⓐ for

🅑 boy

Ⓒ fast

Ⓓ take

11 Ⓐ tipi

 Ⓑ high

 Ⓒ many

 Ⓓ under

12 Ⓕ wabash river

 Ⓖ Wabash river

 Ⓗ wabash River

 Ⓙ Wabash River

13 Ⓐ Little Turtle

 Ⓑ Little Turtles

 Ⓒ Little Turtle's

 Ⓓ Little Turtlies

14 Ⓕ pony

 Ⓖ ponys

 Ⓗ pony's

 Ⓙ ponies

STOP

GRAMMAR

DIRECTIONS Read the sentences. Choose the best way to write each underlined part, or choose "Correct as it is." Mark your answer.
(3 points each)

Miki Schwartz traveled to <u>america from germany</u>. <u>Miki</u> family
　　　　　　　　　　　　　　　★Sample　　　　　　　　15
spoke German.

　　Miki and her family lived on a farm near <u>Omaha, Nebraska</u>. A tribe of
　　　　　　　　　　　　　　　　　　　　　　　16
Sioux people lived near the <u>familys</u> farm. Miki wanted to talk to the Sioux
　　　　　　　　　　　　　　17
children, but they didn't speak German. So, Miki and the Sioux children

spoke to each other with their <u>handes</u>. They used sign language to
　　　　　　　　　　　　　　　18
communicate.

★Sample

Ⓐ america from Germany

Ⓑ America from germany

● America from Germany

Ⓓ Correct as it is

15 Ⓐ Mikis

　　Ⓑ Miki's

　　Ⓒ Mikies

　　Ⓓ Correct as it is

16 Ⓕ omaha, nebraska

　　Ⓖ omaha, Nebraska

　　Ⓗ Omaha, nebraska

　　Ⓙ Correct as it is

17 Ⓐ family's

　　Ⓑ familys'

　　Ⓒ families

　　Ⓓ Correct as it is

18 Ⓕ hand

　　Ⓖ hands

　　Ⓗ hand's

　　Ⓙ Correct as it is

STOP

COMPREHENSION / CRITICAL THINKING

DIRECTIONS Read the two selections. Then read each item.
Choose the best answer. Mark your answer. *(3 points each)*

Grandmother Spider

Long ago, many animals lived in darkness because the sun was far away on the other side of the world.

"I will go find the sun and bring back a piece of it," said Fox.

Fox traveled to the other side of the world and grabbed a piece of the sun in his mouth. However, the sun was so hot that Fox dropped it and came back without it.

Then Squirrel said "I will go find the sun and bring back a piece of it."

Squirrel found the sun and broke off a chunk. She hid the chunk in her bushy tail. However, the sun was so hot that Squirrel dropped it and returned without it.

Grandmother Spider wondered how she could help. Was her web strong enough to hold a piece of the sun? Grandmother Spider made the journey to the sun, broke off a piece, and put it in her web. The sun was very hot, but it did not burn through the web. Grandmother Spider brought the sun to the animals.

Now the sun shines every day, and all the animals are happy.

© Hampton-Brown

GO ON ▶

Rabbit's Tale

Long ago, many animals lived in darkness near the sea. The sun did not like the sea and stayed far away.

arrow

Rabbit

"I will go to the sun and bring it here," said Rabbit.

"That is impossible!" said the other animals.

"Nothing is impossible, if you try hard," Rabbit bravely replied.

So, Rabbit went to the sun. She tied a long rope onto an arrow and shot it at the sun, but the sun burned up the rope and arrow.

Rabbit shot more arrows, but the sun destroyed every one. Rabbit began to weep. Soon the rest of the arrows and rope were soaked in tears, but Rabbit did not give up. She shot a wet arrow and hit the sun, but the sun could not burn the wet rope and arrow!

Rabbit pulled the sun toward the animals. The animals cheered when they saw the light. After a while, Rabbit became tired and stopped running. The sun sank into the sea, and the animals were in darkness again.

The next day, Rabbit pulled the sun out of the sea again.

"Now we can have light every day and rest at night," she said.

The animals saw that Rabbit was right, and they were happy.

GO ON ➡

COMPREHENSION / CRITICAL THINKING

19 **What is the problem in both selections?**

Ⓐ The sun does not like the sea.

Ⓑ Many animals live in darkness.

Ⓒ Many animals need to rest at night.

Ⓓ The sun burns the arrows and rope.

20 **In the first selection, what happens when Squirrel tries to solve the problem?**

Ⓕ Squirrel returns without the sun.

Ⓖ Squirrel carries the sun in her mouth.

Ⓗ Squirrel lets the sun sink into the sea.

Ⓙ Squirrel brings the sun to the animals.

21 **How does Grandmother Spider try to solve the problem?**

Ⓐ She hides the sun.

Ⓑ She runs away from the sun.

Ⓒ She puts a piece of the sun in a web.

Ⓓ She moves the sun to the top of a mountain.

22 **In the second selection, how does Rabbit try to solve the problem?**

Ⓕ She shoots arrows at the sun.

Ⓖ She cuts off a piece of the sun.

Ⓗ She puts a piece of the sun in her tail.

Ⓙ She carries the sun high up into the sky.

23 **What lesson does Rabbit teach the animals?**

Ⓐ Never give up.

Ⓑ Always keep running.

Ⓒ Use dry arrows and rope.

Ⓓ The sun does not like the sea.

24 **Both Grandmother Spider and Rabbit are —**

Ⓕ sad and alone

Ⓖ angry and tired

Ⓗ smart and brave

Ⓙ beautiful and funny

© Hampton-Brown

GO ON ➤

DIRECTIONS Read the selection. Then read each item. Choose the best answer. Mark your answer. *(3 points each)*

Sarah Winnemucca: Voice of Her People

1   Sarah Winnemucca was a Native American. Her people were called the Northern Paiute. She was born in 1844 in a desert area we now call Nevada. There was very little rainfall, and few things grew there. The Paiute people ate pine nuts from the trees and hunted deer and rabbits.

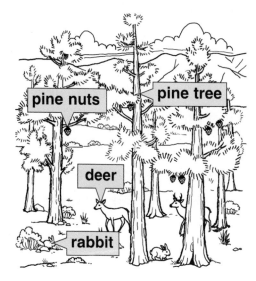

Nevada before the English settlers came

2   Then life for the Paiute people changed forever. When Sarah was a little girl, new people came to settle on the land where the Paiute nation lived. The settlers spoke English and did not live in the Paiute way. They cut down trees to build fences for their ranches. Now cattle lived on the land, but the trees, deer, and rabbits were gone. The Paiute people were hungry.

3   Some of the Paiute people wanted to fight with the settlers. They wanted to make the settlers leave. But Sarah's grandfather had a different idea. He believed that the Paiute people and the settlers could be friends.

Nevada after the English settlers came

© Hampton-Brown

GO ON ➡

Sarah Winnemucca: Voice of Her People, continued

4   Sarah's grandfather sent Sarah to live with a family that spoke English. He wanted her to learn their language and their way of life. Sarah learned fast, and soon she could read and write English very well.

5   More and more settlers came to the land where the Paiute nation lived and took away things that the Paiute people needed. Sarah wanted to help her people. She knew she could do one thing better than anyone else. She could use the English language to convince the government of the United States to help her people.

6   Sarah Winnemucca spent her life trying to help the Paiute nation and the United States settlers understand each other. Because she spoke for the Paiute nation, people called her "the voice of her people."

GO ON ➡

COMPREHENSION / CRITICAL THINKING

25 Look at the chart. What can you tell about the Paiute people and the settlers?

Ⓐ Both ate pine nuts.

Ⓑ Both spoke the Paiute language.

Ⓒ The Paiute people lived in a desert, but the settlers lived in a forest.

Ⓓ The settlers raised cattle, but the Paiute people hunted deer and rabbits.

Comparison Chart

	Land	Food	Language
Paiute People	desert pine trees	pine nuts deer rabbits	Paiute
Settlers	desert fences ranches	cattle	English

26 How was the land different after the settlers came?

Ⓕ The desert flooded.

Ⓖ All the rivers dried up.

Ⓗ The trees disappeared.

Ⓙ A new forest started to grow.

27 What is paragraph 2 mostly about?

Ⓐ Sarah was a little girl.

Ⓑ Cattle lived on the land.

Ⓒ The settlers built fences.

Ⓓ Life changed for the Paiute people.

28 What is paragraph 4 mostly about?

Ⓕ Sarah learned English.

Ⓖ Sarah helped the settlers.

Ⓗ Sarah went to live with her grandfather.

Ⓙ The Paiute people wanted to fight the settlers.

29 Both Sarah and her grandfather —

Ⓐ built fences for their ranch

Ⓑ wanted the settlers to leave the area

Ⓒ believed the Paiute people should give the settlers the land

Ⓓ wanted the Paiute people and the settlers to understand each other

30 Read this main idea.

Sarah Winnemucca had special skills.

Which of these details tells more about this main idea?

Ⓕ Sarah was born in 1844.

Ⓖ Sarah spoke two languages.

Ⓗ There was very little rainfall.

Ⓙ More settlers came to the land.

STOP

Unit 2 • Answer Key

ⓑ Beginning Progress Test

VOCABULARY
(4 points each)

1 Ⓐ   4 Ⓕ
2 Ⓗ   5 Ⓒ
3 Ⓑ   6 Ⓙ

GRAMMAR
(4 points each)

7 Ⓓ   11 Ⓑ
8 Ⓙ   12 Ⓗ
9 Ⓒ   13 Ⓐ
10 Ⓗ

COMPREHENSION / CRITICAL THINKING
(6 points each)

14 Ⓙ   18 Ⓗ
15 Ⓒ   19 Ⓐ
16 Ⓖ   20 Ⓖ
17 Ⓐ   21 Ⓐ

ⓘ Intermediate Progress Test

VOCABULARY
(4 points each)

1 Ⓒ   6 Ⓗ
2 Ⓖ   7 Ⓓ
3 Ⓒ   8 Ⓖ
4 Ⓗ   9 Ⓑ
5 Ⓐ   10 Ⓙ

GRAMMAR
(3 points each)

11 Ⓐ   15 Ⓓ
12 Ⓙ   16 Ⓕ
13 Ⓒ   17 Ⓑ
14 Ⓙ   18 Ⓖ

COMPREHENSION / CRITICAL THINKING
(3 points each)

19 Ⓒ   25 Ⓓ
20 Ⓗ   26 Ⓖ
21 Ⓑ   27 Ⓓ
22 Ⓕ   28 Ⓙ
23 Ⓑ   29 Ⓒ
24 Ⓗ   30 Ⓙ

ⓐ Advanced Progress Test

VOCABULARY
(4 points each)

1 Ⓒ   6 Ⓗ
2 Ⓖ   7 Ⓑ
3 Ⓓ   8 Ⓖ
4 Ⓗ   9 Ⓐ
5 Ⓐ   10 Ⓙ

GRAMMAR
(3 points each)

11 Ⓐ   15 Ⓑ
12 Ⓙ   16 Ⓙ
13 Ⓒ   17 Ⓐ
14 Ⓙ   18 Ⓖ

COMPREHENSION / CRITICAL THINKING
(3 points each)

19 Ⓑ   25 Ⓓ
20 Ⓕ   26 Ⓗ
21 Ⓒ   27 Ⓓ
22 Ⓕ   28 Ⓕ
23 Ⓐ   29 Ⓓ
24 Ⓗ   30 Ⓖ

Unit 2 • Self-Assessment

I Can Speak English!

1. I can tell my opinions and give reasons for them.

   I think plays are _____

   because _____ .

2. I can tell how two things are alike or different.

   A play is different from a story

   because _____ .

My New Words

I Can Read in English!

3. I can find ways things are alike and different.

   ☐ yes   ☐ not yet

4. I can tell the problem and solution in a story.

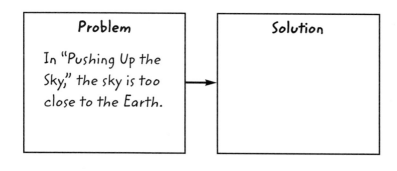

Problem	Solution
In "Pushing Up the Sky," the sky is too close to the Earth.	

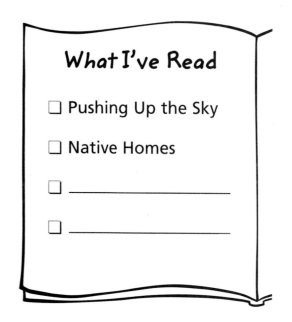

What I've Read

☐ Pushing Up the Sky

☐ Native Homes

☐ _____

☐ _____

Distribute the test pages. Before students begin each subtest, read aloud the directions and use the script to work through each sample item.

VOCABULARY

Read aloud the directions on page 23. Then work through the sample item. Say:

Sample

Look at the pictures in the box. Which picture shows a jacket? Point to the picture. (Pause.) *The second bubble is filled in because the second picture shows a jacket.*

Items 1–6

Read each question aloud. Provide time for students to mark their answers.

GRAMMAR

Read aloud the directions on page 25. Then work through the sample item. Say:

Sample

Look at the picture in the box. Look at the sentence. There is a word missing. Let's try each word. Listen:

> The weather is *very hot today.*
> The weather be *very hot today.*
> The weather are *very hot today.*
> The weather has *very hot today.*

The first bubble is filled in because is *is the best answer.*

Items 7–13

Read each item aloud. Repeat the sentence with the blank, inserting each answer choice so that students can hear the answer choice in context. Provide time for students to mark their answers.

COMPREHENSION / CRITICAL THINKING

Selection 1 and Items 14–17

Read aloud the directions on page 27. Say: *Now listen to the selection. The title is:*

A Storm at Night

Look at Picture 1. Snap! Boom! Crackle! Something outside wakes Luisa up. She calls to her sister, "Teresa, I'm scared!"

Look at Picture 2. The light goes on. Teresa asks, "What's wrong?"
"I am afraid of the noise," Luisa says.

Look at Picture 3. "The storm will not hurt you," Teresa says. She closes the window. "You are safe."

Look at Picture 4. Then Teresa says, "I will stay here until the storm ends." Soon Luisa goes to sleep.

Then read each question aloud. Provide time for students to mark their answers.

Selection 2 and Items 18–21

Read aloud the directions on page 29. Say: *Now listen to the selection. The title is:*

A Spring Blizzard

Look at the first picture. On March 31, 1997, people in New England have a surprise. It is spring. A blizzard arrives during the night.

Look at the next picture. The wind blows down trees and power lines. Many people do not have power.

Look at the next picture. Workers cannot clear the deep snow. Snowplows get stuck. Roads close. Cars and buses cannot go anywhere. On April 1, schools and airports close.

Look at the last picture. The blizzard stops on April 3. Finally, workers can clear the roads. They fix the power lines, too. People go back to work and to school.

Then read each question aloud. Provide time for students to mark their answers.

© Hampton-Brown

Unit 3 • Directions for ❶ and Ⓐ Progress Tests

Distribute the test pages. Before students begin each subtest, read aloud the directions and use the script to work through each sample item.

VOCABULARY

Read aloud the directions on page 23. Then work through the sample item. Say:

Sample

Read the sentence in the box. (Pause.) *Which word goes in the blank? Let's try each one:*

> Carlo wears his new car *to school.*
> Carlo wears his new book *to school.*
> Carlo wears his new jacket *to school.*
> Carlo wears his new building *to school.*

The third bubble is filled in because jacket *is the best answer.*

Items 1–6

Tell students to complete the remaining items in the same way. Provide time for students to mark their answers.

Read aloud the directions on page 24. Then work through the sample item. Say:

Sample

Read the sentence in the box. (Pause.) *In this sentence, what does the word* bat *mean? Read the three choices.* (Pause.) *The third bubble is filled in because in this sentence* bat *means* a small, furry animal with wings.

Items 7–10

Tell students to complete the remaining items in the same way. Provide time for them to mark their answers.

GRAMMAR

Read aloud the directions on page 25. Then work through the sample item. Say:

Sample

Read the sentence. (Pause.) *Which word goes in the blank? Let's try each one:*

> Lisa car *to school every morning.*
> Lisa fast *to school every morning.*
> Lisa walks *to school every morning.*
> Lisa above *to school every morning.*

The third bubble is filled in because walks *is the best answer.*

Items 11–14

Tell students to complete the remaining items in the same way. Provide time for them to mark their answers.

Read aloud the directions on page 26. Then work through the sample item. Say:

Sample

Read the sentence. (Pause.) *What is the best way to write the underlined part? Look at the four choices. The fourth bubble is filled in because the underlined part in the sentence is written correctly. It is* Correct as it is.

Items 15–18

Tell students to complete the remaining items in the same way. Provide time for them to mark their answers.

COMPREHENSION / CRITICAL THINKING

Selections and Items 19–30

Read aloud the directions for each selection. Provide time for students to read the selection and mark their answers.

Unit 3 • Student Profile for Beginning Progress Test

DIRECTIONS Record the student's name and test date. Use the **Answer Key** on page 32a to score the student's test. Then, in the Student Profile, circle the item number of each correct answer and circle the plus or minus sign to indicate mastery. Calculate the subtest scores and then the total test score. To help you group students for reteaching, transfer the minus sign for any unmastered skill to the **Class Profile** (page 23f).

Student Name _____ **Date** _____

| Subtest | Tested Skills | ITEM ANALYSIS | | TEST SCORES |
		Item Numbers	Mastery	No. Correct × Points = Score
VOCABULARY	Key Words	1 2 3 4 5 6	5 out of 6 + −	_____ × 4 = ⬚/24
GRAMMAR	Verbs	7 8 9 10 11 12 13	6 out of 7 + −	_____ × 4 = ⬚/28
COMPREHENSION / CRITICAL THINKING	Analyze Story Elements (plot, setting)	14 15 16 17	3 out of 4 + −	_____ × 6 = ⬚/48
	Identify Sequence	18 19 20 21	3 out of 4 + −	
			TOTAL UNIT 3 PROGRESS TEST	⬚/100

DIRECTIONS Record the student's name and test date. Use the **Answer Key** on page 32a to score the student's test. Then, in the Student Profile, circle the item number of each correct answer and circle the plus or minus sign to indicate mastery. Calculate the subtest scores and then the total test score. To help you group students for reteaching, transfer the minus sign for any unmastered skill to the **Class Profile** (page 23f).

Student Name _____ Date _____

Subtest	Tested Skills	ITEM ANALYSIS		TEST SCORES
		Item Numbers	Mastery	No. Correct × Points = Score
VOCABULARY	Key Words	1 2 3 4 5 6	5 out of 6 + −	_____ × 4 = ⧄/40
	Context Clues	7 8 9 10	3 out of 4 + −	
GRAMMAR	Verbs	11 12 13 14 15 16 17 18	6 out of 8 + −	_____ × 3 = ⧄/24
COMPREHENSION / CRITICAL THINKING	Analyze Story Elements (plot, setting)	25 26 27 28	3 out of 4 + −	_____ × 3 = ⧄/36
	Identify Sequence	19 20 21 22	3 out of 4 + −	
	Summarize	23 24 29 30	3 out of 4 + −	
			TOTAL UNIT 3 PROGRESS TEST	⧄/100

© Hampton-Brown

Unit 3 • Student Profile for Advanced Progress Test

DIRECTIONS Record the student's name and test date. Use the **Answer Key** on page 32a to score the student's test. Then, in the Student Profile, circle the item number of each correct answer and circle the plus or minus sign to indicate mastery. Calculate the subtest scores and then the total test score. To help you group students for reteaching, transfer the minus sign for any unmastered skill to the **Class Profile** (page 23f).

Student Name _____   **Date** _____

Subtest	Tested Skills	ITEM ANALYSIS		TEST SCORES
		Item Numbers	Mastery	No. Correct × Points = Score
VOCABULARY	Key Words	1 2 3 4 5 6	5 out of 6 + −	
	Context Clues	7 8 9 10	3 out of 4 + −	____ × 4 = ⬜/40
GRAMMAR	Verbs	11 12 13 14 15 16 17 18	6 out of 8 + −	____ × 3 = ⬜/24
COMPREHENSION / CRITICAL THINKING	Analyze Story Elements (plot, setting)	25 26 27 28	3 out of 4 + −	
	Identify Sequence	19 20 21 22	3 out of 4 + −	____ × 3 = ⬜/36
	Summarize	23 24 29 30	3 out of 4 + −	
			TOTAL UNIT 3 PROGRESS TEST	⬜/100

© Hampton-Brown

Unit 3 • Class Profile

Date _____

DIRECTIONS Use the **Unit 3 Student Profiles** to complete this chart. In each row, write the student's name, fill in the bubble for the test form taken, and mark a minus sign (–) for any skill not yet mastered. Then group students and use the reteaching ideas and practice exercises to help students reach mastery.

Student Name	Test Form	Key Words	Context Clues	Verbs	Analyze Story Elements (plot, setting)	Identify Sequence	Summarize
	Ⓑ Ⓘ Ⓐ						
	Ⓑ Ⓘ Ⓐ						
	Ⓑ Ⓘ Ⓐ						
	Ⓑ Ⓘ Ⓐ						
	Ⓑ Ⓘ Ⓐ						
	Ⓑ Ⓘ Ⓐ						
	Ⓑ Ⓘ Ⓐ						
	Ⓑ Ⓘ Ⓐ						
	Ⓑ Ⓘ Ⓐ						
	Ⓑ Ⓘ Ⓐ						
	Ⓑ Ⓘ Ⓐ						
	Ⓑ Ⓘ Ⓐ						
	Ⓑ Ⓘ Ⓐ						
	Ⓑ Ⓘ Ⓐ						
	Ⓑ Ⓘ Ⓐ						
	Ⓑ Ⓘ Ⓐ						
	Ⓑ Ⓘ Ⓐ						
	Ⓑ Ⓘ Ⓐ						
	Ⓑ Ⓘ Ⓐ						
	Ⓑ Ⓘ Ⓐ						
	Ⓑ Ⓘ Ⓐ						
	Ⓑ Ⓘ Ⓐ						
RETEACHING RESOURCES		Ⓑ Ⓘ Ⓐ AH T38	Ⓘ Ⓐ LB TG	Ⓑ AH T40 Ⓘ Ⓐ EAYC 258, 261	Ⓑ Ⓘ Ⓐ LB TG	Ⓑ Ⓘ Ⓐ LB TG	Ⓘ Ⓐ LB TG
PRACTICE EXERCISES		PB 35, 45	PB 47	EAYC 392–393	PB 41	PB 49	PB 42–43

Unit 3 | Once Upon a Storm

KEY: **AH:** Assessment Handbook   **EAYC:** English at Your Command!
LB TG: Leveled Books Teacher's Guide   **PB:** Practice Book

23f

Unit 3 • Once Upon a Storm

VOCABULARY

DIRECTIONS Listen to each question. Then choose the correct picture.
Mark your answer. *(4 points each)*

⭐**Sample**

Which picture shows a <u>jacket</u>?

Ⓐ   Ⓑ   Ⓒ   Ⓓ

1 Which picture shows <u>lightning</u>?

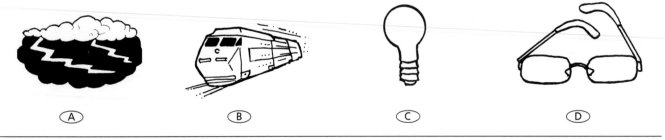

Ⓐ   Ⓑ   Ⓒ   Ⓓ

2 Which picture shows <u>hail</u>?

Ⓕ   Ⓖ   Ⓗ   Ⓙ

3 Which picture shows a <u>tornado</u>?

Ⓐ   Ⓑ   Ⓒ   Ⓓ

GO ON ➡

© Hampton-Brown

VOCABULARY

4 Which picture shows a <u>blizzard</u>?

F G H J

5 Which picture shows a <u>cellar</u>?

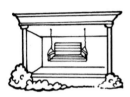 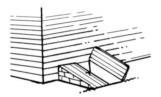  

A B C D

6 Which of these shows the <u>temperature</u>?

F G H J

STOP

GRAMMAR

DIRECTIONS Look at the picture. Listen to the sentence with each answer. Choose the word or words that complete the sentence correctly. Mark your answer. *(4 points each)*

⭐Sample

The weather _____ very hot today.

- Ⓐ is
- Ⓑ be
- Ⓒ are
- Ⓓ has

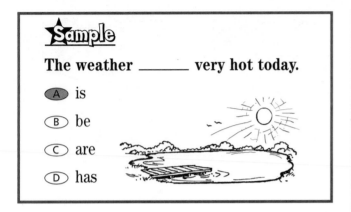

---

7 Lena _____ a big hat.

- Ⓐ is
- Ⓑ be
- Ⓒ has
- Ⓓ have

---

8 The hat _____ the sun off her face.

- Ⓕ keep
- Ⓖ keeps
- Ⓗ to keep
- Ⓙ keeping

---

9 Marta _____ sunglasses to cover her eyes.

- Ⓐ big
- Ⓑ high
- Ⓒ wind
- Ⓓ wears

---

10 Lucas says, "I _____ too hot."

- Ⓕ is
- Ⓖ be
- Ⓗ am
- Ⓙ are

GO ON ➡

© Hampton-Brown

GRAMMAR

B

11 He _____ into the lake.

    Ⓐ jump

    Ⓑ jumps

    Ⓒ to jump

    Ⓓ jumping

12 The girls _____ in the water, too.

    Ⓕ play

    Ⓖ plays

    Ⓗ to play

    Ⓙ playing

13 All the children _____ a great day.

    Ⓐ are

    Ⓑ has

    Ⓒ have

    Ⓓ being

COMPREHENSION / CRITICAL THINKING

DIRECTIONS Listen to the selection. Then listen to each question.
Choose the best answer. Mark your answer. *(6 points each)*

A Storm at Night

1

Snap! Boom! Crackle! Something outside wakes Luisa up. She calls to her sister, "Teresa, I'm scared!"

2

The light goes on. Teresa asks, "What's wrong?"
"I am afraid of the noise," Luisa says.

3

"The storm will not hurt you," Teresa says. She closes the window. "You are safe."

4

Then Teresa says, "I will stay here until the storm ends."
Soon Luisa goes to sleep.

GO ON ▶

COMPREHENSION / CRITICAL THINKING

14 When does the selection take place?

at night   in the morning   at noon   in the afternoon

Ⓕ   Ⓖ   Ⓗ   Ⓙ

15 Where does the selection take place?

Ⓐ   Ⓑ   Ⓒ   Ⓓ

16 What wakes Luisa in the beginning of the selection?

  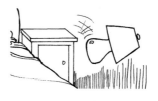 

Ⓕ   Ⓖ   Ⓗ   Ⓙ

17 Which of these shows how Luisa feels?

 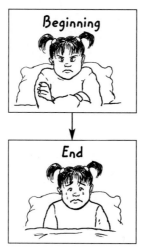  

Ⓐ   Ⓑ   Ⓒ   Ⓓ

GO ON →

© Hampton-Brown

COMPREHENSION / CRITICAL THINKING

DIRECTIONS Listen to the selection. Then listen to each question. Choose the best answer. Mark your answer. *(6 points each)*

A Spring Blizzard

On March 31, 1997, people in New England have a surprise. It is spring. A blizzard arrives during the night.

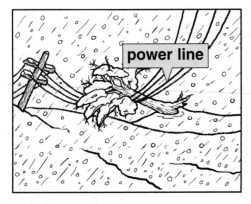

The wind blows down trees and power lines. Many people do not have power.

Workers cannot clear the deep snow. Snowplows get stuck. Roads close. Cars and buses cannot go anywhere. On April 1, schools and airports close.

The blizzard stops on April 3. Finally, workers can clear the roads. They fix the power lines, too. People go back to work and to school.

GO ON ➡

© Hampton-Brown

COMPREHENSION / CRITICAL THINKING

18 What happens first in the selection?

    F   G   H   J

19 What happens next in the selection?

    A   B   C   D

20 When do the schools close?

March 31   April 1   April 3

    F   G   H

21 What happens at the end of the selection?

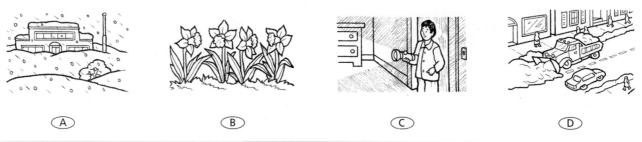

    A   B   C   D

STOP

Unit 3 • Once Upon a Storm

VOCABULARY

DIRECTIONS Read the sentence. Choose the word or words that go in the blank. Mark your answer. *(4 points each)*

⭐ **Sample**

Carlo wears his new _____ to school.

Ⓐ car

Ⓑ book

🅒 jacket

Ⓓ building

---

1 The weather _____ said, "It will snow today."

Ⓐ police

Ⓑ author

Ⓒ neighbor

Ⓓ forecaster

---

2 The _____ flashed across the dark sky.

Ⓕ puddle

Ⓖ thunder

Ⓗ lightning

Ⓙ cold front

---

3 Many pieces of icy _____ fell from the sky.

Ⓐ hail

Ⓑ wind

Ⓒ steam

Ⓓ clouds

---

4 A _____ is a snowstorm with strong winds.

Ⓕ region

Ⓖ blizzard

Ⓗ barometer

Ⓙ temperature

---

5 Icy roads can be very _____.

Ⓐ dry

Ⓑ proud

Ⓒ cloudy

Ⓓ dangerous

---

6 Look at the spinning cloud. A _____ is coming!

Ⓕ train

Ⓖ cellar

Ⓗ spring

Ⓙ tornado

STOP

© Hampton-Brown

VOCABULARY

DIRECTIONS Read the sentence in the box. Choose the meaning of the underlined word. Mark your answer. *(4 points each)*

Sample

A gray bat flies out of the cave.

In this sentence, bat means —

Ⓐ to hit something

Ⓑ to have a turn in baseball

Ⓒ a small, furry animal with wings

7

Grandma likes to rock in her chair.

In this sentence, rock means —

Ⓐ piece of stone

Ⓑ a kind of music

Ⓒ to move back and forth

8

The plant is one foot tall.

In this sentence, foot means —

Ⓕ 12 inches

Ⓖ a kind of ball

Ⓗ the end part of the leg

9

This box is light and easy to carry.

In this sentence, light means —

Ⓐ not dark

Ⓑ not pretty

Ⓒ not heavy

10

Does the shirt match the skirt?

In this sentence, match means —

Ⓕ a game or contest

Ⓖ to go together well

Ⓗ something that helps start a fire

STOP

GRAMMAR

DIRECTIONS Read the sentences. Choose the word or words that go in each blank. Mark your answer. *(3 points each)*

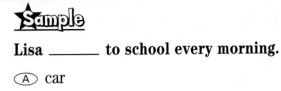

Lisa _____ to school every morning.

Ⓐ car

Ⓑ fast

● walks

Ⓓ above

11 On rainy days, Lisa _____ an umbrella.

Ⓐ too

Ⓑ tall

Ⓒ time

Ⓓ takes

12 It _____ dry under the umbrella.

Ⓕ is

Ⓖ be

Ⓗ am

Ⓙ are

13 Lisa _____ in too many puddles.

Ⓐ step

Ⓑ steps

Ⓒ to step

Ⓓ stepping

14 Her feet _____ always wet!

Ⓕ is

Ⓖ be

Ⓗ am

Ⓙ are

STOP

GRAMMAR

DIRECTIONS Read the sentences. Choose the best way to write each underlined part, or choose "Correct as it is." Mark your answer.

(3 points each)

Sample

Snow <u>falls</u> **only in cold weather.**

Ⓐ fall

Ⓑ to fall

Ⓒ falling

🅓 Correct as it is

---

15 **The cold air** <u>freezing</u> **the rainwater to make snow.**

Ⓐ freeze

Ⓑ freezes

Ⓒ to freeze

Ⓓ Correct as it is

16 **People** <u>has</u> **a lot of fun in the snow.**

Ⓕ be

Ⓖ am

Ⓗ have

Ⓙ Correct as it is

17 **My uncle** <u>make</u> **a house of snow.**

Ⓐ makes

Ⓑ making

Ⓒ to make

Ⓓ Correct as it is

18 **He** <u>slides</u> **down the hill on a sled.**

Ⓕ slide

Ⓖ sliding

Ⓗ to slide

Ⓙ Correct as it is

STOP

COMPREHENSION / CRITICAL THINKING

DIRECTIONS Read the selection. Then read each item. Choose the best answer. Mark your answer. *(3 points each)*

Snow covered the cars.

Power lines and trees fell over.

Roads were closed.

The Spring Blizzard

On the night of March 31, 1997, a blizzard blew into the Northeast. As the storm began, strong winds blew over trees and power lines. Thousands of people had no power for lights and heat.

The snow fell quickly. It covered cars on the roads. Some people could not drive home and had to sleep in their cars that night. Trucks tried to clean up the snow. Then they got stuck.

The next day was April Fool's Day, a day to play jokes. Nature's joke was a winter storm in the spring. On April 1, schools, roads, and airports closed.

The blizzard lasted through April 3. There were more than three feet of snow in some places. Then workers cleaned up the mess. They cleared the roads and turned on the power. The joke was over at last.

GO ON ➡

COMPREHENSION / CRITICAL THINKING

19 Look at the time line.

Time Line

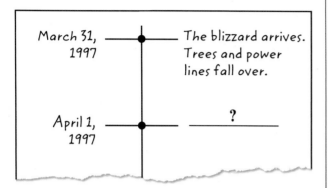

March 31, 1997 — The blizzard arrives. Trees and power lines fall over.

April 1, 1997 — ?

Which of these goes in the blank?

Ⓐ Workers cleaned up the snow.

Ⓑ Workers turned the power on.

Ⓒ Spring rains flooded the streets.

Ⓓ Schools, roads, and airports closed.

20 When did the blizzard end?

Ⓕ March 31

Ⓖ April 1

Ⓗ April 2

Ⓙ April 3

21 Which of these happened first?

Ⓐ Schools closed.

Ⓑ The power went out.

Ⓒ April Fool's Day came.

Ⓓ People slept in their cars.

22 Which of these happened after the blizzard ended?

Ⓕ It started to rain.

Ⓖ Workers cleared the roads.

Ⓗ Trucks got stuck in the snow.

Ⓙ Thousands of people had no power.

23 What is the selection mostly about?

Ⓐ Workers fixed power lines.

Ⓑ People slept in their cars all night.

Ⓒ April Fool's Day is a day to play jokes.

Ⓓ In 1997, there was a blizzard in the Northeast.

24 Which of these belongs in a good summary of the selection?

Ⓕ Trucks are used to clear roads.

Ⓖ The storm lasted for three days.

Ⓗ The Northeast always has storms.

Ⓙ Sometimes snow falls in the spring.

GO ON

© Hampton-Brown

COMPREHENSION / CRITICAL THINKING

DIRECTIONS Read the selection. Then read each item. Choose the best answer. Mark your answer. *(3 points each)*

Bossy Carlos

Carlos and his brother Roberto lived near a lake. They went sailing together one Saturday in the summer. Carlos was telling Roberto what to do. Roberto thought Carlos was being bossy.

At first, the boys were fighting and didn't see the clouds. Then, Carlos saw the storm. He yelled, "We have to get home now!"

The boys tried to sail home, but the wind pushed the boat over. The boys tried to turn the boat back over, but they couldn't. Carlos screamed, "Leave the boat! Start swimming!"

Roberto started to cry. Carlos shouted, "You can do it!"

The boys swam to shore. Dad was there and pulled them out of the water.

Later, at home, Roberto whispered to Carlos, "It's a good thing you are so bossy. Your shouting really helped me."

© Hampton-Brown

GO ON ➡

COMPREHENSION / CRITICAL THINKING

25 Where does the selection take place?

Ⓐ in a car

Ⓑ on a lake

Ⓒ in a store

Ⓓ on a truck

26 When does the selection take place?

Ⓕ at night

Ⓖ in the fall

Ⓗ on a Saturday

Ⓙ during January

27 Which of these best shows what happens in the selection?

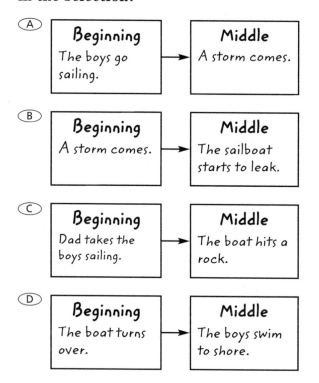

Ⓐ
| Beginning | Middle |
| The boys go sailing. | A storm comes. |

Ⓑ
| Beginning | Middle |
| A storm comes. | The sailboat starts to leak. |

Ⓒ
| Beginning | Middle |
| Dad takes the boys sailing. | The boat hits a rock. |

Ⓓ
| Beginning | Middle |
| The boat turns over. | The boys swim to shore. |

28 Which of these tells how the selection ends?

Ⓕ Roberto starts to cry.

Ⓖ Carlos and Roberto fight.

Ⓗ Strong winds blow across the lake.

Ⓙ Dad pulls the boys out of the water.

29 Which of these belongs in a good summary of the selection?

Ⓐ The boys know how to swim.

Ⓑ The wind pushes the sailboat over.

Ⓒ Carlos sails a lot during the summer.

Ⓓ Dad buys a new sailboat for Carlos and Roberto.

30 Which of these tells what the selection is mostly about?

Ⓕ Carlos yells at Roberto a lot.

Ⓖ Roberto is younger than Carlos.

Ⓗ Roberto and Carlos are good sailors.

Ⓙ Carlos helps Roberto during a storm.

© Hampton-Brown

STOP

Unit 3 • Once Upon a Storm

VOCABULARY

DIRECTIONS Read the sentence. Choose the word or words that go in the blank. Mark your answer. *(4 points each)*

Carlo wears his new _____ to school.

- Ⓐ car
- Ⓑ book
- 🄲 jacket
- Ⓓ building

---

1 During the storm, Dad and I stayed in the _____.

- Ⓐ pole
- Ⓑ style
- Ⓒ cellar
- Ⓓ damage

2 We saw the _____ flash across the dark sky.

- Ⓕ puddle
- Ⓖ thunder
- Ⓗ lightning
- Ⓙ cold front

3 Large pieces of icy _____ fell from the sky.

- Ⓐ hail
- Ⓑ wind
- Ⓒ mass
- Ⓓ twister

4 A lot of snow falls during a _____.

- Ⓕ region
- Ⓖ blizzard
- Ⓗ barometer
- Ⓙ temperature

5 Icy roads can be very _____.

- Ⓐ dry
- Ⓑ proud
- Ⓒ cloudy
- Ⓓ dangerous

6 When we saw the spinning cloud, we knew a _____ was coming.

- Ⓕ train
- Ⓖ spring
- Ⓗ tornado
- Ⓙ forecaster

STOP

VOCABULARY

DIRECTIONS Read the sentence in the box. Choose the meaning of the underlined word. Mark your answer. *(4 points each)*

Sample

| A gray <u>bat</u> flies out of the cave. |

In this sentence, <u>bat</u> means —

Ⓐ to hit something

Ⓑ to have a turn in baseball

● a small, furry animal with wings

---

7 | Grandma likes to <u>rock</u> in her chair. |

In this sentence, <u>rock</u> means —

Ⓐ a kind of music

Ⓑ to move back and forth

Ⓒ a large, heavy piece of stone

8 | The plant was one <u>foot</u> tall. |

In this sentence, <u>foot</u> means —

Ⓕ 12 inches

Ⓖ a kind of ball

Ⓗ the end part of the leg

9 | The girl's dress was <u>light</u> blue. |

In this sentence, <u>light</u> means —

Ⓐ not dark

Ⓑ not heavy

Ⓒ not careful

10 | "Do those pants <u>match</u> my jacket?" asked Miguel. |

In this sentence, <u>match</u> means —

Ⓕ a game or contest

Ⓖ to go together well

Ⓗ something that helps start a fire

STOP

GRAMMAR

DIRECTIONS Read the sentences. Choose the word or words that go in each blank. Mark your answer. *(3 points each)*

Lisa __★Sample__ to school every morning. On rainy days, she ___11___ an

umbrella to stay dry. She has a problem, though. She steps in so many

puddles that her feet ___12___ always wet.

One day, Aunt Angela ___13___ Lisa a box.

"This gift ___14___ for you," says Aunt Angela. "These boots will keep

your feet dry when you walk through the puddles."

★Sample

Ⓐ car

Ⓑ fast

● walks

Ⓓ above

11 Ⓐ too

Ⓑ tall

Ⓒ time

Ⓓ takes

12 Ⓕ is

Ⓖ be

Ⓗ am

Ⓙ are

13 Ⓐ give

Ⓑ gives

Ⓒ giving

Ⓓ to give

14 Ⓕ is

Ⓖ be

Ⓗ am

Ⓙ are

STOP

GRAMMAR

DIRECTIONS Read the sentences. Choose the best way to write each underlined part, or choose "Correct as it is." Mark your answer.

(3 points each)

Snow <u>falls</u> only in cold weather. When water <u>freezing</u> in the cold air,

Sample   **15**

we get snowflakes instead of rain. Did you know that no two snowflakes

look alike? Every snowflake is different.

Snow can bring a lot of trouble, but people <u>has</u> fun in the snow, too.

                                                    16

My uncle <u>make</u> a house of snow. Then he <u>slides</u> down the hill on a sled.

       17   **18**

⭐Sample

(A) fall

(B) to fall

(C) falling

(**D**) Correct as it is

---

15 (A) freeze

(B) freezes

(C) to freeze

(D) Correct as it is

16 (F) be

(G) am

(H) have

(J) Correct as it is

17 (A) makes

(B) making

(C) to make

(D) Correct as it is

18 (F) slide

(G) sliding

(H) to slide

(J) Correct as it is

STOP

DIRECTIONS Read the selection. Then read each item. Choose the best answer. Mark your answer. *(3 points each)*

The Big Flood

In 1993, the Midwest had a wet spring. The ground was so wet it could not hold any more water. For days, water ran off the wet land into the Mississippi River until it was about to flood over its banks.

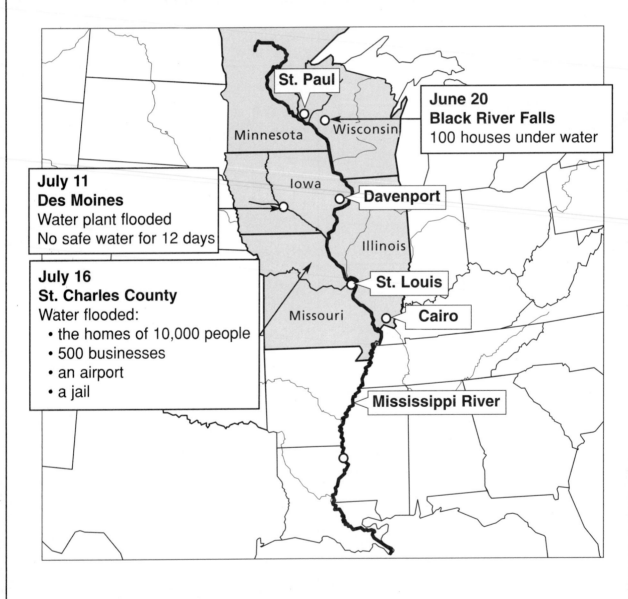

St. Paul

June 20
Black River Falls
100 houses under water

Minnesota Wisconsin

July 11
Des Moines
Water plant flooded
No safe water for 12 days

Iowa

Davenport

Illinois

July 16
St. Charles County
Water flooded:
• the homes of 10,000 people
• 500 businesses
• an airport
• a jail

Missouri

St. Louis

Cairo

Mississippi River

© Hampton-Brown

GO ON ➡

The Big Flood, continued

Then, on June 10, eight inches of rain fell in Wisconsin and Minnesota. In some places more rain fell in one day than usually falls in a month! This started the worst flood in U.S. history.

Rain kept falling day after day. On June 20, a dam broke, and water covered 100 houses near the town of Black River Falls, Wisconsin. Part of the Mississippi River became unsafe, and more than 200 miles of the river were closed to boats.

On July 5, a bridge across the Mississippi River at Keokuk, Iowa, was closed. A few days later another bridge was closed. By then the river was closed for 830 miles, from St. Paul, Minnesota, to Cairo, Illinois.

On July 8, a huge thunderstorm hit Iowa. Ten inches of rain poured into the Raccoon River. On July 11, the water plant in Des Moines was flooded. For twelve days, 250,000 people in Des Moines had no clean water for drinking. They had to catch rainwater or get water from other towns.

On July 16, dirty water flooded St. Charles County, Missouri. Ten thousand people had to leave their homes. Two weeks later, water from the river poured into another part of St. Charles County. This time it flooded 500 businesses, an airport, and a jail.

By August 24, everyone thought the floods were finally over. The Mississippi River opened to boats. Then, on August 30, more rain fell on Des Moines, Iowa. That was the last of the giant storms. The flood was almost over. Then people started the big job of cleaning up the mess it left behind.

GO ON ➤

19 **Which of these happened before June 20?**

Ⓐ A bridge closed.

Ⓑ The river was closed to boats.

Ⓒ Eight inches of rain fell in Wisconsin.

Ⓓ A dam broke on the Mississippi River.

20 **Look at the time line.**

Time Line

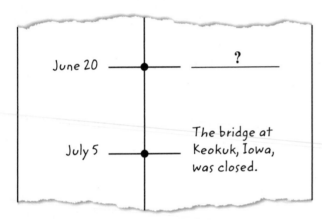

Which of these goes in the blank?

Ⓕ A dam broke in Wisconsin.

Ⓖ The river was about to flood.

Ⓗ A huge thunderstorm hit Iowa.

Ⓙ Everyone thought the floods were over.

21 **What happened on July 16?**

Ⓐ More rain fell on Des Moines.

Ⓑ A bridge closed in Keokuk, Iowa.

Ⓒ People in Des Moines got clean water.

Ⓓ Dirty water flooded St. Charles County, Missouri.

22 **Which of these happened last?**

Ⓕ A water plant was flooded.

Ⓖ People started to clean up the mess.

Ⓗ The Mississippi River opened to boats.

Ⓙ Water covered 100 houses near Black River Falls, Wisconsin.

23 **Which sentence tells what the selection is mostly about?**

Ⓐ A huge thunderstorm hit Iowa.

Ⓑ Cleaning up after a flood is a big job.

Ⓒ In 1993, there was a big flood along the Mississippi River.

Ⓓ In Missouri, 500 businesses, an airport, and a jail were flooded.

24 **Which of these belongs in a good summary of the selection?**

Ⓕ The flood water was very dirty.

Ⓖ Black River Falls is in Wisconsin.

Ⓗ July was a very wet month in Iowa.

Ⓙ The flood of 1993 was the worst in U.S. history.

© Hampton-Brown

GO ON ▶

DIRECTIONS Read the selection. Then read each item. Choose the best answer. Mark your answer. *(3 points each)*

Ashley's Adventure

Ashley Turner lived beside a little river in Iowa called Honey Creek. Ashley and her brother, Kurt, loved to go fishing in the creek. Their dog, Brutus, liked to watch from the shore as Ashley and Kurt waited for the fish to bite.

One Saturday, Ashley and Kurt went down to the creek with their lunch. It was a bright spring morning and they were excited about the fish they might catch.

"Watch the sky," their mother warned. "In April, you never know when a storm will come up. Come home the minute you see clouds in the west."

"We'll watch, Mom!" Kurt replied.

GO ON

Ashley's Adventure, continued

Ashley and Kurt caught seven fish before they stopped to eat their lunch. As Ashley opened the lunch bag, she looked up to see some enormous dark clouds in the west. Trees began to move in the wind and a few drops of rain dropped into the boat.

"Quick! Row toward the shore!" Ashley yelled at Kurt.

Mom saw the storm and ran toward the creek. She yelled at Ashley and Kurt. They both rowed as hard as they could, but they weren't getting any closer to the shore.

"Help!" Ashley called. "Mom! The boat won't move!"

Mom grabbed a branch and held it toward the boat. Ashley reached, but she couldn't grab the branch.

"I'll call 9-1-1," Mom screamed.

Suddenly Ashley felt the boat move toward the shore. She knew that she and Kurt were not that strong. What was moving the boat? Then she saw Brutus swimming ahead of the boat. In his mouth, he held a rope attached to the front of the boat.

"We're getting close!" Kurt cried. "We're going to make it!"

Ashley heard a crunching sound as the boat touched the shore. It was the best sound she had heard in a long time. Kurt and Ashley scrambled out and pulled the boat onto the shore.

"We made it! Or, should I say, Brutus made it!" Ashley said happily. "What a hero you are," she whispered, and she hugged Brutus as hard as she could.

GO ON ▶

COMPREHENSION / CRITICAL THINKING

25 **When does this selection take place?**

Ⓐ in July

Ⓑ at night

Ⓒ on a spring day

Ⓓ on a winter morning

26 **Where does most of the selection take place?**

Ⓕ in a creek

Ⓖ near a city

Ⓗ inside a house

Ⓙ near a mountain

27 **When Ashley sees the clouds, she —**

Ⓐ calls 9-1-1

Ⓑ hugs Brutus

Ⓒ yells at Kurt

Ⓓ starts fishing

28 **Which of these best shows what happens in the selection?**

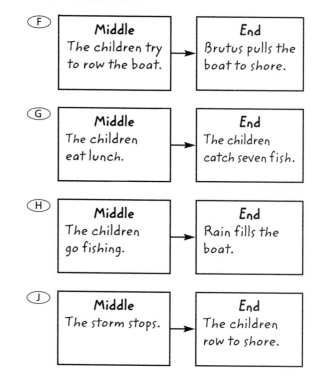

Ⓕ
| Middle | End |
| The children try to row the boat. | Brutus pulls the boat to shore. |

Ⓖ
| Middle | End |
| The children eat lunch. | The children catch seven fish. |

Ⓗ
| Middle | End |
| The children go fishing. | Rain fills the boat. |

Ⓙ
| Middle | End |
| The storm stops. | The children row to shore. |

29 **Which of these belongs in a good summary of the selection?**

Ⓐ A big storm comes up.

Ⓑ Ashley carries lunch to the boat.

Ⓒ The little river is called Honey Creek.

Ⓓ The children love to fish in the creek.

30 **Which sentence tells what the selection is mostly about?**

Ⓕ Brutus swims beside the boat.

Ⓖ Mom holds a branch toward the boat.

Ⓗ Ashley and Kurt go fishing on a Saturday.

Ⓙ Brutus saves Ashley and Kurt during a storm.

STOP

Unit 3 • Answer Key

B Beginning Progress Test

VOCABULARY
(4 points each)

1 (A)   4 (G)
2 (J)   5 (B)
3 (C)   6 (F)

GRAMMAR
(4 points each)

7 (C)   11 (B)
8 (G)   12 (F)
9 (D)   13 (C)
10 (H)

COMPREHENSION / CRITICAL THINKING
(6 points each)

14 (F)   18 (H)
15 (C)   19 (C)
16 (J)   20 (G)
17 (A)   21 (D)

I Intermediate Progress Test

VOCABULARY
(4 points each)

1 (D)   6 (J)
2 (H)   7 (C)
3 (A)   8 (F)
4 (G)   9 (C)
5 (D)   10 (G)

GRAMMAR
(3 points each)

11 (D)   15 (B)
12 (F)   16 (H)
13 (B)   17 (A)
14 (J)   18 (J)

COMPREHENSION / CRITICAL THINKING
(3 points each)

19 (D)   25 (B)
20 (J)   26 (H)
21 (B)   27 (A)
22 (G)   28 (J)
23 (D)   29 (B)
24 (G)   30 (J)

A Advanced Progress Test

VOCABULARY
(4 points each)

1 (C)   6 (H)
2 (H)   7 (B)
3 (A)   8 (F)
4 (G)   9 (A)
5 (D)   10 (G)

GRAMMAR
(3 points each)

11 (D)   15 (B)
12 (J)   16 (H)
13 (B)   17 (A)
14 (F)   18 (J)

COMPREHENSION / CRITICAL THINKING
(3 points each)

19 (C)   25 (C)
20 (F)   26 (F)
21 (D)   27 (C)
22 (G)   28 (F)
23 (C)   29 (A)
24 (J)   30 (J)

© Hampton-Brown

Unit 3 • Self-Assessment

I Can Speak English!

1. I learned to describe events.

There was a storm in _____. It _____.

2. I can give information.

To stay safe in a storm, people _____.

My New Words

_____

_____

_____

_____

_____

_____

_____

_____

_____

I Can Read in English!

3. I can retell events in the right order.

☐ yes   ☐ not yet

4. I can tell what happens in the beginning, middle, and end of a story.

☐ yes   ☐ not yet

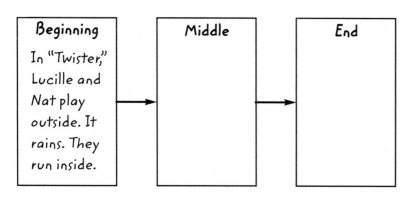

Beginning	Middle	End
In "Twister," Lucille and Nat play outside. It rains. They run inside.		

What I've Read

☐ Twister

☐ The Big Storm

☐ _____

☐ _____

Unit 4 • Directions for ⓑ Progress Test

Distribute the test pages. Before students begin each subtest, read aloud the directions and use the script to work through each sample item.

Read aloud the directions on page 34. Then work through the sample item. Say:

Sample
Look at the pictures in the box. Which picture shows a jacket? Point to the picture. (Pause.) *The second bubble is filled in because the second picture shows a jacket.*

Items 1–6
Read each question aloud. Provide time for students to mark their answers.

GRAMMAR

Read aloud the directions on page 36. Then work through the sample item. Say:

Sample
Look at the picture in the box. (Pause.) *Look at the sentence. There is a word missing. Let's try each word. Listen:*

> *I have* two *pet fish.*
> *I have* bed *pet fish.*
> *I have* could *pet fish.*
> *I have* where *pet fish.*

The first bubble is filled in because two *is the best answer.*

Items 7–13
Read aloud each sentence with its answer choices. Provide time for students to mark their answers.

COMPREHENSION / CRITICAL THINKING

Selection 1 and Items 14–17
Read aloud the directions on page 38. Say: *Now listen to the selection. The title is:*

Marcos Goes Fishing

Look at Picture 1.   Marcos wants fish so he can feed his family. He gets in his boat and rows out to sea. Then he stops to eat a sandwich.

Look at Picture 2.   After he eats, Marcos catches three good fish. He is happy. Then he waits for another fish.

Look at Picture 3.   Finally, Marcos catches another fish. This fish is very big and strong! It pulls the boat through the water!

Look at Picture 4.   This fish is dangerous! Marcos cuts the line, and the fish swims away. Marcos takes home the three small fish.

Then read each question aloud. Provide time for students to mark their answers.

Selection 2 and Items 18–21
Read aloud the directions on page 40. Say: *Now listen to the selection and look at the pictures.*

There are many kinds of seaweeds. Seaweeds can be many colors. Some are green or blue. Others are red or brown.

Seaweeds grow in seawater and on rocks. They need sunlight to grow. They do not make flowers or seeds.

Some seaweeds are very small, but others are large. A giant kelp plant can grow to more than 200 feet long!

People use seaweeds for many things. Some people eat dried seaweeds. People use parts of seaweeds in foods, medicine, and paint.

Then read each question aloud. Provide time for students to mark their answers.

© Hampton-Brown

Distribute the test pages. Before students begin each subtest, read aloud the directions and use the script to work through each sample item.

VOCABULARY

Read aloud the directions on page 34. Then work through the sample item. Say:

Sample

Read the sentence in the box. (Pause.) *Which word goes in the blank? Let's try each one:*

> Carlo wears his new car *to school.*
> Carlo wears his new book *to school.*
> Carlo wears his new jacket *to school.*
> Carlo wears his new building *to school.*

The third bubble is filled in because jacket *is the best answer.*

Items 1–6

Tell students to complete the remaining items in the same way. Provide time for students to mark their answers.

Read aloud the directions on page 35. Then work through the sample item. Say:

Sample

Read the sentence in the box. (Pause.) *Which word goes in the blank? Let's try each one:*

> Gina walks slowly *through the park.*
> Gina walks slower *through the park.*
> Gina walks slowing *through the park.*
> Gina walks slowness *through the park.*

The first bubble is filled in because slowly *is the best answer.*

Items 7–10

Tell students to complete the remaining items in the same way. Provide time for them to mark their answers.

GRAMMAR

Read aloud the directions on page 36. Then work through the sample item. Say:

Sample

Read the sentence. (Pause.) *Which word goes in the blank? Let's try each one:*

> I love to go to the beach on a shine *day.*
> I love to go to the beach on a sunny *day.*
> I love to go to the beach on a quickly *day.*
> I love to go to the beach on a happen *day.*

The second bubble is filled in because sunny *is the best answer.*

Items 11–16

Tell students to complete the remaining items in the same way. Provide time for them to mark their answers.

Read aloud the directions on page 37. Then work through the sample item. Say:

Sample

Read the sentence. (Pause.) *What is the best way to write the underlined part? Look at the four chioces. The second bubble is filled in because* good day *is the best way to write the words.*

Items 17–22

Tell students to complete the remaining items in the same way. Provide time for them to mark their answers.

COMPREHENSION / CRITICAL THINKING

Selections and Items 23–31

Read aloud the directions for the selections. Clarify that Intermediate students are to read each selection separately and then complete its items, while Advanced students are to read the paired selections and then complete all the items. Provide time for students to mark their answers.

DIRECTIONS Record the student's name and test date. Use the **Answer Key** on page 43a to score the student's test. Then, in the Student Profile, circle the item number of each correct answer and circle the plus or minus sign to indicate mastery. Calculate the subtest scores and then the total test score. To help you group students for reteaching, transfer the minus sign for any unmastered skill to the **Class Profile** (page 34f).

Student Name _____ **Date** _____

| Subtest | Tested Skills | ITEM ANALYSIS | | TEST SCORES |
		Item Numbers	Mastery	No. Correct × Points = Score
VOCABULARY	Key Words	1 2 3 4 5 6	5 out of 6 + −	_____ × 4 = ⬚/24
GRAMMAR	Adjectives	7 8 9 10 11 12 13	6 out of 7 + −	_____ × 4 = ⬚/28
COMPREHENSION / CRITICAL THINKING	Analyze Story Elements (characters)	14 15 16 17	3 out of 4 + −	_____ × 6 = ⬚/48
	Relate Main Idea and Details	18 19 20 21	3 out of 4 + −	

TOTAL UNIT 4 PROGRESS TEST ⬚/100

DIRECTIONS Record the student's name and test date. Use the **Answer Key** on page 43a to score the student's test. Then, in the Student Profile, circle the item number of each correct answer and circle the plus or minus sign to indicate mastery. Calculate the subtest scores and then the total test score. To help you group students for reteaching, transfer the minus sign for any unmastered skill to the **Class Profile** (page 34f).

Student Name _____ **Date** _____

Subtest	Tested Skills	ITEM ANALYSIS		TEST SCORES
		Item Numbers	Mastery	No. Correct × Points = Score
VOCABULARY	Key Words	1 2 3 4 5 6	5 out of 6 + −	_____ × 4 = ⬜ /40
	Prefixes and Suffixes	7 8 9 10	3 out of 4 + −	
GRAMMAR	Adjectives	12 14 17 18 19 20 21 22	6 out of 8 + −	_____ × 2 = ⬜ /24
	Comparative and Superlative Adjectives	11 13 15 16	3 out of 4 + −	
COMPREHENSION / CRITICAL THINKING	Analyze Story Elements (characters)	28 29 30 31	3 out of 4 + −	_____ × 4 = ⬜ /36
	Relate Main Idea and Details	23 24 25 26 27	4 out of 5 + −	

TOTAL UNIT 4 PROGRESS TEST ⬜ /100

© Hampton-Brown

Unit 4 • Student Profile for Advanced Progress Test

DIRECTIONS Record the student's name and test date. Use the **Answer Key** on page 43a to score the student's test. Then, in the Student Profile, circle the item number of each correct answer and circle the plus or minus sign to indicate mastery. Calculate the subtest scores and then the total test score. To help you group students for reteaching, transfer the minus sign for any unmastered skill to the **Class Profile** (page 34f).

Student Name _____ Date _____

| Subtest | Tested Skills | ITEM ANALYSIS | | TEST SCORES |
		Item Numbers	Mastery	No. Correct × Points = Score
VOCABULARY	Key Words	1 2 3 4 5 6	5 out of 6 + −	_____ × 4 = ⬚/40
	Prefixes and Suffixes	7 8 9 10	3 out of 4 + −	
GRAMMAR	Adjectives	12 13 14 18 19 20 21 22	6 out of 8 + −	_____ × 2 = ⬚/24
	Comparative and Superlative Adjectives	11 15 16 17	3 out of 4 + −	
COMPREHENSION / CRITICAL THINKING	Analyze Story Elements (characters)	27 28 29 30	3 out of 4 + −	_____ × 4 = ⬚/36
	Relate Main Idea and Details	23 24 25 26 31	4 out of 5 + −	
			TOTAL UNIT 4 PROGRESS TEST	⬚/100

Unit 4 • Class Profile

Date _____

DIRECTIONS Use the **Unit 4 Student Profiles** to complete this chart. In each row, write the student's name, fill in the bubble for the test form taken, and mark a minus sign (–) for any skill not yet mastered. Then group students and use the reteaching ideas and practice exercises to help students reach mastery.

Student Name	Test Form	TESTED SKILLS				
		Key Words	Prefixes and Suffixes	Adjectives	Analyze Story Elements (characters)	Relate Main Idea and Details
	Ⓑ Ⓘ Ⓐ					
	Ⓑ Ⓘ Ⓐ					
	Ⓑ Ⓘ Ⓐ					
	Ⓑ Ⓘ Ⓐ					
	Ⓑ Ⓘ Ⓐ					
	Ⓑ Ⓘ Ⓐ					
	Ⓑ Ⓘ Ⓐ					
	Ⓑ Ⓘ Ⓐ					
	Ⓑ Ⓘ Ⓐ					
	Ⓑ Ⓘ Ⓐ					
	Ⓑ Ⓘ Ⓐ					
	Ⓑ Ⓘ Ⓐ					
	Ⓑ Ⓘ Ⓐ					
	Ⓑ Ⓘ Ⓐ					
	Ⓑ Ⓘ Ⓐ					
	Ⓑ Ⓘ Ⓐ					
	Ⓑ Ⓘ Ⓐ					
	Ⓑ Ⓘ Ⓐ					
	Ⓑ Ⓘ Ⓐ					
	Ⓑ Ⓘ Ⓐ					
	Ⓑ Ⓘ Ⓐ					
	Ⓑ Ⓘ Ⓐ					
RETEACHING RESOURCES		Ⓑ Ⓘ Ⓐ AH T38	Ⓘ Ⓐ EAYC 48–53	Ⓑ AH T40 Ⓘ Ⓐ EAYC 252–257	Ⓑ Ⓘ Ⓐ LB TG	Ⓑ Ⓘ Ⓐ LB TG
PRACTICE EXERCISES		PB 53, 61	PB 54, 58–59	EAYC 389–391	PB 57	PB 67

KEY: **AH:** Assessment Handbook   **EAYC:** English at Your Command!
       LB TG: Leveled Books Teacher's Guide   **PB:** Practice Book

Name _____ Date _____ B BEGINNING PROGRESS TEST

Unit 4 • Watery World

VOCABULARY

DIRECTIONS Listen to each question. Then choose the correct picture.
Mark your answer. *(4 points each)*

Sample

Which picture shows a jacket?

Ⓐ   Ⓑ   Ⓒ   Ⓓ

1 Find the arrow in each picture. Which arrow points to a backbone?

Ⓐ   Ⓑ   Ⓒ   Ⓓ

2 The boy wears something backward. Which picture shows this?

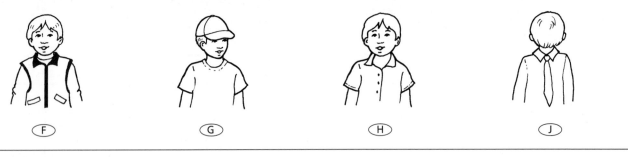

Ⓕ   Ⓖ   Ⓗ   Ⓙ

3 Which picture shows a creature?

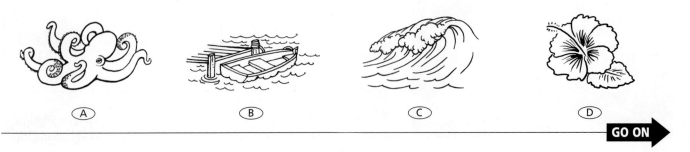

Ⓐ   Ⓑ   Ⓒ   Ⓓ

GO ON

© Hampton-Brown

VOCABULARY

4 Which picture shows a <u>shelter</u>?

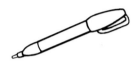

F   G   H   J

5 The girl <u>captures</u> **something. Which picture shows this?**

A   B   C   D

6 Which picture shows <u>camouflage</u>?

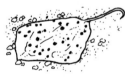

F   G   H   J

STOP

GRAMMAR

DIRECTIONS Look at the picture. Listen to the sentence with each
answer. Choose the word or words that complete the sentence correctly.
Mark your answer. *(4 points each)*

⭐Sample

I have _____ pet fish.

Ⓐ two
Ⓑ bed
Ⓒ could
Ⓓ where

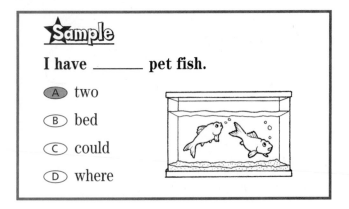

7 Gene has _____ hair.

Ⓐ soil
Ⓑ dark
Ⓒ water
Ⓓ branch

8 Yamaya is a _____ girl.

Ⓕ six
Ⓖ tall
Ⓗ from
Ⓙ signal

9 This shell is _____.

Ⓐ soft
Ⓑ high
Ⓒ loud
Ⓓ round

© Hampton-Brown

GO ON ➡

10 Juan runs on the _____ beach.

Ⓕ fast

Ⓖ over

Ⓗ sandy

Ⓙ young

11 She holds _____.

Ⓐ one shell

Ⓑ shell one

Ⓒ many shells

Ⓓ shells many

12 The shell feels _____.

Ⓕ very

Ⓖ down

Ⓗ under

Ⓙ rough

13 He goes to the beach on a _____.

Ⓐ days

Ⓑ sunny

Ⓒ sunny day

Ⓓ day sunny

STOP

COMPREHENSION / CRITICAL THINKING

DIRECTIONS Listen to the selection. Then listen to each question. Choose the best answer. Mark your answer. *(6 points each)*

Marcos Goes Fishing

1

Marcos wants fish so he can feed his family. He gets in his boat and rows out to sea. Then he stops to eat a sandwich.

2

After he eats, Marcos catches three good fish. He is happy. Then he waits for another fish.

3

Finally, Marcos catches another fish. This fish is very big and strong! It pulls the boat through the water!

4

This fish is dangerous! Marcos cuts the line, and the fish swims away. Marcos takes home the three small fish.

© Hampton-Brown

GO ON ➡

COMPREHENSION / CRITICAL THINKING

14 Why does Marcos go out to sea?

to read	to swim	to fish	to sleep
F	G	H	J

15 Marcos catches three good fish. How does he feel?

happy	scared	angry
A	B	C

16 The big fish pulls the boat through the water. How does Marcos feel?

happy	scared	angry
F	G	H

17 Marcos cuts the line because the fish is too —

big	little	long	fat
A	B	C	D

GO ON ➡

COMPREHENSION / CRITICAL THINKING

DIRECTIONS Listen to the selection. Then listen to each question. Choose the best answer. Mark your answer. *(6 points each)*

There are many kinds of seaweeds. Seaweeds can be many colors. Some are green or blue. Others are red or brown.

Seaweeds grow in seawater and on rocks. They need sunlight to grow. They do not make flowers or seeds.

Some seaweeds are very small, but others are large. A giant kelp plant can grow to more than 200 feet long!

People use seaweeds for many things. Some people eat dried seaweeds. People use parts of seaweeds in foods, medicines, and paint.

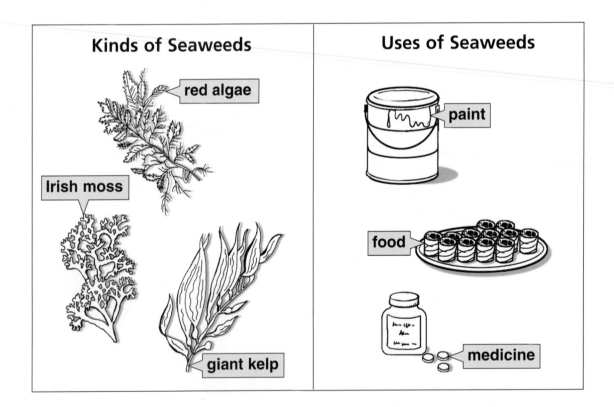

Kinds of Seaweeds

red algae

Irish moss

giant kelp

Uses of Seaweeds

paint

food

medicine

GO ON ▶

COMPREHENSION / CRITICAL THINKING

18 **What is the selection mostly about?**

(F)

(G)

(H)
(J)

19 **Some seaweeds are large. Which seaweed grows to more than 200 feet long?**

red algae
(A)

giant kelp
(B)

Irish moss
(C)

20 **People use seaweeds. What do they make from seaweeds?**

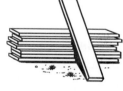

tires
(F)

paint
(G)

wood
(H)

tools
(J)

21 **What is a good title for the selection?**

How to
Cook Seaweeds
(A)

Flowers
from Seaweeds
(B)

Seaweeds
and Sunshine
(C)

Seaweeds
and Their Uses
(D)

STOP

Unit 4 • Watery World

DIRECTIONS Read the sentence. Choose the word that goes in the blank. **Mark your answer.** *(4 points each)*

 Sample

Carlo wears his new _____ to school.

- Ⓐ car
- Ⓑ book
- ⬤ jacket
- Ⓓ building

---

1 Frank studies fish. He is _____ about them.

- Ⓐ quick
- Ⓑ angry
- Ⓒ strange
- Ⓓ curious

---

2 Oh, no! The "S" on the sign is _____.

- Ⓕ hidden
- Ⓖ backward
- Ⓗ downstairs
- Ⓙ comfortable

FOR SALE

---

3 Jill _____ an insect in a jar.

- Ⓐ chases
- Ⓑ breaks
- Ⓒ captures
- Ⓓ celebrates

---

4 Animals use _____ to hide from each other.

- Ⓕ hail
- Ⓖ safety
- Ⓗ lightning
- Ⓙ camouflage

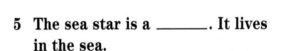

---

5 The sea star is a _____. It lives in the sea.

- Ⓐ signal
- Ⓑ shelter
- Ⓒ twister
- Ⓓ creature

---

6 No one can find Maria's shells. She hides them in a _____ place.

- Ⓕ wet
- Ⓖ dirty
- Ⓗ secret
- Ⓙ dangerous

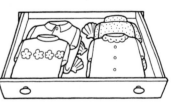

STOP

VOCABULARY

DIRECTIONS Read the sentence. Choose the word that goes in the blank. Mark your answer. *(4 points each)*

⭐ **Sample**

Gina walks _____ through the park.

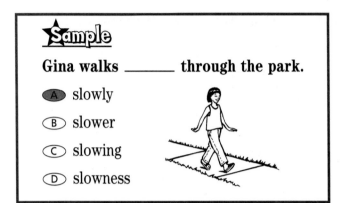

- (A) slowly
- (B) slower
- (C) slowing
- (D) slowness

---

7 A fish is _____ a bear.

- (A) alike
- (B) likely
- (C) unlike
- (D) likeness

8 The water bottle was empty.
I can _____ it.

- (F) fills
- (G) refill
- (H) filler
- (J) filling

9 A glass is _____.

- (A) break
- (B) breaks
- (C) rebreak
- (D) breakable

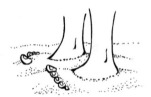

10 The _____ beach feels soft.

- (F) sandy
- (G) sands
- (H) sanding
- (J) sandiness

STOP

GRAMMAR

DIRECTIONS Read the sentences. Choose the word or words that go in each blank. Mark your answer. *(2 points each)*

Sample

I love to go to the beach on
a _____ day.

Ⓐ shine

Ⓑ sunny

Ⓒ quickly

Ⓓ happen

---

11 Everything feels warm. The sand feels the _____ of all.

Ⓐ warm

Ⓑ warmer

Ⓒ warmest

Ⓓ most warm

12 I watch _____ crabs dig in the sand.

Ⓕ tiny

Ⓖ softly

Ⓗ waves

Ⓙ makes

13 The birds are _____ during the day than they are at night.

Ⓐ noisier

Ⓑ noisiest

Ⓒ more noisier

Ⓓ most noisiest

14 I like the moonlight. It shines on the _____ water at night.

Ⓕ run

Ⓖ over

Ⓗ dark

Ⓙ sand

15 The ocean seems _____ at night than during the day.

Ⓐ peacefuller

Ⓑ peacefullest

Ⓒ most peaceful

Ⓓ more peaceful

16 Of all the places I go, I am _____ at the ocean.

Ⓕ calm

Ⓖ calmer

Ⓗ calmest

Ⓙ most calmest

© Hampton-Brown

STOP

GRAMMAR

DIRECTIONS Read the sentences. Choose the best way to write each underlined part, or choose "Correct as it is." Mark your answer.

(2 points each)

⭐ **Sample**

Manuel wanted a <u>goodly day</u> to go fishing.

- Ⓐ day good
- ⬤Ⓑ good day
- Ⓒ day goodly
- Ⓓ Correct as it is

---

17 "I hope we catch <u>not any</u> fish!" said Grandpa.

- Ⓐ none
- Ⓑ some
- Ⓒ a one
- Ⓓ Correct as it is

18 Manuel wanted to catch more than <u>three fish</u>.

- Ⓕ fish three
- Ⓖ threes fish
- Ⓗ fish threes
- Ⓙ Correct as it is

19 Manuel and Grandpa put two <u>longs poles</u> in the boat.

- Ⓐ long poles
- Ⓑ poles long
- Ⓒ longs pole
- Ⓓ Correct as it is

20 They rowed to the middle of the <u>deep</u> lake.

- Ⓕ tall
- Ⓖ sailed
- Ⓗ across
- Ⓙ Correct as it is

21 It was a <u>spot quiet</u> to fish.

- Ⓐ quiet spot
- Ⓑ spots quiet
- Ⓒ quiet spots
- Ⓓ Correct as it is

22 They caught so <u>lot</u> fish that they filled their boat!

- Ⓕ one
- Ⓖ few
- Ⓗ many
- Ⓙ Correct as it is

⬤ **STOP**

COMPREHENSION / CRITICAL THINKING

DIRECTIONS Read the selection. Then read each item. Choose the best answer. Mark your answer. *(4 points each)*

Salt and Its Uses

1   Many fish need the salty ocean to live. Do you know that we need salt to help us live, too?

2   Most people like the taste of salt. Salt adds flavor to food. Many people put salt in foods as they cook. Some people add even more salt to food at the table.

3   People use salt to keep food from spoiling. Meat or fish packed in salt will stay safe to eat for a long time.

4   In the winter, salt helps make roads and highways safe. In cold places, workers spread it on roads to melt snow and ice. That way cars and trucks won't slide into each other.

5   Factories use salt to make many things. Salt is used to make glass, soap, paper, and plastics.

6   We may not need salt as much as fish do, but it does help us live!

People add salt to make their food taste better.

People pack meat and fish in salt.

Workers spread salt on icy roads.

People use salt to make soap and other things.

© Hampton-Brown

GO ON

COMPREHENSION / CRITICAL THINKING

23 **What is the selection mostly about?**

Ⓐ Fish live in the ocean.

Ⓑ Salt costs a lot of money.

Ⓒ Salt is important to people.

Ⓓ People keep salt on the table.

24 **Look at the cluster.**

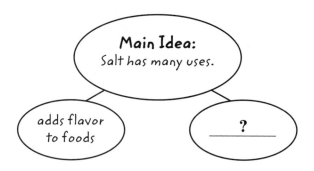

Which of these goes in the blank?

Ⓕ is easy to pour

Ⓖ keeps roads safe

Ⓗ is white and grainy

Ⓙ comes from the ocean

25 **What is the main idea of paragraph 2?**

Ⓐ People buy a lot of salt.

Ⓑ Some foods are very salty.

Ⓒ People like the taste of salt.

Ⓓ Some people are good cooks.

26 **Read this main idea.**

Salt keeps food from spoiling.

Which of these tells about this main idea?

Ⓕ The ocean is very salty.

Ⓖ Fish cannot live without salt.

Ⓗ Workers eat a lot of salty food in the winter.

Ⓙ Meat packed in salt stays safe to eat for a long time.

27 **Read this main idea.**

Factories use salt to make things.

Which of these tells about this main idea?

Ⓐ Fish need the salty ocean to live.

Ⓑ Some plastics are made with salt.

Ⓒ Some people add even more salt to food.

Ⓓ Salt keeps cars from sliding into each other.

© Hampton-Brown

GO ON ➡

COMPREHENSION / CRITICAL THINKING

DIRECTIONS Read the selection. Then read each item. Choose the best answer. Mark your answer. *(4 points each)*

Abdul's Wish

Abdul the fisherman sells fish at the market. Every morning Abdul goes to fish in the sea. He takes the fish he catches back to sell. Today he catches a big fish and pulls it into the boat.

The big fish looks at Abdul and says, "Please let me go. I will give you one wish. You may wish for anything you want."

Abdul knows he needs salt to pack his fish for market. Salt costs a lot, too. So he says, "I wish for enough salt to fill my boat and three others!"

The fish smiles and says, "Yes, you may have the salt."

Abdul lets the fish go free. Suddenly the boat fills with salt! Then it sinks into the sea. Abdul has to swim back to shore.

Today salt still pours from the boat beneath the sea. That is why the sea is so salty.

© Hampton-Brown

GO ON ➡

COMPREHENSION / CRITICAL THINKING

28 **Abdul goes fishing because he —**

    Ⓕ is lonely

    Ⓖ is hungry

    Ⓗ needs fish to sell

    Ⓙ likes to talk to fish

29 **The fish gives Abdul a wish because it —**

    Ⓐ wants to be free

    Ⓑ is afraid of Abdul's boat

    Ⓒ wants the sea to be salty

    Ⓓ is happy that Abdul caught it

30 **Why does Abdul wish for salt?**

    Ⓕ He wants some salt to sell.

    Ⓖ He needs salt to pack his fish.

    Ⓗ He likes to put salt on his food.

    Ⓙ He hopes the salt will sink his boat.

31 **Abdul lets the fish go free. This shows that Abdul —**

    Ⓐ is afraid

    Ⓑ is strong

    Ⓒ likes to swim

    Ⓓ keeps his promises

© Hampton-Brown

STOP

Unit 4 • Watery World

VOCABULARY

DIRECTIONS Read the sentence. Choose the word that goes in the blank.
Mark your answer. *(4 points each)*

☆Sample

Carlo wears his new _____ to school.

- Ⓐ car
- Ⓑ book
- **Ⓒ jacket**
- Ⓓ building

---

1 Jill _____ insects in a jar so she can study them.

- Ⓐ minds
- Ⓑ forgets
- Ⓒ reminds
- Ⓓ captures

2 Many animals use _____ to hide from their enemies.

- Ⓕ safety
- Ⓖ boldness
- Ⓗ backbones
- Ⓙ camouflage

3 Frank asks a lot of questions about fish because he is _____.

- Ⓐ quick
- Ⓑ curious
- Ⓒ outgrown
- Ⓓ traditional

4 Maria keeps her shells in a _____ place no one else knows about.

- Ⓕ cold
- Ⓖ silent
- Ⓗ secret
- Ⓙ dangerous

5 Some _____ chase their enemies away.

- Ⓐ shelters
- Ⓑ defenses
- Ⓒ materials
- Ⓓ creatures

6 Dad _____ to take us to the lake on Saturday.

- Ⓕ judged
- Ⓖ noticed
- Ⓗ promised
- Ⓙ discovered

STOP

VOCABULARY

DIRECTIONS Read the sentence. Choose the word that goes in the blank. Mark your answer. *(4 points each)*

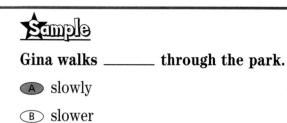

Sample

Gina walks _____ through the park.

- Ⓐ slowly
- Ⓑ slower
- Ⓒ slowing
- Ⓓ slowness

7 A fish is _____ a bear.

- Ⓐ alike
- Ⓑ likely
- Ⓒ unlike
- Ⓓ likeness

8 Please wash your cup so you can _____ it later.

- Ⓕ using
- Ⓖ reuse
- Ⓗ useful
- Ⓙ useless

9 Some fish are very _____ and bright.

- Ⓐ colors
- Ⓑ colorful
- Ⓒ coloring
- Ⓓ colorless

10 The _____ beach feels soft under my feet.

- Ⓕ sandy
- Ⓖ sands
- Ⓗ sandly
- Ⓙ sandness

STOP

GRAMMAR

DIRECTIONS Read the sentences. Choose the word or words that go in each blank. Mark your answer. *(2 points each)*

I love to go to the beach on a ___Sample___ day. The sand is the ___11___ of all then. I listen to the ___12___ birds. Sometimes I see ___13___ dig holes in the sand.

At night, I watch the silver moonlight shine on the ___14___ water. The ocean seems ___15___ at night than it is during the day. It is ___16___ then, too.

⭐Sample

Ⓐ shine

Ⓑ sunny

Ⓒ quickly

Ⓓ happen

11 Ⓐ warm

Ⓑ warmer

Ⓒ warmest

Ⓓ most warmest

12 Ⓕ fly

Ⓖ noisy

Ⓗ below

Ⓙ across

13 Ⓐ small crabs

Ⓑ crabs small

Ⓒ smalls crabs

Ⓓ crabs smalls

14 Ⓕ run

Ⓖ over

Ⓗ dark

Ⓙ sand

15 Ⓐ calm

Ⓑ calmer

Ⓒ most calm

Ⓓ more calmer

16 Ⓕ peacefuller

Ⓖ peacefullest

Ⓗ most peaceful

Ⓙ more peaceful

STOP

© Hampton-Brown

GRAMMAR

DIRECTIONS Read the sentences. Choose the best way to write each underlined part, or choose "Correct as it is." Mark your answer.

(2 points each)

Manuel wanted a <u>goodly day</u> to go fishing. Friday was the <u>cloudy</u> day
        ⭐Sample   **17**
of the week, and Grandpa said, "This is good fishing weather."

"I hope we catch <u>few</u> fish today," Manuel said. "We need at least
                    18

<u>three fish</u> for dinner!"
   19

Manuel and Grandpa got two <u>longs pole</u> and left in the boat. Soon
                              20

they stopped in a <u>quiet</u> spot. They caught so <u>lot</u> fish they filled the boat.
                     21   **22**

⭐Sample

Ⓐ day good

🅱 good day

Ⓒ day goodly

Ⓓ Correct as it is

17 Ⓐ cloudier

Ⓑ cloudiest

Ⓒ less cloudy

Ⓓ Correct as it is

18 Ⓕ no

Ⓖ none

Ⓗ some

Ⓙ Correct as it is

19 Ⓐ fish three

Ⓑ threes fish

Ⓒ fish threes

Ⓓ Correct as it is

20 Ⓕ long poles

Ⓖ poles long

Ⓗ longs poles

Ⓙ Correct as it is

21 Ⓐ was

Ⓑ with

Ⓒ down

Ⓓ Correct as it is

22 Ⓕ one

Ⓖ few

Ⓗ many

Ⓙ Correct as it is

STOP

DIRECTIONS Read the selections. Then read each item. Choose the best answer. Mark your answer. *(4 points each)*

Salt and Its Uses

1   You know that some fish live in the salty ocean, but do you know how important salt is to people and other animals? Long ago, Roman soldiers got a little salt each day to keep them healthy. In parts of Africa, salt was worth so much that people used it for money.

2   Today, many people add salt to food at the table. Most cooks put salt in foods, too. Salt makes food taste better, but there are more reasons why salt is important.

3   People need salt to keep food from spoiling. Meat or fish packed in salt will stay safe to eat for a long time. Sometimes people soak vegetables in salty water. When there are no fresh vegetables around, people can eat these "pickled" vegetables to stay healthy.

People add salt to food.

© Hampton-Brown

GO ON ➡

COMPREHENSION / CRITICAL THINKING

Salt and Its Uses, continued

4   Animals need salt, too. Salt keeps animals from getting so thirsty when the weather is hot and dry. It also helps keep animals' blood healthy. Many farmers put blocks of salt where their animals can lick them and get the salt they need.

5   In the winter, salt helps make roads and highways safe. When there is snow or ice, workers spread salt on roads. The salt melts the snow and ice so cars and trucks don't slide around and crash.

Animals get salt from salt blocks.

Trucks spread salt on icy roads.

6   Factories use salt when they make things, such as glass, soap, paper, and plastics. We may not use salt as money today, but it is still important to everyone.

GO ON ▶

Why the Sea Is Salty

Pedro the fisherman worked hard every day. On good days Pedro caught many fish, but on bad days he caught only one or two. Then one day Pedro came home with no fish at all, and that night he was hungry.

The next day, Pedro rowed far, far out to sea looking for fish. No other fisherman had gone that far before. Many miles from land, Pedro was surprised to discover an island.

On the island, Pedro found a strange box with a handle on one side. When Pedro turned the handle, salt poured out of the box. He was excited because he knew that people in his village always needed salt. Pedro had found a secret salt maker! Quickly he filled a bucket with salt, lifted it into his boat, and rowed home to share his good luck.

GO ON ➡

Why the Sea Is Salty, continued

Pedro gave most of the salt to his neighbors and kept some salt for himself. When the salt was gone, he returned to the island. This time Pedro filled three buckets with salt. Again he shared one bucket of salt, but he sold the salt in the other two buckets. He decided that selling salt was much easier than catching fish!

Now Pedro's life was easy! Once a week, he rowed to the island and brought back salt to sell. With no work to do, Pedro grew lazy and did not want to row to the island every week. Then he got an idea.

"I will go to the island once more," he said. "I will bring the salt maker home, and I will never have to row my boat again."

Pedro rowed to the island, grabbed the salt maker, and started to row home. Soon the wind began to blow and waves bumped the little boat up and down. Suddenly a big wave hit the boat, and the salt maker fell into the sea!

Now Pedro has to work hard at fishing again. But at the bottom of the sea, the secret salt maker keeps working every day and that is why the ocean is salty!

GO ON ➡

COMPREHENSION / CRITICAL THINKING

Use "Salt and Its Uses" on pages 38–39 to answer items 23–26.

---

23 Look at the cluster.

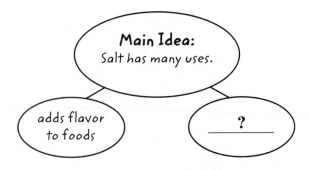

Which of these goes in the blank?

Ⓐ is easy to pour

Ⓑ comes from the ocean

Ⓒ does not cost very much

Ⓓ keeps roads safe in winter

24 What is paragraph 1 mostly about?

Ⓕ Fish live in the ocean.

Ⓖ Salt makes food taste better.

Ⓗ Salt is important to people and animals.

Ⓙ Roman soldiers ate a little salt every day.

25 Read this main idea.

> Salt keeps food from spoiling.

Which of these tells more about this main idea?

Ⓐ Some plastics are made with salt.

Ⓑ Salt has been important for a long time.

Ⓒ Road workers use a lot of salt in the winter.

Ⓓ Fish packed in salt stays safe to eat for a long time.

26 What is the main idea of paragraph 4?

Ⓕ Salt blocks are only for cows.

Ⓖ Animals like very hot weather.

Ⓗ Salt helps keep animals healthy.

Ⓙ Farm animals are always thirsty.

© Hampton-Brown

GO ON ➡

> Use "Why the Sea Is Salty" on pages 40–41 to answer items 27–30.

27 Why does Pedro row so far out to sea?

Ⓐ He knows he can find salt there.

Ⓑ He wants to win a fishing contest.

Ⓒ He is hungry and needs to catch some fish.

Ⓓ He remembers where there is a good fishing spot.

28 Pedro finds some salt. He is excited because —

Ⓕ salt is easy to carry

Ⓖ fish like salty water

Ⓗ people in his village need salt

Ⓙ he can put plenty of salt on his food

29 Why does Pedro stop fishing?

Ⓐ All the fish are gone.

Ⓑ It is easier to sell salt.

Ⓒ He forgets how to fish.

Ⓓ The wind blows too hard.

30 Which of these actions shows that Pedro cares about other people?

Ⓕ Pedro gets a good idea.

Ⓖ Pedro works hard every day.

Ⓗ Pedro tries to row his boat home.

Ⓙ Pedro shares his salt with his neighbors.

> Use "Salt and Its Uses" and "Why the Sea Is Salty" to answer item 31.

31 Both of the selections will be published in one book. Which of these is the best title for the book?

Ⓐ The Salty Ocean

Ⓑ Pedro Finds Salt

Ⓒ Salt: In the Sea and on the Land

Ⓓ How Salt Makes Food Taste Good

© Hampton-Brown

STOP

Unit 4 • Answer Key

ⒷBeginning Progress Test

VOCABULARY
(4 points each)

1 B	4 H
2 J	5 D
3 A	6 G

GRAMMAR
(4 points each)

7 B	11 C
8 G	12 J
9 D	13 C
10 H	

COMPREHENSION / CRITICAL THINKING
(6 points each)

14 H	18 F
15 A	19 B
16 G	20 G
17 A	21 D

ⒾIntermediate Progress Test

VOCABULARY
(4 points each)

1 D	6 H
2 G	7 C
3 C	8 G
4 J	9 D
5 D	10 F

GRAMMAR
(2 points each)

11 C	17 B
12 F	18 J
13 A	19 A
14 H	20 J
15 D	21 A
16 H	22 H

COMPREHENSION / CRITICAL THINKING
(4 points each)

23 C	28 H
24 G	29 A
25 C	30 G
26 J	31 D
27 B	

ⒶAdvanced Progress Test

VOCABULARY
(4 points each)

1 D	6 H
2 J	7 C
3 B	8 G
4 H	9 B
5 D	10 F

GRAMMAR
(2 points each)

11 C	17 B
12 G	18 H
13 A	19 D
14 H	20 F
15 B	21 D
16 J	22 H

COMPREHENSION / CRITICAL THINKING
(4 points each)

23 D	28 H
24 H	29 B
25 D	30 J
26 H	31 C
27 C	

Unit 4 • Self-Assessment

I Can Speak English!

1. I learned to describe a place.

 The beach is _____.

2. I can give more details about that place.

The beach also _____.

My New Words

_____
_____
_____
_____
_____
_____
_____
_____
_____

I Can Read in English!

3. I can tell what a character does and why he or she does it.

☐ yes   ☐ not yet

4. I can tell the main idea and supporting details.

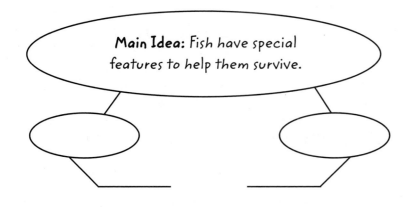

Main Idea: Fish have special features to help them survive.

What I've Read

☐ The Secret Footprints

☐ Hello, Fish!

☐ _____

☐ _____

Unit 5 • Directions for Ⓑ Progress Test

Distribute the test pages. Before students begin each subtest, read aloud the directions and use the script to work through each sample item.

VOCABULARY

Read aloud the directions on page 45. Then work through the sample item. Say:

Sample

Look at the pictures in the box. Which picture shows a jacket? Point to the picture. (Pause.) *The second bubble is filled in because the second picture shows a jacket.*

Items 1–6

Read each question aloud. Provide time for students to mark their answers.

GRAMMAR

Read aloud the directions on page 47. Then work through the sample item. Say:

Sample

Look at the picture in the box. Look at the sentences. There is a word missing in the second sentence. Look at the four choices. Let's try each one. Listen:

> *Dara plays basketball. It has the ball.*
> *Dara plays basketball. He has the ball.*
> *Dara plays basketball. Him has the ball.*
> *Dara plays basketball. They has the ball.*

The second bubble is filled in because He *is the best answer.*

Items 7–13

Read aloud each sentence with its answer choices. Provide time for students to mark their answers.

COMPREHENSION / CRITICAL THINKING

Selection 1 and Items 14–17

Read aloud the directions on page 49. Say: *Now listen to the selection. The title is:*

How to Make Gazpacho

Look at Picture 1.	*Our neighbor Corazón loves to make a soup called* gazpacho. *She makes it the same way she made it at home in Spain.*
Look at Picture 2.	*Now she teaches me how to make it. First I cut up a cucumber. I cut up a tomato, a green pepper, and an onion, too.*
Look at Picture 3.	*Next, we mix the vegetables with tomato juice. Corazón adds oil and vinegar. Then I mix in salt, pepper, and spices.*
Look at Picture 4.	*Corazón adds ice cubes. Gazpacho tastes great on a hot day!*

Then read each question aloud. Provide time for students to mark their answers.

Selection 2 and Items 18–21

Read aloud the directions on page 51. Say: *Now listen to the selection. The title is:*

Bette Bao Lord

Look at the first picture.	*Bette Bao was born in China in 1938. Eight years later, her parents took her to the United States. Baby sister Sansan was too small to go with them then.*
Look at the next picture.	*Finally, Sansan moved to the United States, too. Bette and Sansan talked and talked. Then Bette began to write a book about Sansan's life called* Eighth Moon.
Look at the next picture.	*Bette had a very happy year in 1963. She married a man named Winston Lord.*
Look at the last picture.	*The next year,* Eighth Moon *was published. Many people read the book and liked it. Today, Bette Bao Lord is a famous author.*

Then read each question aloud. Provide time for students to mark their answers.

Unit 5 • Directions for ① and Ⓐ Progress Tests

Distribute the test pages. Before students begin each subtest, read aloud the directions and use the script to work through each sample item.

VOCABULARY

Read aloud the directions on page 45. Then work through the sample item. Say:

Sample

Read the sentence in the box. (Pause.) Which word goes in the blank? Let's try each one:

Carlo wears his new car *to school.*
Carlo wears his new book *to school.*
Carlo wears his new jacket *to school.*
Carlo wears his new building *to school.*

The third bubble is filled in because jacket *is the best answer.*

Items 1–10

Tell students to complete the remaining items in the same way. Provide time for students to mark their answers.

GRAMMAR

Read aloud the directions on page 47. Then work through the sample item. Say:

Sample

Look at the sentences. The first sentence says:
Look at this beautiful quilt! *Which word goes in the next sentence? Look at the four choices. Let's try each one:*

Aunt Lil made I *for me.*
Aunt Lil made it *for me.*
Aunt Lil made we *for me.*
Aunt Lil made they *for me.*

The second bubble is filled in because it *is the best answer.*

Items 11–14

Tell students to complete the remaining items in the same way. Provide time for them to mark their answers.

GRAMMAR continued

Read aloud the directions on page 48. Then work through the sample item. Say:

Sample

Read the sentence. (Pause.) What is the best way to write the underlined part? Look at the four choices. The first bubble is filled in because his *is the best answer.*

Items 15–18

Tell students to complete the remaining items in the same way. Provide time for them to mark their answers.

COMPREHENSION / CRITICAL THINKING

Selections and Items 19–30

Read aloud the directions for each selection. Provide time for students to read the selection and mark their answers.

DIRECTIONS Record the student's name and test date. Use the **Answer Key** on page 54a to score the student's test. Then, in the Student Profile, circle the item number of each correct answer and circle the plus or minus sign to indicate mastery. Calculate the subtest scores and then the total test score. To help you group students for reteaching, transfer the minus sign for any unmastered skill to the **Class Profile** (page 45f).

Student Name _____   Date _____

| Subtest | Tested Skills | ITEM ANALYSIS | | TEST SCORES |
		Item Numbers	Mastery	No. Correct × Points = Score
VOCABULARY	Key Words	1 2 3 4 5 6	5 out of 6 + −	_____ × 4 = /24
GRAMMAR	Nouns and Pronouns	7 8 9 10 11 12 13	6 out of 7 + −	_____ × 4 = /28
COMPREHENSION / CRITICAL THINKING	Identify Sequence	14 15 18 19	3 out of 4 + −	_____ × 6 = /48
	Draw Conclusions	16 17 20 21	3 out of 4 + −	

TOTAL UNIT 5 PROGRESS TEST   /100

DIRECTIONS Record the student's name and test date. Use the **Answer Key** on page 54a to score the student's test. Then, in the Student Profile, circle the item number of each correct answer and circle the plus or minus sign to indicate mastery. Calculate the subtest scores and then the total test score. To help you group students for reteaching, transfer the minus sign for any unmastered skill to the **Class Profile** (page 45f).

Student Name _____   Date _____

Subtest	Tested Skills	ITEM ANALYSIS		TEST SCORES
		Item Numbers	Mastery	No. Correct × Points = Score
VOCABULARY	Key Words	1 2 3 4 5 6 7 8 9 10	8 out of 10 + −	_____ × 4 = /40
GRAMMAR	Nouns and Pronouns	11 12 13 14 15 16 17 18	6 out of 8 + −	_____ × 3 = /24
COMPREHENSION / CRITICAL THINKING	Identify Sequence	20 21 25 26	3 out of 4 + −	
	Draw Conclusions	22 23 27 28	3 out of 4 + −	_____ × 3 = /36
	Distinguish Literary Forms and Purposes	19 24 29 30	3 out of 4 + −	
			TOTAL UNIT 5 PROGRESS TEST	/100

© Hampton-Brown

Unit 5 • Student Profile for Advanced Progress Test

DIRECTIONS Record the student's name and test date. Use the **Answer Key** on page 54a to score the student's test. Then, in the Student Profile, circle the item number of each correct answer and circle the plus or minus sign to indicate mastery. Calculate the subtest scores and then the total test score. To help you group students for reteaching, transfer the minus sign for any unmastered skill to the **Class Profile** (page 45f).

Student Name _____ **Date** _____

Subtest	Tested Skills	ITEM ANALYSIS		TEST SCORES
		Item Numbers	**Mastery**	**No. Correct × Points = Score**
VOCABULARY	**Key Words**	1 2 3 4 5 6 7 8 9 10	8 out of 10 + −	_____ × 4 = ⬜/40
GRAMMAR	**Nouns and Pronouns**	11 12 13 14 15 16 17 18	6 out of 8 + −	_____ × 3 = ⬜/24
COMPREHENSION / CRITICAL THINKING	**Identify Sequence**	20 21 25 26	3 out of 4 + −	_____ × 3 = ⬜/36
	Draw Conclusions	22 23 27 28	3 out of 4 + −	
	Distinguish Literary Forms and Purposes	19 24 29 30	3 out of 4 + −	
			TOTAL UNIT 5 PROGRESS TEST	⬜/100

© Hampton-Brown

Unit 5 • Class Profile

Date _____

DIRECTIONS Use the **Unit 5 Student Profiles** to complete this chart. In each row, write the student's name, fill in the bubble for the test form taken, and mark a minus sign (–) for any skill not yet mastered. Then group students and use the reteaching ideas and practice exercises to help students reach mastery.

Student Name	Test Form	TESTED SKILLS				
		Key Words	**Nouns and Pronouns**	**Identify Sequence**	**Draw Conclusions**	**Distinguish Literary Forms and Purposes**
	Ⓑ Ⓘ Ⓐ					
	Ⓑ Ⓘ Ⓐ					
	Ⓑ Ⓘ Ⓐ					
	Ⓑ Ⓘ Ⓐ					
	Ⓑ Ⓘ Ⓐ					
	Ⓑ Ⓘ Ⓐ					
	Ⓑ Ⓘ Ⓐ					
	Ⓑ Ⓘ Ⓐ					
	Ⓑ Ⓘ Ⓐ					
	Ⓑ Ⓘ Ⓐ					
	Ⓑ Ⓘ Ⓐ					
	Ⓑ Ⓘ Ⓐ					
	Ⓑ Ⓘ Ⓐ					
	Ⓑ Ⓘ Ⓐ					
	Ⓑ Ⓘ Ⓐ					
	Ⓑ Ⓘ Ⓐ					
	Ⓑ Ⓘ Ⓐ					
	Ⓑ Ⓘ Ⓐ					
	Ⓑ Ⓘ Ⓐ					
	Ⓑ Ⓘ Ⓐ					
	Ⓑ Ⓘ Ⓐ					
	Ⓑ Ⓘ Ⓐ					
RETEACHING RESOURCES		Ⓑ Ⓘ Ⓐ AH T38	Ⓑ AH T40 Ⓘ Ⓐ EAYC 244, 246–249	Ⓑ Ⓘ Ⓐ LB TG	Ⓑ Ⓘ Ⓐ LB TG	Ⓘ Ⓐ LB TG
PRACTICE EXERCISES		PB 71, 79	EAYC 386, 387–389	PB 75	PB 76–77	

KEY: **AH:** Assessment Handbook **EAYC:** English at Your Command! **LB TG:** Leveled Books Teacher's Guide **PB:** Practice Book

© Hampton-Brown

Unit 5 • Cultural Ties

VOCABULARY

DIRECTIONS Listen to each question. Then choose the correct picture.
Mark your answer. (4 points each)

⭐Sample

Which picture shows a <u>jacket</u>?

Ⓐ   Ⓑ   Ⓒ   Ⓓ

1   Which picture shows a <u>throne</u>?

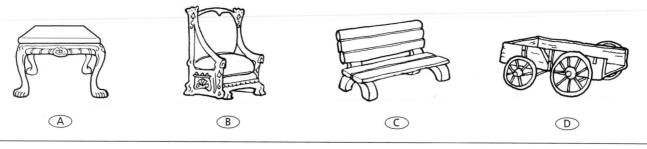

Ⓐ   Ⓑ   Ⓒ   Ⓓ

2   Which picture shows a <u>bloom</u>?

Ⓕ   Ⓖ   Ⓗ   Ⓙ

3   The girl feels <u>pride</u>. Which picture shows this?

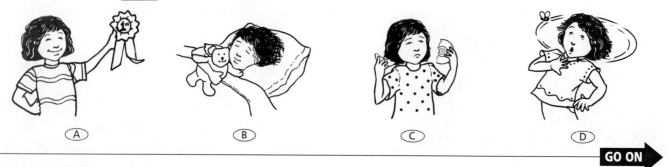

Ⓐ   Ⓑ   Ⓒ   Ⓓ

GO ON ➡

VOCABULARY

4 Which picture shows a lotus?

Ⓕ   Ⓖ   Ⓗ   Ⓙ

5 The man arrives home. Which picture shows this?

Ⓐ   Ⓑ   Ⓒ   Ⓓ

6 Which person is an emperor?

  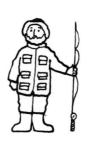 

Ⓕ   Ⓖ   Ⓗ   Ⓙ

© Hampton-Brown

STOP

GRAMMAR

DIRECTIONS Look at the picture. Listen to the sentence with each answer. Choose the word that completes the sentence correctly. **Mark your answer.** *(4 points each)*

> ★**Sample**
>
> Dara plays basketball.
> _____ has the ball.
>
> Ⓐ It
> **Ⓑ He**
> Ⓒ Him
> Ⓓ They

7 Dara throws _____ to Kim.

Ⓐ it
Ⓑ he
Ⓒ she
Ⓓ him

8 _____ catches the ball.

Ⓕ It
Ⓖ She
Ⓗ Her
Ⓙ They

9 _____ brother and I play, too.

Ⓐ I
Ⓑ Me
Ⓒ My
Ⓓ Him

10 _____ are all on a team.

Ⓕ It
Ⓖ We
Ⓗ She
Ⓙ Them

GO ON ➡

© Hampton-Brown

GRAMMAR

B 48

11 Our _____ name is the Bobcats.

(A) teams

(B) teams'

(C) team's

(D) teams's

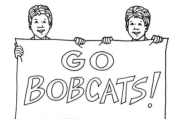

13 We learn about the game from _____.

(A) he

(B) his

(C) they

(D) them

12 Our coaches teach _____.

(F) us

(G) my

(H) we

(J) they

STOP

© Hampton-Brown

COMPREHENSION / CRITICAL THINKING

DIRECTIONS Listen to the selection. Then listen to each question. Choose the best answer. Mark your answer. *(6 points each)*

How to Make Gazpacho

1

Our neighbor Corazón loves to make a soup called *gazpacho*. She makes it the same way she made it at home in Spain.

2

Now she teaches me how to make it. First I cut up a cucumber. I cut up a tomato, a green pepper, and an onion, too.

3

Next, we mix the vegetables with tomato juice. Corazón adds oil and vinegar. Then I mix in salt, pepper, and spices.

4

Corazón adds ice cubes. *Gazpacho* tastes great on a hot day!

© Hampton-Brown

GO ON ➡

COMPREHENSION / CRITICAL THINKING

14 What does the boy do first?

adds tomato juice
Ⓕ

adds salt
Ⓖ

cuts vegetables
Ⓗ

15 What does Corazón do last?

mixes vegetables
Ⓐ

adds ice cubes
Ⓑ

adds pepper
Ⓒ

reads the directions
Ⓓ

16 Where did Corazón learn to make *gazpacho*?

in Spain
Ⓕ

in Mexico
Ⓖ

in the U.S.
Ⓗ

in Japan
Ⓙ

17 Where should you keep *gazpacho*?

Ⓐ

Ⓑ

Ⓒ

GO ON ➡

COMPREHENSION / CRITICAL THINKING

DIRECTIONS Listen to the selection. Then listen to each question. Choose the best answer. Mark your answer. *(6 points each)*

Bette Bao Lord

Bette Bao was born in China in 1938. Eight years later, her parents took her to the United States. Baby sister Sansan was too small to go with them then.

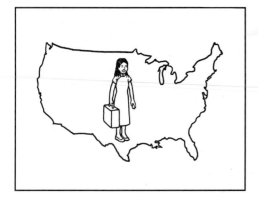

Finally, Sansan moved to the United States, too. Bette and Sansan talked and talked. Then Bette began to write a book about Sansan's life called *Eighth Moon*.

Bette had a very happy year in 1963. She married a man named Winston Lord.

The next year, *Eighth Moon* was published. Many people read the book and liked it. Today, Bette Bao Lord is a famous author.

© Hampton-Brown

GO ON ➡

COMPREHENSION / CRITICAL THINKING

18 Which of these happened first?

Bette left China.
Ⓕ

Bette got married.
Ⓖ

Sansan came to the U.S.
Ⓗ

19 Which of these happened last?

Bette got married.
Ⓐ

Bette and Sansan talked.
Ⓑ

Bette finished her book.
Ⓒ

20 From the selection, you can tell that Bette's book is about —

life in China
Ⓕ

Chinese letters
Ⓖ

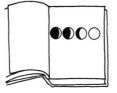
the Moon
Ⓗ

21 Bette is a good writer. How do you know?

Many people liked Bette's book.
Ⓐ

Bette married Winston Lord.
Ⓑ

Bette and Sansan talked and talked.
Ⓒ

Bette called her book *Eighth Moon*.
Ⓓ

STOP

Unit 5 • Cultural Ties

VOCABULARY

DIRECTIONS Read the sentence. Choose the word or words that go
in the blank. Mark your answer. *(4 points each)*

Sample

Carlo wears his new _____ to school.

Ⓐ car

Ⓑ book

Ⓒ jacket

Ⓓ building

1 My plant has one big _____.

Ⓐ collar

Ⓑ bloom

Ⓒ family

Ⓓ garden

2 Komar was in such a hurry, he _____
his homework!

Ⓕ sent

Ⓖ forgot

Ⓗ carried

Ⓙ noticed

3 Niki _____ at school at 7:30.

Ⓐ rides

Ⓑ drives

Ⓒ arrives

Ⓓ celebrates

4 My clothes _____ Vietnam.

Ⓕ put on

Ⓖ look at

Ⓗ pick out

Ⓙ come from

5 My grandmother gave me this ring.
It is very _____.

Ⓐ sad

Ⓑ proud

Ⓒ wrong

Ⓓ special

GO ON ➡

VOCABULARY

6 A _____ grows in the water.

Ⓕ map

Ⓖ pole

Ⓗ tribe

Ⓙ lotus

7 The _____ ruled Vietnam for 50 years.

Ⓐ actor

Ⓑ father

Ⓒ teacher

Ⓓ emperor

8 Golnar's team won.
Golnar feels a lot of _____.

Ⓕ fear

Ⓖ pride

Ⓗ anger

Ⓙ sadness

9 He sits on a beautiful _____.

Ⓐ plate

Ⓑ shelf

Ⓒ frame

Ⓓ throne

10 The twins _____ their tenth birthday party.

Ⓕ find

Ⓖ drop

Ⓗ order

Ⓙ remember

STOP

GRAMMAR

DIRECTIONS Read the sentences. Choose the word that goes in each blank. Mark your answer. *(3 points each)*

Look at this beautiful quilt!
Aunt Lil made _____ for me.

(A) I

(B) it

(C) we

(D) they

11 Aunt Lil used _____ old dresses.

(A) my

(B) me

(C) him

(D) hers

12 She used _____ old dresses, too.

(F) Mother

(G) Mothers

(H) Mothers'

(J) Mother's

13 Aunt Lil cut _____ into small pieces.

(A) he

(B) my

(C) they

(D) them

14 Then, _____ sewed the pieces together.

(F) us

(G) her

(H) she

(J) them

© Hampton-Brown

STOP

GRAMMAR

DIRECTIONS Read the sentences. Choose the best way to write each underlined part, or choose "Correct as it is." Mark your answer.

(3 points each)

 Sample

When Pasha was nine, <u>they's</u> family immigrated to the United States.

- Ⓐ his
- Ⓑ him
- Ⓒ he's
- Ⓓ Correct as it is

---

15 **They liked <u>them's</u> new home.**

- Ⓐ they
- Ⓑ their
- Ⓒ them
- Ⓓ Correct as it is

16 **Pasha missed his uncle. In Russia, Pasha saw <u>he</u> every day.**

- Ⓕ she
- Ⓖ him
- Ⓗ they
- Ⓙ Correct as it is

17 **Pasha loved <u>Uncle Vanya's</u> stories.**

- Ⓐ Uncle Vanya
- Ⓑ Uncle Vanyas
- Ⓒ Uncle Vanyas'
- Ⓓ Correct as it is

18 **Now <u>him</u> calls Uncle Vanya every week.**

- Ⓕ he
- Ⓖ her
- Ⓗ they
- Ⓙ Correct as it is

STOP

COMPREHENSION / CRITICAL THINKING

DIRECTIONS Read the selection. Then read each item. Choose the best answer. Mark your answer. *(3 points each)*

The Story of Bette Bao Lord

Bette Bao was born in China in 1938. When she was eight, she moved to New York City with her parents. The Bao family had to leave baby Sansan behind. She was too small to go with them.

Bette did not see Sansan for 16 years. Then, Sansan came to the United States, too. Bette wrote a book about Sansan's life in China. She called the book *Eighth Moon*.

In 1963, Bette married Winston Lord. The next year, she became a U.S. citizen and *Eighth Moon* was published. Many people read her book and liked it.

After that, Bette wrote more books about China. In 1984, she finished a book about Bandit, a girl from China. Bandit moves to New York City. She does not speak English at first. The book is called *In the Year of the Boar and Jackie Robinson*.

Time Line of Bette Bao Lord's Life

Bette and her parents moved to New York City. 1946

Bette married Winston Lord. 1963

1938 Bette was born in China.

1962 Sansan came to the U.S.

1964 *Eighth Moon* was published.

1984 Bette finished *In the Year of the Boar and Jackie Robinson*.

© Hampton-Brown

GO ON ➡

COMPREHENSION / CRITICAL THINKING

19 **The author wrote the selection to —**

(A) entertain you

(B) express feelings

(C) give you information

(D) explain how to do something

20 **Which of these events happened first?**

(F) Bette got married.

(G) Bette wrote a book.

(H) Bette became a U.S. citizen.

(J) Bette moved to New York City.

21 **Sansan came to the U.S. —**

(A) before Bette was born

(B) before Bette got married

(C) after Bette wrote *Eighth Moon*

(D) after Bette wrote a book about Bandit

22 **From the selection, you can tell that Bette —**

(F) lives in China

(G) does not speak English

(H) writes books in Chinese

(J) knows a lot about China

23 **How can you tell that Bette is a good writer?**

(A) Her family lived in New York City.

(B) She married Winston Lord in 1963.

(C) She did not see Sansan for 16 years.

(D) Many people read and liked *Eighth Moon*.

24 **The selection is a —**

(F) poem

(G) folk tale

(H) biography

(J) news report

GO ON ▶

DIRECTIONS Read the selection. Then read each item. Choose the best answer. Mark your answer. *(3 points each)*

Good Food, Good Friends

Grandpa is a great cook. He is teaching me to cook Filipino food. Last week, we made *pancit* with meat and noodles.

I had an idea. "Grandpa, let's invite our neighbors to dinner."

"That's a good idea, Alina," Grandpa said to me.

I went next door. Mrs. López opened the door. "Please come to eat with my family tonight," I said.

"My family would love to come," Mrs. López said.

That evening the López family came to our house. They brought *arroz con pollo,* or rice with chicken.

We had a terrific time. We ate and talked and laughed.

The next day, Mrs. López wrote a poem for us. It said,

We came as neighbors and left as friends.
I hope our friendship never ends!

GO ON ➡️

COMPREHENSION / CRITICAL THINKING

25 **Look at the sequence chain. Which of these goes in the blank for number 25?**

Ⓐ Everyone eats.

Ⓑ The children play games.

Ⓒ Alina and Grandpa cook *pancit*.

Ⓓ The López family comes to Alina's house.

26 **Look at the sequence chain. Which of these goes in the blank for number 26?**

Ⓕ The *pancit* smells good.

Ⓖ Mrs. López writes a poem.

Ⓗ Mrs. López comes to the door.

Ⓙ The neighbors bring *arroz con pollo*.

Sequence Chain

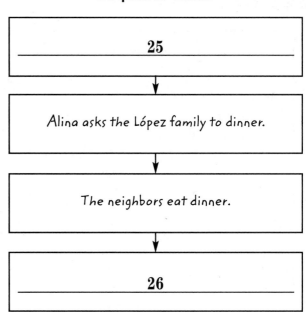

27 **From the selection, you can tell that Alina —**

Ⓐ does not like games

Ⓑ likes to make new friends

Ⓒ does not like her grandfather

Ⓓ likes *pancit* better than *arroz con pollo*

28 **The neighbors like each other. How do you know?**

Ⓕ Mrs. López opens the door.

Ⓖ Everyone eats *arroz con pollo*.

Ⓗ Grandpa and Alina cook Filipino food.

Ⓙ The López family, Alina, and Grandpa talk and laugh together.

29 **The selection is a —**

Ⓐ story

Ⓑ poem

Ⓒ science article

Ⓓ thank-you note

30 **The author wrote the selection to —**

Ⓕ entertain you

Ⓖ explain how to play games

Ⓗ give information about cooking

STOP

Unit 5 • Cultural Ties

VOCABULARY

DIRECTIONS Read the sentence. Choose the word or words that go in the blank. Mark your answer. *(4 points each)*

⭐ **Sample**

Carlo wears his new _____ to school.

Ⓐ car

Ⓑ book

Ⓒ jacket

Ⓓ building

1 The flower's _____ was dark red.

Ⓐ collar

Ⓑ bloom

Ⓒ creature

Ⓓ backbone

2 Komar left so quickly that he _____ his homework.

Ⓕ sent

Ⓖ forgot

Ⓗ noticed

Ⓙ published

3 Niki's bus _____ at school every morning at 7:30.

Ⓐ loses

Ⓑ sleeps

Ⓒ arrives

Ⓓ celebrates

4 This ring is _____ because my grandmother gave it to me.

Ⓕ proud

Ⓖ wrong

Ⓗ special

Ⓙ deadly

5 When Manu moved to the United States, he had to _____ to a new country.

Ⓐ reply

Ⓑ adjust

Ⓒ refuse

Ⓓ explain

© Hampton-Brown

GO ON ➡

6 We believe that red is a lucky color. That is part of our _____.

- Ⓕ job
- Ⓖ class
- Ⓗ sport
- Ⓙ culture

7 The _____ ruled his people for 50 years.

- Ⓐ actor
- Ⓑ father
- Ⓒ teacher
- Ⓓ emperor

8 Golnar feels a lot of _____ because his team always wins.

- Ⓕ fear
- Ⓖ pride
- Ⓗ anger
- Ⓙ sadness

9 The queen sat on a blue and gold _____.

- Ⓐ lotus
- Ⓑ shelf
- Ⓒ plate
- Ⓓ throne

10 A good education will help me have a _____.

- Ⓕ nice friend
- Ⓖ tasty recipe
- Ⓗ small house
- Ⓙ better future

STOP

GRAMMAR

DIRECTIONS Read the sentences. Choose the word that goes
in each blank. Mark your answer. *(3 points each)*

Look at this beautiful quilt! Aunt Lil made __Sample__ for me. First, she
collected some old clothes and cut __11__ into small pieces. When Aunt Lil
had enough pieces, __12__ sewed them together into a detailed pattern.
Aunt Lil used __13__ old dresses for parts of the quilt. She used
__14__ dresses for some parts of it, too. It is a wonderful quilt!

Sample
- Ⓐ I
- Ⓑ it
- Ⓒ we
- Ⓓ they

11
- Ⓐ he
- Ⓑ her
- Ⓒ they
- Ⓓ them

12
- Ⓕ he
- Ⓖ her
- Ⓗ she
- Ⓙ they

13
- Ⓐ Mother
- Ⓑ Mothers
- Ⓒ Mothers'
- Ⓓ Mother's

14
- Ⓕ my
- Ⓖ me
- Ⓗ him
- Ⓙ hers

STOP

GRAMMAR

DIRECTIONS Read the sentences. Choose the best way to write each underlined part, or choose "Correct as it is." Mark your answer.
(3 points each)

> When Pasha was nine, they's family immigrated to the United States.
> **Sample**
>
> Pasha'a family enjoyed them's new home, but Pasha missed his uncle. In
> **15**
>
> Russia, Uncle Vanya lived nearby, so Pasha visited he every day. Pasha
> **16**
>
> loved Uncle Vanya's collection of old Russian books. Him hoped Uncle
> **17** **18**
>
> Vanya would come to the United States someday.

★Sample

Ⓐ his
Ⓑ him
Ⓒ he's
Ⓓ Correct as it is

15 Ⓐ they
Ⓑ their
Ⓒ them
Ⓓ Correct as it is

16 Ⓕ it
Ⓖ him
Ⓗ they
Ⓙ Correct as it is

17 Ⓐ Uncle Vanya
Ⓑ Uncle Vanyas
Ⓒ Uncle Vanyas'
Ⓓ Correct as it is

18 Ⓕ He
Ⓖ She
Ⓗ They
Ⓙ Correct as it is

STOP

© Hampton-Brown

DIRECTIONS Read the selection. Then read each item. Choose the best answer. Mark your answer. *(3 points each)*

Bette Bao as a young girl

Bette Bao Lord in 1998

The Story of Bette Bao Lord

In 1938, a baby girl was born in Shanghai, China. Today she is a famous writer named Bette Bao Lord.

When Bette Bao was eight years old, her father moved to the United States to work. Bette and her mother came, too, but Bette's baby sister was too small to travel. Baby Sansan stayed with another family in China. Her family expected to go back to China soon, but they were not able to return.

The Bao family settled in New York City. Bette went to school and worked to help her family. She got her first job when she was 12 years old. Bette finished high school and then went to college. After that, she went to another school to study law.

The years passed, and Bette's sister stayed in China. Bette did not see Sansan for 16 years. Then, at last, Sansan came to the United States to be with her family. After Sansan and Bette talked for many hours, Bette decided to write a book about her sister's life in China. She called the book *Eighth Moon*.

GO ON ➡

The Story of Bette Bao Lord, continued

In 1963, Bette Bao married a man named Winston Lord. The next year Bette Bao Lord became a U.S. citizen and published *Eighth Moon*. Many, many people read the book and liked it.

In 1973, Mrs. Lord returned to China for the first time. She then wrote many books for adults about China. In 1984, Mrs. Lord finished a book for children called *In the Year of the Boar and Jackie Robinson*. It tells the story of a girl named Bandit who moves with her parents from China to New York. Bandit cannot speak any English at first, but she soon learns the language and makes new friends.

Time Line of Bette Bao Lord's Life

- 1938 — Bette was born in Shanghai, China.
- 1946 — Bette and her parents came to the U.S.
- 1950 — Bette got her first job.
- 1955 — Bette started college.
- 1962 — Sansan came to the U.S.
- 1963 — Bette married Winston Lord.
- 1964 — Bette became a U.S. citizen. Eighth Moon was published.
- 1973 — Bette returned to China for the first time.
- 1984 — Bette finished In the Year of the Boar and Jackie Robinson.

© Hampton-Brown

GO ON ➡

COMPREHENSION / CRITICAL THINKING

19 **The author wrote this selection to —**

Ⓐ entertain you

Ⓑ express feelings

Ⓒ give you information

Ⓓ explain how to do something

20 **Before Bette started college, she —**

Ⓕ got a job

Ⓖ wrote a book

Ⓗ returned to China

Ⓙ married Winston Lord

21 **When did Sansan come to the U.S.?**

Ⓐ after Bette got married

Ⓑ before Bette started college

Ⓒ after Bette returned to China

Ⓓ before Bette became a U.S. citizen

22 **From the selection, you can tell that Bette Bao Lord —**

Ⓕ wants to move to China

Ⓖ writes books in Chinese

Ⓗ cannot speak any English

Ⓙ knows a lot about life in China

23 **Bette got writing ideas from her own experiences. How do you know?**

Ⓐ Bette married in 1963.

Ⓑ Bette is a famous writer.

Ⓒ Bette went to another school to study law.

Ⓓ Bette wrote a book about a girl who moved from China to New York.

24 **This selection is a —**

Ⓕ poem

Ⓖ folk tale

Ⓗ biography

Ⓙ news report

© Hampton-Brown

GO ON

COMPREHENSION / CRITICAL THINKING

DIRECTIONS Read the selection. Then read each item. Choose the best answer. Mark your answer. *(3 points each)*

Good Food, Good Friends!

Grandpa is the best chef in the world. He learned to cook at home in the Philippines, and now he is teaching me.

Last week, we made our favorite dish called *pancit*. *Pancit* is full of tasty things like pork and noodles. While we cooked, our apartment smelled so good that it gave me a great idea. "Grandpa, let's invite our neighbors to eat *pancit* with us."

"That's a good idea, Alina," Grandpa said to me. "Ask our neighbors to come tonight. We have plenty of food."

In our building, there are four apartments. First I went to invite Mr. Sahni. He was cooking, too, but he said, "I will come and bring lamb curry, a dish from India."

Next, I invited the Nguyen family. They were cooking beef and rice noodles. "We will come, and we will bring *pho*, a delicious Vietnamese stew," they said.

GO ON ▶

COMPREHENSION / CRITICAL THINKING

Good Food, Good Friends!, continued

Then, I went to the last apartment, where a new family lived, and a lady opened the door. "Please come to eat with my family tonight," I said.

"We would love to come," the lady said.

Soon our apartment was full of people. The last person to come was our new neighbor, Mrs. López. She brought *arroz con pollo*, or rice with chicken, from Cuba.

Everyone had a terrific time. We ate and talked and laughed, and the children played games. It was late when everyone went home.

The next day, Grandpa found a piece of paper under our door. "This is for you," Grandpa said. "It's from Mrs. López. Read it."

Grandpa saw my big smile and said, "You are a good cook and a good neighbor, too. In one day, you turned neighbors into friends."

Morning Neighbors, Evening Friends

The food was good; we ate it all.
None of our bites were very small!

Our games were fun; some lost, some won.
But now those games are over and done.

We came as neighbors and left as friends.
I hope our friendship never ends!

Morning neighbors, evening friends.

Mrs. López

© Hampton-Brown

GO ON

COMPREHENSION / CRITICAL THINKING

25 **Look at the sequence chain. Which of these goes in the blank for number 25?**

Ⓐ Mrs. López writes to Alina.

Ⓑ The apartment is full of people.

Ⓒ Alina and Grandpa cook *pancit*.

Ⓓ The Nguyens say they will bring some *pho*.

26 **Look at the sequence chain. Which of these goes in the blank for number 26?**

Ⓕ Alina invites Mr. Sahni.

Ⓖ Alina goes to the last apartment.

Ⓗ Grandpa and Alina start to cook.

Ⓙ Grandpa finds a paper under the door.

Sequence Chain

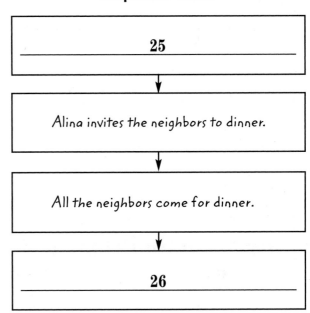

25

↓

Alina invites the neighbors to dinner.

↓

All the neighbors come for dinner.

↓

26

27 **The neighbors like each other. How do you know?**

Ⓐ A lady opens the door.

Ⓑ The apartment smells good.

Ⓒ Grandpa learned to cook in the Philippines.

Ⓓ The families talk, laugh, and play games together.

28 **Which of these is true about Alina?**

Ⓕ She likes to eat alone.

Ⓖ She likes to make new friends.

Ⓗ She does not like to play games.

Ⓙ She likes *pancit* better than *arroz con pollo*.

29 **To thank Alina and Grandpa, Mrs. López writes a —**

Ⓐ poem

Ⓑ folk tale

Ⓒ biography

Ⓓ news article

30 **The author wrote this selection to —**

Ⓕ explain how to cook

Ⓖ entertain you with a story

Ⓗ give you facts about Filipino food

STOP

© Hampton-Brown

Unit 5 • Answer Key

B Beginning Progress Test

VOCABULARY
(4 points each)

1 B	4 H
2 J	5 D
3 A	6 G

GRAMMAR
(4 points each)

7 A	11 C
8 G	12 F
9 C	13 D
10 G	

**COMPREHENSION /
CRITICAL THINKING**
(6 points each)

14 H	18 F
15 B	19 C
16 F	20 F
17 B	21 A

I Intermediate Progress Test

VOCABULARY
(4 points each)

1 B	6 J
2 G	7 D
3 C	8 G
4 J	9 D
5 D	10 J

GRAMMAR
(3 points each)

11 A	15 B
12 J	16 G
13 D	17 D
14 H	18 F

**COMPREHENSION /
CRITICAL THINKING**
(3 points each)

19 C	25 C
20 J	26 G
21 B	27 B
22 J	28 J
23 D	29 A
24 H	30 F

A Advanced Progress Test

VOCABULARY
(4 points each)

1 B	6 J
2 G	7 D
3 C	8 G
4 H	9 D
5 B	10 J

GRAMMAR
(3 points each)

11 D	15 B
12 H	16 G
13 D	17 D
14 F	18 F

**COMPREHENSION /
CRITICAL THINKING**
(3 points each)

19 C	25 C
20 F	26 J
21 D	27 D
22 J	28 G
23 D	29 A
24 H	30 G

Unit 5 • Self-Assessment

I Can Speak English!

1. I can tell what I think and how I feel.

💬 I feel _____ when my family _____.

2. I can tell how two things are alike and different.

💬 In the United States, people like

to _____. In _____, people

like to _____.

My New Words

_____
_____
_____
_____
_____
_____
_____
_____
_____
_____

I Can Read in English!

3. I can retell the events in a story in order.

☐ yes   ☐ not yet

4. I can tell the difference between facts and opinions.

Facts	Opinions
Rogelio came to the U.S. when he was seven.	He misses his friends.
_____	_____

What I've Read

☐ The Lotus Seed

☐ Where We Come From

☐ _____

☐ _____

Unit 6 • Directions for Ⓑ Progress Test

Distribute the test pages. Before students begin each subtest, read aloud the directions and use the script to work through each sample item.

VOCABULARY

Read aloud the directions on page 56. Then say:

Sample
Look at the pictures in the box. Which picture shows a jacket? (Pause.) *The third bubble is filled in because the third picture shows a* jacket.

Items 1–7
Read each question aloud. Provide time for students to mark their answers.

GRAMMAR

Read aloud the directions on page 58. Then say:

Sample
Look at the picture in the box. The first sentence says: We have a new house. *Which word goes in the next sentence? Let's try each one:*

> *Yesterday Dad* plant *a rosebush.*
> *Yesterday Dad* plants *a rosebush.*
> *Yesterday Dad* planted *a rosebush.*
> *Yesterday Dad* planting *a rosebush.*

The third bubble is filled in because planted *is correct.*

Items 8–11
Read aloud each sentence with each answer choice. Provide time for students to mark their answers.

Read aloud the directions on page 59. Then say:

Sample
Look at the picture in the box. Look at the sentence. There is a word missing. Let's try each word:

> *I am* see the ship from here!
> *I can* see the ship from here!
> *I are* see the ship from here!
> *I has* see the ship from here!

The second bubble is filled in because can *is correct.*

Items 12–15
Read aloud each sentence with each answer choice. Provide time for students to mark their answers.

COMPREHENSION / CRITICAL THINKING

Selection 1 and Items 16–19
Read aloud the directions on page 60. Say: *Now listen to the selection. The title is:*

Johnny Appleseed

Look at Picture 1. John Chapman walked many miles. He carried a bag of apple seeds. People called him Johnny Appleseed.

Look at Picture 2. When Johnny found a good spot, he dug holes in the soil. Then he planted apple seeds.

Look at Picture 3. Johnny cared for the apple trees for a while. They grew taller and taller.

Look at Picture 4. Then, Johnny gave his trees to farmers. Soon there were apple trees everywhere.

Then read each question aloud. Provide time for students to mark their answers.

Selection 2 and Items 20–23
Read aloud the directions on page 62. Say: *Now listen to the selection. The title is:*

A Redwood Grows

Look at the first picture. A squirrel sits on a redwood tree. It eats seeds from a redwood cone. Some seeds fall to the ground.

Look at the next picture. A redwood seed lands in good soil. Roots grow down into the soil. A new tree starts to grow.

Look at the next picture. The new redwood tree grows tall. It might be 300 feet high! It has many branches. Now squirrels, birds, and raccoons can live in the tree. After 5 years, it begins to make cones.

Look at the last picture. A redwood tree can live 3,000 years. Then it falls to the forest floor. New trees grow from its seeds.

Then read each question aloud. Provide time for students to mark their answers.

© Hampton-Brown

Distribute the test pages. Before students begin each subtest, read aloud the directions and use the script to work through each sample item.

VOCABULARY

Read aloud the directions on page 56. Then work through the sample item. Say:

Sample

Read the sentence in the box. (Pause.) *Which word goes in the blank? Let's try each one:*

> *Carlo wears his new car to school.*
> *Carlo wears his new book to school.*
> *Carlo wears his new jacket to school.*
> *Carlo wears his new building to school.*

The third bubble is filled in because jacket *is the best answer.*

Items 1–6

Tell students to complete the remaining items in the same way. Provide time for students to mark their answers.

Items 7–10

Read aloud the directions on page 57. Then point out the entry words, parts of speech, and definitions on the dictionary page. Tell students to complete the items. Provide time for students to mark their answers.

GRAMMAR

Read aloud the directions on page 58. Then work through the sample item. Say:

Sample

Read the sentence. (Pause.) *Which word goes in the blank? Let's try each one:*

> *Yesterday, Noah wrote a letter to the governor.*
> *Yesterday, Noah writed a letter to the governor.*
> *Yesterday, Noah writes a letter to the governor.*
> *Yesterday, Noah writing a letter to the governor.*

The first bubble is filled in because wrote *is the best answer.*

Items 11–14

Tell students to complete the remaining items in the same way. Provide time for them to mark their answers.

Read aloud the directions on page 59. Then work through the sample item. Say:

Sample

Read the sentence. (Pause.) *What is the best way to write the underlined part? Look at the four choices. The fourth bubble is filled in because the underlined part in the sentence is* Correct as it is.

Items 15–18

Tell students to complete the remaining items in the same way. Provide time for them to mark their answers.

COMPREHENSION / CRITICAL THINKING

Selections and Items 19–30

Read aloud the directions for each selection. Provide time for students to read the selection and mark their answers.

Unit 6 • Student Profile for Beginning Progress Test

DIRECTIONS Record the student's name and test date. Use the **Answer Key** on page 65a to score the student's test. Then, in the Student Profile, circle the item number of each correct answer and circle the plus or minus sign to indicate mastery. Calculate the subtest scores and then the total test score. To help you group students for reteaching, transfer the minus sign for any unmastered skill to the **Class Profile** (page 56f).

Student Name _____   **Date** _____

Subtest	Tested Skills	ITEM ANALYSIS		TEST SCORES
		Item Numbers	Mastery	No. Correct × Points = Score
VOCABULARY	Key Words	1 2 3 4 5 6 7	6 out of 7 + −	____ × 4 = / 28
GRAMMAR	Verb Tense (present, past, future)	8 9 10 11	3 out of 4 + −	____ × 4 = / 32
	Modals	12 13 14 15	3 out of 4 + −	
COMPREHENSION / CRITICAL THINKING	Relate Steps in a Process	16 17 21 23	3 out of 4 + −	____ × 5 = / 40
	Relate Cause and Effect	18 19 20 22	3 out of 4 + −	
			TOTAL UNIT 6 PROGRESS TEST	/ 100

© Hampton-Brown

DIRECTIONS Record the student's name and test date. Use the **Answer Key** on page 65a to score the student's test. Then, in the Student Profile, circle the item number of each correct answer and circle the plus or minus sign to indicate mastery. Calculate the subtest scores and then the total test score. To help you group students for reteaching, transfer the minus sign for any unmastered skill to the **Class Profile** (page 56f).

Student Name _____ Date _____

| Subtest | Tested Skills | ITEM ANALYSIS | | TEST SCORES |
		Item Numbers	Mastery	No. Correct × Points = Score
VOCABULARY	Key Words	1 2 3 4 5 6	5 out of 6 + −	_____ × 4 = ⬜ /40
VOCABULARY	Confirm Word Meaning (dictionary)	7 8 9 10	3 out of 4 + −	
GRAMMAR	Verb Tense (present, past, future)	11 12 13 14	3 out of 4 + −	_____ × 3 = ⬜ /24
GRAMMAR	Modals	15 16 17 18	3 out of 4 + −	
COMPREHENSION / CRITICAL THINKING	Relate Steps in a Process	22 26 27 28	3 out of 4 + −	_____ × 3 = ⬜ /36
COMPREHENSION / CRITICAL THINKING	Relate Cause and Effect	19 20 29 30	3 out of 4 + −	
COMPREHENSION / CRITICAL THINKING	Determine Author's Purpose, Point of View, and Logic	21 23 24 25	3 out of 4 + −	

TOTAL UNIT 6 PROGRESS TEST ⬜ /100

© Hampton-Brown

DIRECTIONS Record the student's name and test date. Use the **Answer Key** on page 65a to score the student's test. Then, in the Student Profile, circle the item number of each correct answer and circle the plus or minus sign to indicate mastery. Calculate the subtest scores and then the total test score. To help you group students for reteaching, transfer the minus sign for any unmastered skill to the **Class Profile** (page 56f).

Student Name _____ Date _____

| Subtest | Tested Skills | ITEM ANALYSIS | | TEST SCORES |
		Item Numbers	Mastery	No. Correct × Points = Score
VOCABULARY	Key Words	1 2 3 4 5 6	5 out of 6 + −	_____ × 4 = ◻/40
	Confirm Word Meaning (dictionary)	7 8 9 10	3 out of 4 + −	
GRAMMAR	Verb Tense (present, past, future)	11 12 13 14	3 out of 4 + −	_____ × 3 = ◻/24
	Modals	15 16 17 18	3 out of 4 + −	
COMPREHENSION / CRITICAL THINKING	Relate Steps in a Process	19 20 27 30	3 out of 4 + −	_____ × 3 = ◻/36
	Relate Cause and Effect	25 26 28 29	3 out of 4 + −	
	Determine Author's Purpose, Point of View, and Logic	21 22 23 24	3 out of 4 + −	

TOTAL UNIT 6 PROGRESS TEST ◻/100 Ⓐ

© Hampton-Brown

Unit 6 • Class Profile

Date _____

DIRECTIONS Use the **Unit 6 Student Profiles** to complete this chart. In each row, write the student's name, fill in the bubble for the test form taken, and mark a minus sign (–) for any skill not yet mastered. Then group students and use the reteaching ideas and practice exercises to help students reach mastery.

Student Name	Test Form	TESTED SKILLS						
		Key Words	**Confirm Word Meaning** (dictionary)	**Verb Tense** (present, past, future)	**Modals**	**Relate Steps in a Process**	**Relate Cause and Effect**	**Determine Author's Purpose, Point of View, and Logic**
	ⒷⒾⒶ							
	ⒷⒾⒶ							
	ⒷⒾⒶ							
	ⒷⒾⒶ							
	ⒷⒾⒶ							
	ⒷⒾⒶ							
	ⒷⒾⒶ							
	ⒷⒾⒶ							
	ⒷⒾⒶ							
	ⒷⒾⒶ							
	ⒷⒾⒶ							
	ⒷⒾⒶ							
	ⒷⒾⒶ							
	ⒷⒾⒶ							
	ⒷⒾⒶ							
	ⒷⒾⒶ							
	ⒷⒾⒶ							
	ⒷⒾⒶ							
	ⒷⒾⒶ							
	ⒷⒾⒶ							
RETEACHING RESOURCES		Ⓑ Ⓘ Ⓐ AH T38	Ⓘ Ⓐ EAYC 322–325	Ⓑ AH T40 Ⓘ Ⓐ EAYC 261–264	Ⓑ AH T40 Ⓘ Ⓐ EAYC 259	Ⓑ Ⓘ Ⓐ LB TG	Ⓑ Ⓘ Ⓐ LB TG	Ⓘ Ⓐ LB TG
PRACTICE EXERCISES		PB 85, 91	PB 90	EAYC 393–396	EAYC 392	PB 87	PB 96–97	

KEY: **AH:** Assessment Handbook **EAYC:** English at Your Command! **LB TG:** Leveled Books Teacher's Guide **PB:** Practice Book

© Hampton-Brown

Unit 6 • This State of Mine

VOCABULARY

DIRECTIONS Listen to each question. Then choose the correct picture.
Mark your answer. *(4 points each)*

⭐Sample

Which picture shows a <u>jacket</u>?

Ⓐ   Ⓑ   Ⓒ   Ⓓ

1 The girls are in a <u>contest</u>. Which picture shows this?

Ⓐ   Ⓑ   Ⓒ   Ⓓ

2 Which picture shows the <u>capital</u> of the United States?

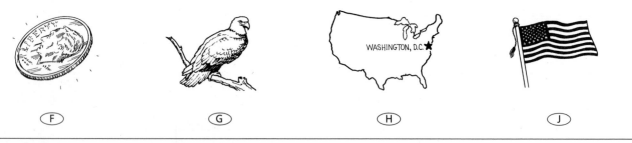

WASHINGTON, D.C.★

Ⓕ   Ⓖ   Ⓗ   Ⓙ

3 The girl makes a <u>sketch</u>. Which picture shows this?

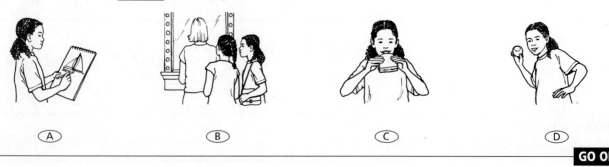

Ⓐ   Ⓑ   Ⓒ   Ⓓ

GO ON ➡

VOCABULARY

4 The boy likes to show his <u>talent</u>. Which picture shows this?

         ...

F   G   H   J

5 Which picture shows a <u>settlement</u>?

Ⓐ   Ⓑ   Ⓒ   Ⓓ

6 Which picture shows a <u>design</u>?

F   G   H   J

7 Find the arrow in each picture. Which arrow points to a <u>boundary</u>?

Ⓐ   Ⓑ   Ⓒ   Ⓓ

STOP

GRAMMAR

DIRECTIONS Look at the picture. Listen to the sentence with each answer. Choose the word that completes the sentence correctly. Mark your answer. *(4 points each)*

⭐**Sample**

We have a new house. Yesterday Dad _____ a rosebush.

Ⓐ plant

Ⓑ plants

Ⓒ planted

Ⓓ planting

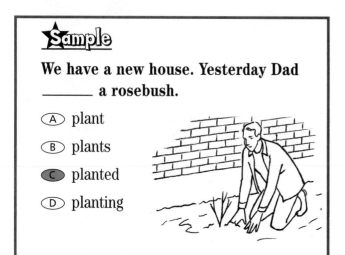

8 He _____ the rosebush from our old house.

Ⓕ bring

Ⓖ bringed

Ⓗ brought

Ⓙ bringing

9 Last year, the flowers _____ all spring and summer.

Ⓐ bloom

Ⓑ blooms

Ⓒ bloomed

Ⓓ blooming

10 Next spring our plant _____ so pretty.

Ⓕ look

Ⓖ looked

Ⓗ looking

Ⓙ will look

11 Dad's rosebush _____ beautiful every year!

Ⓐ is

Ⓑ are

Ⓒ has

Ⓓ have

© Hampton-Brown

STOP

GRAMMAR

DIRECTIONS Look at the picture. Listen to the sentence with each answer. Choose the word that completes the sentence correctly. Mark your answer. *(4 points each)*

⭐**Sample**

I _____ see the ship from here!

Ⓐ am

Ⓑ can

Ⓒ are

Ⓓ has

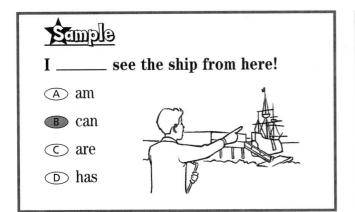

12 I _____ draw a picture of it.

Ⓕ am

Ⓖ has

Ⓗ can

Ⓙ have

13 I _____ add an American flag.

Ⓐ am

Ⓑ has

Ⓒ have

Ⓓ could

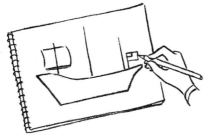

14 I _____ get closer to see the ship better.

Ⓕ be

Ⓖ am

Ⓗ have

Ⓙ must

15 I _____ color the picture to finish it.

Ⓐ be

Ⓑ am

Ⓒ has

Ⓓ should

STOP

COMPREHENSION / CRITICAL THINKING

DIRECTIONS Listen to the selection. Then listen to each question.
Choose the best answer. Mark your answer. *(5 points each)*

Johnny Appleseed

1

John Chapman walked many miles. He carried a bag of apple seeds. People called him Johnny Appleseed.

2

When Johnny found a good spot, he dug holes in the soil. Then he planted apple seeds.

3

Johnny cared for the apple trees for a while. They grew taller and taller.

4

Then, Johnny gave his trees to farmers. Soon there were apple trees everywhere.

© Hampton-Brown

GO ON ➡

COMPREHENSION / CRITICAL THINKING

16 What did Johnny Appleseed do first?

    F   G   H   J

17 Johnny planted seeds. What did he do next?

    A   B   C   D

18 The farmers were happy to see Johnny because he brought them —

apple seeds   apple trees   fresh milk   new songs

    F   G   H   J

19 Because Johnny worked hard, people could —

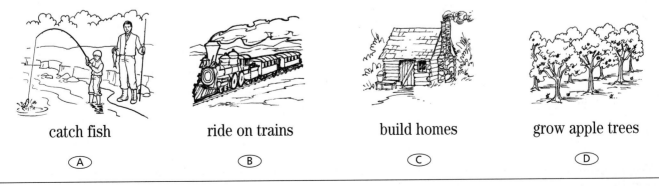

catch fish   ride on trains   build homes   grow apple trees

    A   B   C   D

GO ON ▶

COMPREHENSION / CRITICAL THINKING

DIRECTIONS Listen to the selection. Then listen to each question.
Choose the best answer. Mark your answer. *(5 points each)*

A Redwood Grows

A squirrel sits on a redwood tree. It eats seeds from a redwood cone. Some seeds fall to the ground.

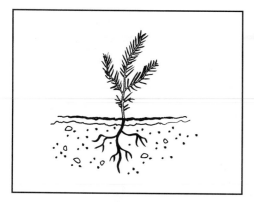

A redwood seed lands in good soil. Roots grow down into the soil. A new tree starts to grow.

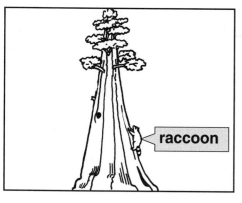

The new redwood tree grows tall. It might be 300 feet high! It has many branches. Now squirrels, birds, and raccoons can live in the tree. After 5 years, it begins to make cones.

A redwood tree can live for 3,000 years. Then it falls to the forest floor. New trees grow from its seeds.

© Hampton-Brown

Name _____ Date _____

COMPREHENSION / CRITICAL THINKING

20 What makes the redwood seeds fall?

Ⓕ   Ⓖ   Ⓗ   Ⓙ

21 Seeds fall to the ground. What happens next?

Ⓐ   Ⓑ   Ⓒ   Ⓓ

22 Because the new redwood tree has many branches, —

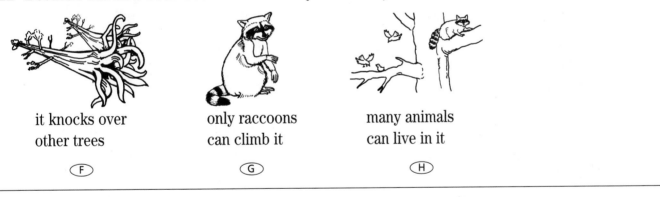

it knocks over   only raccoons   many animals
other trees   can climb it   can live in it

Ⓕ   Ⓖ   Ⓗ

23 After 5 years, the redwood tree starts to —

fall   make cones   lose branches

Ⓐ   Ⓑ   Ⓒ

Ⓢ **STOP**

Unit 6 • This State of Mine

VOCABULARY

DIRECTIONS Read the sentence. Choose the word that goes in the blank.
Mark your answer. *(4 points each)*

⭐ **Sample**

Carlo wears his new _____ to school.

Ⓐ car

Ⓑ book

Ⓒ jacket

Ⓓ building

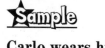

1 This is the _____ for our new gym.

Ⓐ tent

Ⓑ chair

Ⓒ stamp

Ⓓ design

2 Marla has a _____ for making quilts.

Ⓕ fear

Ⓖ state

Ⓗ brush

Ⓙ talent

3 We _____ heroes on this poster.

Ⓐ call

Ⓑ fight

Ⓒ honor

Ⓓ forget

4 Washington, D.C., is the _____ of the United States.

Ⓕ side

Ⓖ coin

Ⓗ throne

Ⓙ capital

5 Fran likes to paint. First she makes a _____.

Ⓐ poem

Ⓑ sketch

Ⓒ report

Ⓓ recipe

6 People built a new _____ near the river.

Ⓕ contest

Ⓖ reporter

Ⓗ problem

Ⓙ settlement

STOP

© Hampton-Brown

Name _____ Date _____

VOCABULARY

DIRECTIONS Use this part of a dictionary page to answer each question. Mark your answer. *(4 points each)*

---

quilt ➤ quote

quilt (**kwilt**) *noun*

A **quilt** is a cover for a bed.

verb To **quilt** is to stitch something together into a pattern.

quince (**kwins**) *noun*

A **quince** is a yellow fruit that grows on a tree.

quip (**kwip**) *noun*

A **quip** is a funny remark.

verb To **quip** is to say something funny.

quit (**kwit**) *verb*

To **quit** is to stop or give up.

quiver (**kwiv**-er) *noun*

A **quiver** is a case for arrows.

verb To **quiver** is to shake gently.

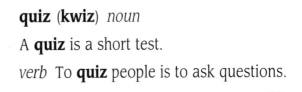

quiz (**kwiz**) *noun*

A **quiz** is a short test.

verb To **quiz** people is to ask questions.

---

7 What is a quince?

- Ⓐ a yellow fruit
- Ⓑ a funny remark
- Ⓒ a cover for a bed
- Ⓓ a case for arrows

8 To quip means to —

- Ⓕ cover a bed
- Ⓖ shake gently
- Ⓗ grow on a tree
- Ⓙ say something funny

9 To quilt means to —

- Ⓐ shake gently
- Ⓑ ask questions
- Ⓒ stitch together
- Ⓓ pick some fruit

10 Read the sentence.

We took a spelling quiz today.

In this sentence, what does quiz mean?

- Ⓕ a tall tree
- Ⓖ a short test
- Ⓗ to ask questions
- Ⓙ to stop or give up

STOP

© Hampton-Brown

GRAMMAR

DIRECTIONS Read the sentences. Choose the word or words that go in each blank. Mark your answer. *(3 points each)*

⭐ **Sample**

Yesterday, Noah _____ a letter to the governor.

(A) wrote

(B) writed

(C) writes

(D) writing

---

11 Noah's letter said, "In the past, our state _____ many forests."

(A) had

(B) have

(C) having

(D) will have

12 "Today, people _____ the trees down."

(F) chop

(G) chops

(H) chopped

(J) chopping

13 "Last year, people _____ many new shopping malls."

(A) built

(B) build

(C) builded

(D) are building

14 "Soon, there _____ too many malls and only a few forests."

(F) be

(G) was

(H) have

(J) will be

STOP

GRAMMAR

DIRECTIONS Read the sentences. Choose the best way to write each underlined part, or choose "Correct as it is." Mark your answer.

(3 points each)

 Sample

My grandma <u>could</u> show you a stamp from almost every state.

(A) is

(B) are

(C) have

(D) Correct as it is

---

15 I <u>am</u> find a new stamp for Grandma.

(A) has

(B) must

(C) have

(D) Correct as it is

16 I <u>have</u> get a butterfly stamp or a rock stamp.

(F) am

(G) are

(H) could

(J) Correct as it is

17 They <u>are</u> keep both stamps at the hobby store.

(A) is

(B) has

(C) should

(D) Correct as it is

18 Maybe I <u>can</u> get two stamps for Grandma!

(F) be

(G) has

(H) have

(J) Correct as it is

STOP

© Hampton-Brown

DIRECTIONS Read the selection. Then read each item. Choose the best answer. Mark your answer. *(3 points each)*

March 7, 2003

To the Editor:

Our science class at Hilltop School is studying redwood trees. That gave us an idea! We want to tell people how special redwoods are. We also want to tell them how they can help save some redwoods.

Redwood trees are huge and live a long time. Some grow more than 300 feet tall and live as long as 3,000 years. Some animals depend on redwoods. Many birds, foxes, and squirrels live in the giant trees. When people cut down redwoods, many animals lose their homes.

Some people in our town want to cut down some redwood trees to build a new road. Some other people want to build the road in a different place to save the redwoods. The road that saves the redwoods will cost more, but people can help pay for it.

Our class started a "Kids Can Make a Difference" club. We plan to make money to help build the road that will save some redwood trees. If you print our letter, maybe other schools will start clubs like ours.

Sincerely,
Kids Can Make a Difference Club
Hilltop School

© Hampton-Brown

GO ON ➡️

COMPREHENSION / CRITICAL THINKING

19 Some people want to cut down some redwood trees so they can —

   Ⓐ start a club

   Ⓑ build a road

   Ⓒ help animals

   Ⓓ clean up the forest

20 What happens when people cut down redwoods?

   Ⓕ The trees grow very tall.

   Ⓖ Newspapers print letters.

   Ⓗ Animals lose their homes.

   Ⓙ Other trees stop growing.

21 The students who wrote the letter —

   Ⓐ do not like clubs

   Ⓑ want more roads

   Ⓒ read a lot of letters

   Ⓓ love redwood trees

22 Which of these happened first?

   Ⓕ The kids started a club.

   Ⓖ The newspaper printed the kids' letter

   Ⓗ The kids made money to save the redwoods.

   Ⓙ The kids' science class studied redwood trees.

23 The money the students make can help —

   Ⓐ pay for clubs in other schools

   Ⓑ pay people to cut down redwoods

   Ⓒ build a road that saves redwoods

   Ⓓ build a bridge across a river near the school

24 Which of these tells why redwood trees are special?

   Ⓕ Please put this letter in your paper!

   Ⓖ Some redwoods are over 3,000 years old.

   Ⓗ We started a "Kids Can Make a Difference" club.

   Ⓙ We plan to make money to help save the redwoods.

25 The letter was written to —

   Ⓐ tell a funny story

   Ⓑ persuade other schools to start a club

   Ⓒ give information about a famous road

   Ⓓ explain the steps in a science experiment

GO ON ➡

COMPREHENSION / CRITICAL THINKING

DIRECTIONS Read the selection. Then read each item. Choose the best answer. Mark your answer. *(3 points each)*

Johnny Appleseed

Johnny Appleseed lived long ago in the Midwest. He wasn't a fancy man. He had no shoes. For a shirt, he wore an old sack that had holes for his head and arms. Johnny always had a bag full of apple seeds, though.

Johnny planted apple trees across the land. First, he walked for miles looking for good places to grow apple trees. When he came to a sunny spot, he stopped to check the soil. If the soil was good, he planted his seeds. He watered them until they grew. Then he would look for other spots for more trees.

One day, Johnny came to a lonely farm. A man and a woman waved at Johnny. They asked him to come in for dinner. Then they brought out a bowl of big, red apples. Johnny grinned. The apples were from a tree he had planted many years before!

© Hampton-Brown

GO ON ➡

COMPREHENSION / CRITICAL THINKING

26 Look at the chart.

Flow Chart

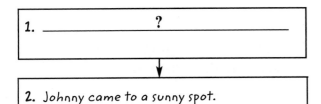

1. _____ **?** _____

2. Johnny came to a sunny spot.

Which of these goes in the blank?

Ⓕ Johnny walked for miles.

Ⓖ Johnny talked to farmers.

Ⓗ Johnny put on some new shoes.

Ⓙ Johnny got a bowl of big, red apples.

27 Johnny came to a sunny spot. What did he do next?

Ⓐ He planted a tree.

Ⓑ He checked the soil.

Ⓒ He talked to the animals.

Ⓓ He looked for some apples.

28 After the trees grew in one spot, Johnny —

Ⓕ ate all the apples

Ⓖ asked a farmer for dinner

Ⓗ planted other kinds of trees

Ⓙ looked for other good places to plant trees

29 Why did Johnny have to walk for miles?

Ⓐ No one would give him a ride.

Ⓑ He needed to meet the farmer.

Ⓒ He wanted to find good places to grow apple trees.

Ⓓ He was not a very fancy man and had no shoes.

30 Johnny grinned because the farmer —

Ⓕ told a funny joke

Ⓖ baked an apple pie

Ⓗ had many cows and chickens

Ⓙ had apples from one of Johnny's trees

STOP

© Hampton-Brown

Unit 6 • This State of Mine

DIRECTIONS Read the sentence. Choose the word that goes in the blank.
Mark your answer. *(4 points each)*

⭐**Sample**

Carlo wears his new _____ to school.

ⓐ car

ⓑ book

🔘 jacket

ⓓ building

---

1 Washington, D.C., is the _____ of the United States.

ⓐ capital

ⓑ throne

ⓒ material

ⓓ boundary

2 Marla has a special _____ for telling stories.

Ⓕ brush

Ⓖ talent

Ⓗ village

Ⓙ backbone

3 Fran likes to draw. Her _____ shows a sailboat on the lake.

ⓐ treaty

ⓑ sketch

ⓒ shelter

ⓓ contest

4 The _____ for our new school shows where the gym will be.

Ⓕ tent

Ⓖ coin

Ⓗ design

Ⓙ defense

5 We made a poster to _____ our state's heroes.

ⓐ mind

ⓑ honor

ⓒ adjust

ⓓ discover

6 People built a new _____ on the land near the river.

Ⓕ region

Ⓖ problem

Ⓗ landform

Ⓙ settlement

STOP

VOCABULARY

DIRECTIONS Use this part of a dictionary page to answer each question. Mark your answer. *(4 points each)*

quilt ➤ quote

quilt (**kwilt**) *noun* A **quilt** is a cover for a bed. *verb* To **quilt** is to stitch something together into a pattern.

quince (**kwins**) *noun* A **quince** is a yellow fruit that grows on a tree.

quip (**kwip**) *noun* A **quip** is a clever or funny remark. *verb* To **quip** is to say something funny or clever.

quit (**kwit**) *verb* To **quit** is to stop or give up.

quiver (**kwiv**-er) *noun* A **quiver** is a case for arrows. *verb* To **quiver** is to shake gently.

quiz (**kwiz**) *noun* A **quiz** is a short test. *verb* To **quiz** people is to ask them questions.

---

7 **What does quince mean?**

Ⓐ a yellow fruit

Ⓑ to cover a bed

Ⓒ a case for arrows

Ⓓ to stop or give up

8 **In which sentence is quip used as a verb?**

Ⓕ Dad makes many quips about saving money.

Ⓖ Mari used a funny quip in her book report.

Ⓗ "That quip about me was very clever," Jorge said.

Ⓙ "On a sunny day, my dog turns into a hot dog," Lionel quips.

9 **Read the sentence.**

Mr. Barnes gave us a quiz.

In this sentence, quiz means —

Ⓐ a tall tree

Ⓑ a short test

Ⓒ to ask questions

Ⓓ to say something funny

10 **Read the sentence.**

My aunt quilts with my mom.

In this sentence, quilt means —

Ⓕ to shake gently

Ⓖ a clever remark

Ⓗ to stitch together

Ⓙ a cover for a bed

STOP

GRAMMAR

DIRECTIONS Read the sentences. Choose the word or words that go in each blank. Mark your answer. *(3 points each)*

Yesterday, Noah __Sample__ a letter to the governor. His letter said,

"Every day I __11__ to school and all I see are shopping malls. I wish I

could see more trees. In the past, forests __12__ our state. Now, most of

the trees are gone. Please help save our forests."

Noah __13__ his letter to school. He showed it to his classmates. Then,

the other students wrote letters to the governor, too. The students hope

the governor __14__ their letters soon.

⭐Sample

- (A) wrote
- (B) writed
- (C) writes
- (D) writing

11
- (A) am
- (B) have
- (C) walk
- (D) walks

12
- (F) cover
- (G) covers
- (H) covered
- (J) covering

13
- (A) take
- (B) took
- (C) taked
- (D) tooked

14
- (F) answer
- (G) answered
- (H) answering
- (J) will answer

STOP

GRAMMAR

DIRECTIONS Read the sentences. Choose the best way to write each underlined part, or choose "Correct as it is." Mark your answer.
(3 points each)

My grandma <u>could</u> show you a stamp from almost every state. I want
Sample
to help Grandma find more stamps for her collection. I promised to get her

a stamp from the state of Vermont, so I <u>am</u> find one.
15

I thought I <u>have</u> get a Vermont stamp at the hobby store. The owner
16

looked and looked. He <u>is</u> keep more stamps of each state in the store. He
17

said, "I <u>can</u> order a Vermont stamp for you, though."
18

"Oh, please do!" I said. I hope it will get here before Grandma's birthday!

⭐ Sample

Ⓐ is

Ⓑ are

Ⓒ have

🄳 Correct as it is

15 Ⓐ has

Ⓑ must

Ⓒ have

Ⓓ Correct as it is

16 Ⓕ am

Ⓖ are

Ⓗ could

Ⓙ Correct as it is

17 Ⓐ has

Ⓑ have

Ⓒ should

Ⓓ Correct as it is

18 Ⓕ be

Ⓖ has

Ⓗ have

Ⓙ Correct as it is

STOP

COMPREHENSION / CRITICAL THINKING

DIRECTIONS Read the selection. Then read each item. Choose the best answer. Mark your answer. *(3 points each)*

The City Daily

Letter to the Editor

Dear Editor,

A story in your newspaper last week said the warehouse between Grove Street and Third Avenue is old and should be torn down. Then there will be an ugly, empty lot right in the center of town.

The kids in our class think that our city would be more beautiful with a park on that block. We also want a place to honor our state heroes. If the warehouse is torn down, we think the City Council should build a Heroes' Park in its place. There could be a lot of benches in the park. The names of state heroes could be written on plaques on the benches. For example, some benches might honor famous heroes like President Jimmy Carter or Dr. Martin Luther King, Jr. Other benches might honor heroes who are not famous, such as teachers, doctors, firefighters, and police officers.

Here's what the City Council should do to build the park: They should hire someone to design the park. Then, the designer should meet with people who live in the city. The people can tell the designer what they want in the park.

© Hampton-Brown

GO ON ➡

COMPREHENSION / CRITICAL THINKING

Letter to the Editor, continued

For example, some kids probably want a baseball diamond. Other kids probably want a duck pond or playground equipment. Adults probably would like big trees and picnic tables.

After the meeting, the designer should make a sketch of the park to show where everything will be. Here's an idea to get started:

bench →
plaque for hero's name

The City Council can look at the sketch and decide what they like about it. Then, they should hire workers to build the park. After the park is finished, the City Council should have a celebration to tell how the park honors the heroes of Georgia.

We think Heroes' Park will make our city a much better place.

Yours truly,

Fourth-grade Students at

Martin Luther King, Jr., Elementary School

GO ON ➡

© Hampton-Brown

COMPREHENSION / CRITICAL THINKING

19 Look at the chart.

Flow Chart

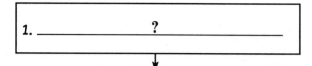

1. _____ ?

2. The designer meets with people who live in the city.

Which of these goes in the blank?

Ⓐ The designer makes a sketch of the park.

Ⓑ The City Council hires workers to build the park.

Ⓒ The City Council hires someone to design the park.

Ⓓ People tell the designer what they want in the park.

20 Which of these is the last step in the students' plan?

Ⓕ The City Council has a celebration.

Ⓖ The class writes a letter to the City Council.

Ⓗ The City Council decides what they like about the sketch.

Ⓙ The adults tell the designer to put picnic tables in the park.

21 Which of these is a good reason to build the park?

Ⓐ The students are in the fourth grade.

Ⓑ The designer needs to make a sketch.

Ⓒ The old warehouse should be destroyed.

Ⓓ The students want a place to honor state heroes.

22 From the letter, you can tell that the students believe it is important to —

Ⓕ get a new City Council

Ⓖ build more playgrounds

Ⓗ have a warehouse on Third Avenue

Ⓙ listen to people who live in the city

23 Which of these gives the best reason why Heroes' Park will make the city a better place?

Ⓐ Some kids probably want a baseball diamond.

Ⓑ Our city would be more beautiful with a park.

Ⓒ We want the City Council to build Heroes' Park.

Ⓓ President Carter and Dr. Martin Luther King, Jr. are famous heroes.

24 The fourth-grade students wrote their letter to —

Ⓕ tell a sad story

Ⓖ make readers laugh

Ⓗ convince the City Council to build a new park

Ⓙ give information about Dr. Martin Luther King, Jr.

© Hampton-Brown

GO ON ➡

COMPREHENSION / CRITICAL THINKING

DIRECTIONS Read the selection. Then read each item. Choose the best answer. Mark your answer. *(3 points each)*

The Giant Sequoia

California's state tree is a kind of redwood called the giant sequoia. It is the largest tree on Earth. A full-grown sequoia can be 150–250 feet tall. It begins its life, however, as a tiny seed. What does the sequoia seed need to develop into a mighty tree?

The Seed Stage

Everything has to be just right for a sequoia seed to grow into a tree. If the weather is too sunny and hot when the seed falls to the ground, the seed will just dry up.

If the soil around the seed is wet enough, the seed cracks open and roots reach out. The roots push down and begin to get food from the soil. The stem of the sequoia pushes up toward the sunlight.

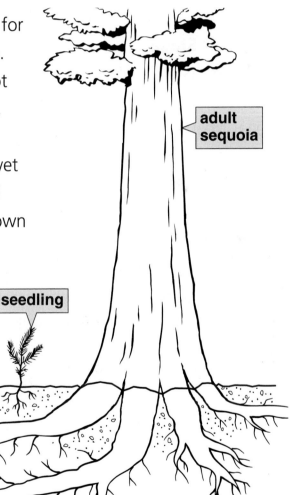

adult sequoia

seedling

stem

root

GO ON ▶

The Giant Sequoia, continued

The Seedling Stage

The sequoia stem pushes upward because it needs sunlight to grow. If more than about one-half inch of soil covers the seed, the stem cannot reach sunlight quickly. Without sunlight, the sequoia will die. If the stem reaches sunlight soon enough, it grows taller and the roots spread farther into the soil. After a few days, the empty shell of the seed pops off and the baby sequoia, called a seedling, stands up.

The Adult Stage

The roots of a sequoia only go a few feet down into the soil, but they spread out as wide as 200 feet. Most of a sequoia's roots are smaller than a human hair. These tiny roots bring food into the plant. At this stage, a few roots get as thick as 2–3 feet across. These larger roots help hold the tree in place.

Once they are past the seedling stage, very few sequoias die. Even a forest fire cannot kill most adult sequoias. One thing that can kill an adult sequoia, though, is a high wind. Because their roots do not reach very deep into the soil, sequoias can be knocked over by a strong wind. After a sequoia dies, a new baby sequoia usually will grow in its place.

Most giant sequoias live a long time. Many are hundreds of years old, and the oldest is more than 3,000 years old.

© Hampton-Brown

GO ON ➡

COMPREHENSION / CRITICAL THINKING

25 **Which of these can cause a sequoia seed to dry up?**

- Ⓐ a lot of wind
- Ⓑ hot, sunny weather
- Ⓒ too many seeds in one place
- Ⓓ too many trees near the seed

26 **If the soil is wet enough —**

- Ⓕ the seed fills with water
- Ⓖ the seedling floats away
- Ⓗ the seedling drops seeds onto the ground
- Ⓙ the seed cracks open and roots grow into the ground

27 **Which of these happens before the seedling stage?**

- Ⓐ The seedling makes seeds.
- Ⓑ The sequoia becomes a giant tree.
- Ⓒ Roots begin to get food from the soil.
- Ⓓ Some roots grow as thick as 2–3 feet across.

28 **Too much soil on top of a sequoia seed is harmful because the —**

- Ⓕ roots grow too deep
- Ⓖ roots can't get enough food
- Ⓗ weight breaks the seed open
- Ⓙ stem can't reach the sunlight soon enough

29 **A sequoia can be knocked over by a high wind because its roots —**

- Ⓐ get too wet
- Ⓑ do not reach very deep
- Ⓒ bring food from the soil
- Ⓓ are all smaller than a human hair

30 **Which of these usually happens after a sequoia dies?**

- Ⓕ Its roots get smaller.
- Ⓖ A new baby sequoia grows.
- Ⓗ It becomes California's state tree.
- Ⓙ The leaves of the tree grow faster.

STOP

B Beginning Progress Test

VOCABULARY
(4 points each)

1 B   5 D
2 H   6 F
3 A   7 C
4 F

GRAMMAR
(4 points each)

8 H   12 H
9 C   13 D
10 J   14 J
11 A   15 D

COMPREHENSION / CRITICAL THINKING
(5 points each)

16 F   20 F
17 B   21 D
18 G   22 H
19 D   23 B

I Intermediate Progress Test

VOCABULARY
(4 points each)

1 D   6 J
2 J   7 A
3 C   8 J
4 J   9 C
5 B   10 G

GRAMMAR
(3 points each)

11 A   15 B
12 F   16 H
13 A   17 C
14 J   18 J

COMPREHENSION / CRITICAL THINKING
(3 points each)

19 B   25 B
20 H   26 F
21 D   27 B
22 J   28 J
23 C   29 C
24 G   30 J

A Advanced Progress Test

VOCABULARY
(4 points each)

1 A   6 J
2 G   7 A
3 B   8 J
4 H   9 B
5 B   10 H

GRAMMAR
(3 points each)

11 C   15 B
12 H   16 H
13 B   17 C
14 J   18 J

COMPREHENSION / CRITICAL THINKING
(3 points each)

19 C   25 B
20 F   26 J
21 D   27 C
22 J   28 J
23 B   29 B
24 H   30 G

Unit 6 • Self-Assessment

I Can Speak English!

1. I can ask for and give information.

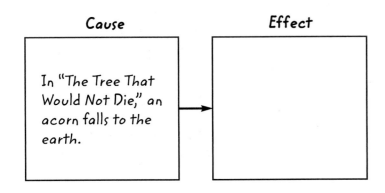 My state is in the _____ region.

_____ is your state?

2. I can persuade someone to do something.

When you visit _____, you should

see _____ .

My New Words

_____

_____

_____

_____

_____

_____

_____

_____

_____

I Can Read in English!

3. I can tell the steps to do or make something.

☐ yes   ☐ not yet

4. I can tell the causes and effects in a story.

Cause		Effect
In "The Tree That Would Not Die," an acorn falls to the earth.	→	

What I've Read

☐ A Quarter's Worth of Fame

☐ The Tree That Would Not Die

☐ _____

☐ _____

Unit 7 • Directions for Ⓑ Progress Test

Distribute the test pages. Before students begin each subtest, read aloud the directions and use the script to work through each sample item.

VOCABULARY

Read aloud the directions on page 67. Then work through the sample item. Say:

Sample

Look at the pictures in the box. Which picture shows a jacket? *Point to the picture.* (Pause.) *The second bubble is filled in because the second picture shows a* jacket.

Items 1–7

Read each question aloud. Provide time for students to mark their answers.

GRAMMAR

Read aloud the directions on page 69. Then work through the sample item. Say:

Sample

Look at the picture in the box. Look at the sentence. Something is missing. Let's try each answer choice. Listen:

> He is read *the newspaper.*
> He reading *the newspaper.*
> He is reading *the newspaper.*
> He are reading *the newspaper.*

The third bubble is filled in because is reading *is the best answer.*

Items 8–11

Read aloud each sentence with each answer choice. Provide time for students to mark their answers.

Read aloud the directions on page 70. Then work through the sample item. Say:

Sample

Look at the picture in the box. Which group of words is a complete sentence? Listen:

> My penny.
> The penny falls.
> The shiny penny.
> Falls on the ground.

GRAMMAR continued

The second bubble is filled in because The penny falls *is a complete sentence.*

Items 12–15

Read aloud the answer choices for each item. Provide time for students to mark their answers.

COMPREHENSION / CRITICAL THINKING

Selection 1 and Items 16–19

Read aloud the directions on page 71. Say: *Now listen to the selection. The title is:*

The Gift

Look at Picture 1. On Saturdays, Jalaal works with his mother and father.

Look at Picture 2. Jalaal gets $5.00 each week. He wants to buy a gift for his father. Jalaal saves his money.

Look at Picture 3. One day, Jalaal sees a good gift for his father.

Look at Picture 4. Jalaal's father reads some of the words. He says, "Thank you, son!"

Then read each question aloud. Provide time for students to mark their answers.

Selection 2 and Items 20–23

Read aloud the directions on page 73. Say: *Now listen to the selection. The title is:*

A Birthday Party for Sue

Look at the first picture. It is Sue's birthday! Her friends have no money for a big party. So, they use what they have.

Look at the next picture. Phuong brings flowers from home. She puts them on the tables. They make the room look beautiful.

Look at the next picture. Kellie and Paco make a poster for Sue. They hang it on the wall. They put up colorful paper.

Look at the last picture. The friends invite other kids to the party. They play music and dance. It is a great birthday party!

Then read each question aloud. Provide time for students to mark their answers.

© Hampton-Brown

Distribute the test pages. Before students begin each subtest, read aloud the directions and use the script to work through each sample item.

VOCABULARY

Read aloud the directions on page 67. Then work through the sample item. Say:

Sample

Read the sentence in the box. (Pause.) Which word goes in the blank? Let's try each one:

> *Carlo wears his new* car *to school.*
> *Carlo wears his new* book *to school.*
> *Carlo wears his new* jacket *to school.*
> *Carlo wears his new* building *to school.*

The third bubble is filled in because jacket *is the best answer.*

Items 1–6

Tell students to complete the remaining items in the same way. Provide time for students to mark their answers.

Read aloud the directions on page 68. Then work through the sample item. Say:

Sample

Read the sentence in the box. (Pause.) Which word goes in the blank? Let's try each one:

> *Gina walks* slowly *through the park.*
> *Gina walks* slower *through the park.*
> *Gina walks* slowing *through the park.*
> *Gina walks* slowness *through the park.*

The first bubble is filled in because slowly *is the best answer.*

Items 7–10

Tell students to complete the remaining items in the same way. Provide time for them to mark their answers.

GRAMMAR

Read aloud the directions on page 69. Then work through the sample item. Say:

Sample

Read the sentence. (Pause.) What is the best way to write the underlined part? Look at the four choices. The third bubble is filled in because are working *is the best way to write the underlined part.*

Items 11–16

Tell students to complete the remaining items in the same way. Provide time for them to mark their answers.

Read aloud the directions on page 70. Then work through the sample item. Say:

Sample

Read each group of words in the box. (Pause.) Which group of words is a complete sentence? Look at the four choices. The second bubble is filled in because Sue eats tacos *is a complete sentence.*

Items 17–22

Tell students to complete the remaining items in the same way. Provide time for them to mark their answers.

COMPREHENSION / CRITICAL THINKING

Selections and Items 23–31

Read aloud the directions for each selection. Provide time for students to read the selection and mark their answers.

Unit 7 • Student Profile for Beginning Progress Test Ⓑ

DIRECTIONS Record the student's name and test date. Use the **Answer Key** on page 76a to score the student's test. Then, in the Student Profile, circle the item number of each correct answer and circle the plus or minus sign to indicate mastery. Calculate the subtest scores and then the total test score. To help you group students for reteaching, transfer the minus sign for any unmastered skill to the **Class Profile** (page 67f).

Student Name _____ **Date** _____

| Subtest | Tested Skills | ITEM ANALYSIS | | TEST SCORES |
		Item Numbers	Mastery	No. Correct × Points = Score
VOCABULARY	Key Words	1 2 3 4 5 6 7	6 out of 7 + −	_____ × 4 = ⬜/28
GRAMMAR	Helping Verbs	8 9 10 11	3 out of 4 + −	_____ × 4 = ⬜/32
	Complete Sentences	12 13 14 15	3 out of 4 + −	
COMPREHENSION / CRITICAL THINKING	Relate Goal and Outcome	16 17 18 19	3 out of 4 + −	_____ × 5 = ⬜/40
	Relate Problem and Solution	20 21 22 23	3 out of 4 + −	

TOTAL UNIT 7 PROGRESS TEST ⬜/100

© Hampton-Brown

Unit 7 • Student Profile for Intermediate Progress Test

DIRECTIONS Record the student's name and test date. Use the **Answer Key** on page 76a to score the student's test. Then, in the Student Profile, circle the item number of each correct answer and circle the plus or minus sign to indicate mastery. Calculate the subtest scores and then the total test score. To help you group students for reteaching, transfer the minus sign for any unmastered skill to the **Class Profile** (page 67f).

Student Name _____ Date _____

| Subtest | Tested Skills | ITEM ANALYSIS | | TEST SCORES |
		Item Numbers	Mastery	No. Correct × Points = Score
VOCABULARY	Key Words	1 2 3 4 5 6	5 out of 6 + −	_____ × 4 = ⧄/40
	Prefixes and Suffixes	7 8 9 10	3 out of 4 + −	
GRAMMAR	Helping Verbs	11 12 13 14 15 16	5 out of 6 + −	_____ × 2 = ⧄/24
	Complete Sentences	17 18 19 20 21 22	5 out of 6 + −	
COMPREHENSION / CRITICAL THINKING	Relate Goal and Outcome	27 28 29 30 31	4 out of 5 + −	_____ × 4 = ⧄/36
	Relate Problem and Solution	23 24 25 26	3 out of 4 + −	
			TOTAL UNIT 7 PROGRESS TEST	⧄/100

© Hampton–Brown

DIRECTIONS Record the student's name and test date. Use the **Answer Key** on page 76a to score the student's test. Then, in the Student Profile, circle the item number of each correct answer and circle the plus or minus sign to indicate mastery. Calculate the subtest scores and then the total test score. To help you group students for reteaching, transfer the minus sign for any unmastered skill to the **Class Profile** (page 67f).

Student Name _____   Date _____

Subtest	Tested Skills	ITEM ANALYSIS		TEST SCORES
		Item Numbers	Mastery	No. Correct × Points = Score
VOCABULARY	Key Words	1 2 3 4 5 6	5 out of 6 + −	____ × 4 = ⬚/40
	Prefixes and Suffixes	7 8 9 10	3 out of 4 + −	
GRAMMAR	Helping Verbs	11 12 13 14 15 16	5 out of 6 + −	____ × 2 = ⬚/24
	Complete Sentences	17 18 19 20 21 22	5 out of 6 + −	
COMPREHENSION / CRITICAL THINKING	Relate Goal and Outcome	23 28 29 30 31	4 out of 5 + −	____ × 4 = ⬚/36
	Relate Problem and Solution	24 25 26 27	3 out of 4 + −	
			TOTAL UNIT 7 PROGRESS TEST	⬚/100

© Hampton-Brown

Unit 7 • Class Profile

Date _____

DIRECTIONS Use the **Unit 7 Student Profiles** to complete this chart. In each row, write the student's name, fill in the bubble for the test form taken, and mark a minus sign (–) for any skill not yet mastered. Then group students and use the reteaching ideas and practice exercises to help students reach mastery.

		TESTED SKILLS					
Student Name	**Test Form**	**Key Words**	**Prefixes and Suffixes**	**Helping Verbs**	**Complete Sentences**	**Relate Goal and Outcome**	**Relate Problem and Solution**
	ⒷⒾⒶ						
	ⒷⒾⒶ						
	ⒷⒾⒶ						
	ⒷⒾⒶ						
	ⒷⒾⒶ						
	ⒷⒾⒶ						
	ⒷⒾⒶ						
	ⒷⒾⒶ						
	ⒷⒾⒶ						
	ⒷⒾⒶ						
	ⒷⒾⒶ						
	ⒷⒾⒶ						
	ⒷⒾⒶ						
	ⒷⒾⒶ						
	ⒷⒾⒶ						
	ⒷⒾⒶ						
	ⒷⒾⒶ						
	ⒷⒾⒶ						
	ⒷⒾⒶ						
	ⒷⒾⒶ						
	ⒷⒾⒶ						
	ⒷⒾⒶ						
RETEACHING RESOURCES		ⒷⒾⒶ AH T38	ⒾⒶ EAYC 48–53	Ⓑ AH T40 ⒾⒶ EAYC 259	Ⓑ AH T40 ⒾⒶ EAYC 236–237	ⒷⒾⒶ LB TG	ⒷⒾⒶ LB TG
PRACTICE EXERCISES		PB 100, 109	PB 108, 119	EAYC 392	EAYC 382	PB 105	PB 116

KEY: **AH:** Assessment Handbook   **EAYC:** English at Your Command!
LB TG: Leveled Books Teacher's Guide   **PB:** Practice Book

Unit 7 • What's It Worth?

DIRECTIONS Listen to each question. Then choose the correct picture.
Mark your answer. *(4 points each)*

⭐**Sample**

Which picture shows a <u>jacket</u>?

1 Which picture shows a <u>coin</u>?

2 Someone has a <u>load</u> of apples. Which picture shows this?

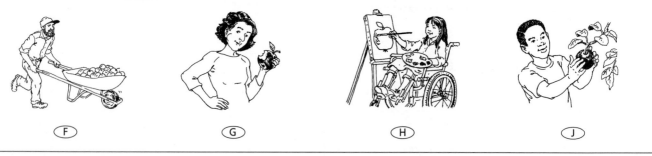

3 A child <u>trades</u> something. Which picture shows this?

GO ON ➡

© Hampton-Brown

VOCABULARY

4 Which picture shows a reward?

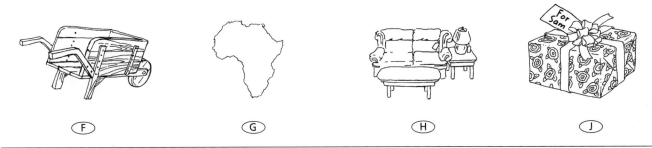

ⓒFⓓ   ⓒGⓓ   ⓒHⓓ   ⓒJⓓ

5 Which picture shows a market?

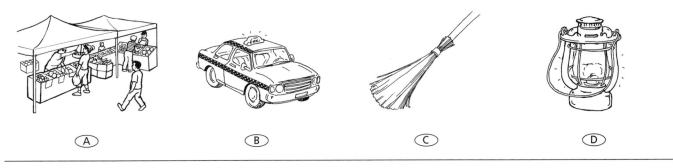

ⒶA   ⒷB   ⒸC   ⒹD

6 Which girl is disappointed?

ⓒFⓓ   ⓒGⓓ   ⓒHⓓ   ⓒJⓓ

7 Which boy does a service?

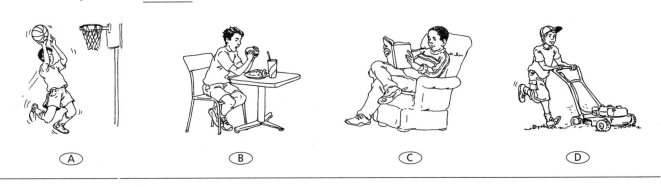

ⒶA   ⒷB   ⒸC   ⒹD

STOP

GRAMMAR

DIRECTIONS Look at the picture. Listen to the sentence with each answer. Choose the word or words that complete the sentence correctly. Mark your answer. *(4 points each)*

Sample

He _____ the newspaper.

Ⓐ is read
Ⓑ reading
Ⓒ is reading
Ⓓ are reading

8 She _____ for lunch.

Ⓕ pay
Ⓖ paying
Ⓗ is paying
Ⓙ are paying

9 They _____ bicycles.

Ⓐ is ride
Ⓑ are ride
Ⓒ is riding
Ⓓ are riding

10 She _____ for a dress.

Ⓕ look
Ⓖ is look
Ⓗ is looking
Ⓙ are looking

11 The boys _____ their money.

Ⓐ is count
Ⓑ are count
Ⓒ is counting
Ⓓ are counting

STOP

GRAMMAR

DIRECTIONS Look at the picture. Read each group of words.
Choose the complete sentence. Mark your answer. *(4 points each)*

⭐**Sample**

Ⓐ My penny.

Ⓑ The penny falls.

Ⓒ The shiny penny.

Ⓓ Falls on the ground.

14

Ⓕ Buys many toys.

Ⓖ She looks at the toys.

Ⓗ Goes to the big market.

Ⓙ A lot of books and toys.

12

Ⓕ The boy buys a cap.

Ⓖ A blue baseball cap.

Ⓗ Buys a baseball cap.

Ⓙ The boy with money.

15

Ⓐ Pays for it now.

Ⓑ Dad buys a gift.

Ⓒ A gift at the store.

Ⓓ Something special for Mom.

13

Ⓐ The big, soft bed.

Ⓑ Counts her money.

Ⓒ The girl on the bed.

Ⓓ She counts her money.

STOP

© Hampton-Brown

COMPREHENSION / CRITICAL THINKING

DIRECTIONS Listen to the selection. Then listen to each question.
Choose the best answer. Mark your answer. *(5 points each)*

The Gift

1

On Saturdays, Jalaal works with his mother and father.

2

Jalaal gets $5.00 each week. He wants to buy a gift for his father. Jalaal saves his money.

3

One day, Jalaal sees a good gift for his father.

4

Jalaal's father reads some of the words. He says, "Thank you, son!"

GO ON ➡

© Hampton-Brown

COMPREHENSION / CRITICAL THINKING

16 What does Jalaal want?

F   G   H   J

17 What does Jalaal do to get what he wants?

A   B   C   D

18 Where does Jalaal go to get what he wants?

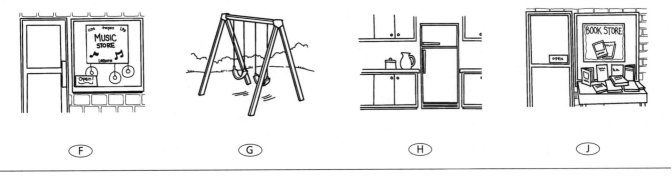

F   G   H   J

19 What finally happens?

A   B   C   D

GO ON ➤

COMPREHENSION / CRITICAL THINKING

DIRECTIONS Listen to the selection. Then listen to each question. Choose the best answer. Mark your answer. *(5 points each)*

A Birthday Party for Sue

It is Sue's birthday! Her friends have no money for a big party. So, they use what they have.

Phuong brings flowers from home. She puts them on the tables. They make the room look beautiful.

Kellie and Paco make a poster for Sue. They hang it on the wall. They put up colorful paper.

The friends invite other kids to the party. They play music and dance. It is a great birthday party!

© Hampton-Brown

COMPREHENSION / CRITICAL THINKING

20 **The friends want a big party for Sue. That's a problem because they have —**

a messy room
Ⓕ

no money
Ⓖ

too much homework
Ⓗ

too many people
Ⓙ

21 **To help solve the problem, Phuong —**

buys flowers
Ⓐ

makes paper flowers
Ⓑ

brings flowers from home
Ⓒ

paints flowers
Ⓓ

22 **How do Kellie and Paco help solve the problem?**

Ⓕ

Ⓖ

Ⓗ

Ⓙ

23 **What happens at the end of the selection?**

Ⓐ

Ⓑ

Ⓒ

Ⓓ

STOP

© Hampton-Brown

Unit 7 • What's It Worth?

VOCABULARY

DIRECTIONS Read the sentence. Choose the word that goes in the blank.
Mark your answer. *(4 points each)*

⭐ **Sample**

Carlo wears his new _____ to school.

- Ⓐ car
- Ⓑ book
- ⬤Ⓒ jacket
- Ⓓ building

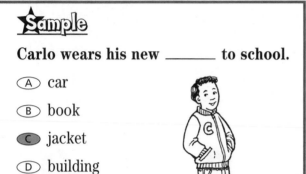

1 Ms. Harmon carried a _____ of apples.

- Ⓐ load
- Ⓑ house
- Ⓒ throne
- Ⓓ pocket

2 He sells a lot of fruit at the _____.

- Ⓕ map
- Ⓖ class
- Ⓗ frame
- Ⓙ market

3 Elaine used all her _____ to buy fruit.

- Ⓐ coins
- Ⓑ boxes
- Ⓒ secrets
- Ⓓ vegetables

4 Jimmy was _____ to save money for a baseball mitt.

- Ⓕ quiet
- Ⓖ afraid
- Ⓗ determined
- Ⓙ disappointed

5 At the bank, Mr. Kane _____ some U.S. dollars for pesos.

- Ⓐ watched
- Ⓑ explained
- Ⓒ exchanged
- Ⓓ remembered

6 Ken collected the most cans so he got a _____.

- Ⓕ cent
- Ⓖ story
- Ⓗ reward
- Ⓙ problem

STOP

© Hampton-Brown

VOCABULARY

DIRECTIONS Read the sentence. Choose the word that goes in the blank.
Mark your answer. *(4 points each)*

⭐ **Sample**

Gina walks _____ through the park.

Ⓐ slowly
Ⓑ slower
Ⓒ slowing
Ⓓ slowness

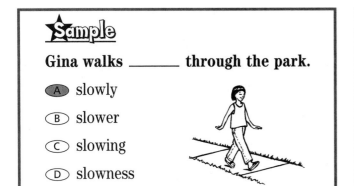

7 John says he ate 20 pancakes.
I think he _____ .

Ⓐ count
Ⓑ counter
Ⓒ counting
Ⓓ miscounted

8 The paper says that 2 + 3 = 4, but the answer is _____ .

Ⓕ correct
Ⓖ correctly
Ⓗ incorrect
Ⓙ correcting

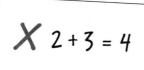

$X \ 2 + 3 = 4$

9 Every morning, a _____ opens the store at nine o'clock.

Ⓐ work
Ⓑ worker
Ⓒ worked
Ⓓ working

10 Saturday was a very _____ day.

Ⓕ rainy
Ⓖ rains
Ⓗ rained
Ⓙ raining

STOP

GRAMMAR

DIRECTIONS Read the sentences. Choose the best way to write each underlined part, or choose "Correct as it is." Mark your answer.
(2 points each)

⭐**Sample**

Teresa and Jun <u>are work</u> hard on our class project.

Ⓐ working

Ⓑ is working

Ⓒ are working

Ⓓ Correct as it is

---

11 They <u>making</u> a budget for the class trip.

Ⓐ are make

Ⓑ is making

Ⓒ are making

Ⓓ Correct as it is

12 Teresa and Jun <u>is study</u> maps every day.

Ⓕ studying

Ⓖ have studied

Ⓗ have studying

Ⓙ Correct as it is

13 Jun <u>have learning</u> that Highway 66 is the best way to get there.

Ⓐ has learn

Ⓑ has learned

Ⓒ are learning

Ⓓ Correct as it is

14 Right now, Teresa <u>is reading</u> about places to eat.

Ⓕ is read

Ⓖ are reading

Ⓗ has reading

Ⓙ Correct as it is

15 She <u>is discovered</u> some good places.

Ⓐ discovering

Ⓑ has discovered

Ⓒ have discovering

Ⓓ Correct as it is

16 Now all the students <u>is getting</u> excited about the trip.

Ⓕ are get

Ⓖ are getting

Ⓗ have getting

Ⓙ Correct as it is

STOP

GRAMMAR

DIRECTIONS Read each group of words. Choose the complete sentence.
Mark your answer. *(2 points each)*

Sample

Ⓐ Sue and Joe.

🅑 Sue eats tacos.

Ⓒ Tacos for lunch.

Ⓓ Always eats tacos.

17　Ⓐ Costs money.

　　Ⓑ Wants a new bike.

　　Ⓒ Jesse saves his money.

　　Ⓓ Saves money for a bike.

18　Ⓕ Looked all day.

　　Ⓖ Looked carefully.

　　Ⓗ Everyone in my family.

　　Ⓙ I looked for my cat all day.

19　Ⓐ That girl.

　　Ⓑ Found a dime.

　　Ⓒ Is in her pocket.

　　Ⓓ Mina found a coin.

20　Ⓕ Paper money.

　　Ⓖ I save pennies.

　　Ⓗ Likes old coins.

　　Ⓙ Nickels and dimes.

21　Ⓐ I don't want that jacket.

　　Ⓑ Not that bright red jacket.

　　Ⓒ The beautiful warm jacket.

　　Ⓓ Wanted a red and blue jacket.

22　Ⓕ No bikes here.

　　Ⓖ Don't cost much.

　　Ⓗ Doesn't sell bikes here.

　　Ⓙ No one sells bikes here.

STOP

© Hampton-Brown

DIRECTIONS Read the selection. Then read each item. Choose the best answer. **Mark your answer.** *(4 points each)*

Diana Saves Money

Diana wants a skateboard, but she doesn't have enough money to buy one. So, she makes a budget. She writes down how much money she gets every week. Then she writes down all the things she buys.

Diana sees that she spends all the money she gets. She thinks about what she wants most, a new skateboard! So, she decides to spend less on candy. Now she can save $5.00 every week.

One day, Diana wants a candy bar after school. She remembers her new budget and decides to follow it. Soon she saves enough money to buy a skateboard.

Diana thinks about what she wants most.

Diana's Budget

Money I Get	
Mom and Dad	$ 5.00
Babysitting	$12.00
TOTAL	$17.00

Money I Spend	
Lunches	$10.00
Candy	$ ~~7.00~~ 2.00
TOTAL	$~~17.00~~ 12.00

GO ON →

COMPREHENSION / CRITICAL THINKING

23 **Look at the problem-and-solution chain. What goes in the blank?**

  Ⓐ She buys lunch.

  Ⓑ She makes a budget.

  Ⓒ She asks her parents for more money.

  Ⓓ She decides to buy something different.

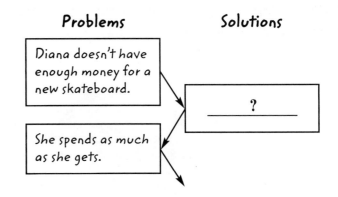

Problems   Solutions

Diana doesn't have enough money for a new skateboard.

She spends as much as she gets.

?

24 **What helps Diana stop spending all the money she gets?**

  Ⓕ She has to pay for her own lunches.

  Ⓖ She gives the money to Mom and Dad.

  Ⓗ She thinks about what she really wants.

  Ⓙ She writes down all the things she buys.

25 **To save money, Diana decides to —**

  Ⓐ buy less candy

  Ⓑ get a second job

  Ⓒ stop buying lunch

  Ⓓ babysit more kids

26 **Diana almost gets a candy bar after school. Instead, she —**

  Ⓕ writes a letter

  Ⓖ changes her budget

  Ⓗ follows her new budget

  Ⓙ gives the candy to her parents

© Hampton-Brown

GO ON ▶

DIRECTIONS Read the selection. Then read each item. Choose the best answer. Mark your answer. *(4 points each)*

The Money Book

Tim and Antonio like to learn about money. They decide to collect money from many countries. They buy a special book and put a U.S. bill on one page. They ask people for more bills.

Antonio's sister has a bill from Mexico, but she is saving it for a trip to Mexico. Antonio's mom gives the boys an old Mexican bill. Tim's dad gives them an old bill from China. The boys put the bills in their book.

Their teacher, Mr. Winn, gives the boys a bill from France. "It is worth five euros," he says. Then Tim's neighbor, Mrs. Feld, gives the boys an old bill from Russia. "Here are ten rubles," she says.

"We are rich in five different ways!" Antonio says.

GO ON ➡

COMPREHENSION / CRITICAL THINKING

27 **The boys' goal is to —**

Ⓐ meet a new neighbor

Ⓑ write a report about money

Ⓒ find someone with a lot of money

Ⓓ collect money from many countries

28 **To reach their goal, the boys —**

Ⓕ go to the library

Ⓖ ask people for bills

Ⓗ travel to different countries

Ⓙ send letters to their neighbors

29 **Which of these events helps Tim and Antonio reach their goal?**

Ⓐ Mrs. Feld gives the boys a book.

Ⓑ Mr. Winn gives the boys five euros.

Ⓒ Antonio's mom tells the boys a story.

Ⓓ Tim's dad tells the boys about China.

30 **Which event does <u>not</u> help the boys reach their goal?**

Ⓕ The boys put bills in their book.

Ⓖ Antonio's sister saves her money.

Ⓗ Mrs. Feld gives the boys ten rubles.

Ⓙ Antonio's mom gives the boys a Mexican bill.

31 **How does the selection end?**

Ⓐ The boys finish their report.

Ⓑ The boys go to five countries.

Ⓒ The boys have bills from five countries.

Ⓓ The boys give Antonio's sister some money.

STOP

Unit 7 • What's It Worth?

VOCABULARY

DIRECTIONS Read the sentence. Choose the word that goes in the blank.
Mark your answer. *(4 points each)*

⭐**Sample**

Carlo wears his new _____ to school.

Ⓐ car

Ⓑ book

🅲 jacket

Ⓓ building

---

1 Ms. Harmon carried a _____ of apples to the truck.

Ⓐ load

Ⓑ treaty

Ⓒ design

Ⓓ throne

2 Farmers sell a lot of vegetables at the _____.

Ⓕ tribe

Ⓖ frame

Ⓗ goods

Ⓙ market

3 Jim was _____ to save enough money to buy a baseball mitt.

Ⓐ silent

Ⓑ afraid

Ⓒ determined

Ⓓ disappointed

4 Elaine used all her _____ to buy some fruit.

Ⓕ coins

Ⓖ secrets

Ⓗ contests

Ⓙ sketches

5 At the bank, Mr. Kane _____ some U.S. dollars for pesos.

Ⓐ blended

Ⓑ captured

Ⓒ exchanged

Ⓓ remembered

6 Ken got a _____ for collecting more cans than anyone else.

Ⓕ style

Ⓖ value

Ⓗ service

Ⓙ reward

STOP

Ⓐ

DIRECTIONS Read the sentence. Choose the word that goes in the blank.
Mark your answer. *(4 points each)*

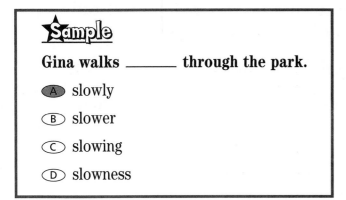

⭐ Sample

Gina walks _____ through the park.

- Ⓐ slowly
- Ⓑ slower
- Ⓒ slowing
- Ⓓ slowness

7 John says he ate 20 pancakes.
I think he _____.

- Ⓐ counter
- Ⓑ recount
- Ⓒ counting
- Ⓓ miscounted

8 I did not check my answer, so it
may be _____.

- Ⓕ incorrect
- Ⓖ correctly
- Ⓗ recorrect
- Ⓙ correction

9 A _____ opens the store at
nine o'clock.

- Ⓐ work
- Ⓑ worker
- Ⓒ worked
- Ⓓ working

10 Saturday was a very _____ day.

- Ⓕ rains
- Ⓖ rainy
- Ⓗ rained
- Ⓙ raining

STOP

GRAMMAR

DIRECTIONS Read the sentences. Choose the best way to write each underlined part, or choose "Correct as it is." Mark your answer. *(2 points each)*

Teresa and Jun <u>are work</u> hard on our class project. They <u>making</u> a
            ★Sample   11

budget for the class trip to the state capital.

Teresa and Jun <u>is study</u> maps every day to see which road we should
            12

take. Jun <u>have learning</u> that Highway 66 is the fastest route.
        13

Right now, Teresa <u>is reading</u> about places to eat along the way. She
                14

<u>is discovered</u> some good places that won't cost too much.
15

This project is fun! All of the students <u>is getting</u> very excited.
                                        16

★**Sample**

Ⓐ working

Ⓑ is working

Ⓒ are working

Ⓓ Correct as it is

---

11 Ⓐ are make

Ⓑ is making

Ⓒ are making

Ⓓ Correct as it is

12 Ⓕ studying

Ⓖ have studied

Ⓗ have studying

Ⓙ Correct as it is

13 Ⓐ has learn

Ⓑ has learned

Ⓒ are learning

Ⓓ Correct as it is

14 Ⓕ is read

Ⓖ are reading

Ⓗ has reading

Ⓙ Correct as it is

15 Ⓐ discovering

Ⓑ has discovered

Ⓒ have discovering

Ⓓ Correct as it is

16 Ⓕ are get

Ⓖ are getting

Ⓗ have getting

Ⓙ Correct as it is

© Hampton-Brown

Name _____ Date _____

GRAMMAR

DIRECTIONS Read each group of words. Choose the complete sentence.
Mark your answer. *(2 points each)*

⭐ **Sample**

Ⓐ Sue and Joe.

🅑 Sue eats tacos.

Ⓒ Tacos for lunch.

Ⓓ Always eats tacos.

---

17 Ⓐ Wants a new bike.

Ⓑ Costs a lot of money.

Ⓒ Jesse saves a lot of money.

Ⓓ Saves some money for a bike.

18 Ⓕ Yesterday my cat.

Ⓖ Have looked carefully.

Ⓗ Looked everywhere for my cat.

Ⓙ I looked for my cat all day yesterday.

19 Ⓐ I found a dime.

Ⓑ Saw a silver coin.

Ⓒ Was in my pocket.

Ⓓ Found it on the ground.

20 Ⓕ I save pennies.

Ⓖ Uses paper money.

Ⓗ The value of money.

Ⓙ Nickels, dimes, and quarters.

21 Ⓐ Don't want a jacket.

Ⓑ Not the blue and yellow.

Ⓒ I don't want a blue jacket.

Ⓓ The beautiful, yellow jacket.

22 Ⓕ No bikes here today.

Ⓖ No one sells bikes here.

Ⓗ Don't cost much money.

Ⓙ Doesn't sell bikes here now.

STOP

COMPREHENSION / CRITICAL THINKING

DIRECTIONS Read the selection. Then read each item. Choose the best answer. Mark your answer. *(4 points each)*

Control Your Money!

Do you control your money? When you want something really special, do you have enough money to buy it? Can you save thirty, forty, or even fifty dollars? You may be able to save money and still buy pizza, get new CDs, and go to the movies. Here's how:

Start with a Budget

You can buy some of the little things you like and save money for bigger things, too. How? Make a budget! A budget is a plan. It shows how much money you get in one week or a month and how you plan to spend it.

To help you follow your budget, picture the thing you want.

To start, figure out your weekly or monthly income, or how much money you will get. Next, list all your expenses, or what you usually spend money on. Then add up how much you spend. If you spend as much or more than you earn, you won't be able to save money.

This is the hard part. If you want to save money, you have to decide what you really need to spend money on and what you can do without. For example, you need to buy lunch every day at school, but you don't really need to buy a soda every day on the way home.

© Hampton-Brown

GO ON ➡

COMPREHENSION / CRITICAL THINKING

Control Your Money!, continued

Follow Your Budget

It isn't always easy to follow a budget. Every day you see all kinds of things that look great, but your budget says that you can't buy everything you want whenever you want it. You have to keep your goal in mind.

Here's something that will help. Imagine yourself with the thing you are saving for. How do you feel? If you like that feeling, it will help you follow your budget. If you follow your budget, you will get another reward, too. You will discover that you really can take control of your money!

Diana wants a new skateboard, but she doesn't have enough money. So, she makes a weekly budget to see how she can save money.

Diana's income and expenses are equal, so she has to cut out some things. She decides to spend less on candy and CDs every week.

Then one day Diana sees a beautiful skirt she wants to buy. She quickly imagines herself on her skateboard and decides to save her money instead.

Diana is following her budget. Soon she'll have enough money to buy a new skateboard!

Diana's Weekly Budget

Income

Mom and Dad	$ 5.00
Babysitting	$12.00
Weeding the garden	$ 8.00
TOTAL	$25.00

Expenses

Library fine	$ 2.00
Candy	$ ~~8.00~~ 4.00
~~New CD~~	~~$15.00~~
TOTAL	~~$25.00~~ 6.00

GO ON ▶

© Hampton-Brown

COMPREHENSION / CRITICAL THINKING

23 If your goal is to save money, which of these is the best way to reach your goal?

Ⓐ Stop babysitting.

Ⓑ Skip lunch some days.

Ⓒ Spend less money on sodas.

Ⓓ Borrow money from a friend.

24 Look at the problem-and-solution chain.

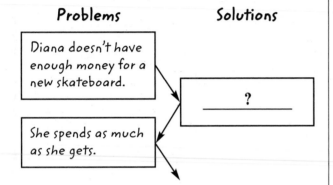

Which of these goes in the blank?

Ⓕ She makes a budget.

Ⓖ She gets another job.

Ⓗ She buys a soda after school.

Ⓙ She asks her parents for money.

25 What helps Diana stop spending all the money she earns?

Ⓐ She has to pay for her own lunches.

Ⓑ She gives the money to Mom and Dad.

Ⓒ She thinks about what she really wants.

Ⓓ She writes down all the things she buys.

26 To save money Diana decides to —

Ⓕ pull more weeds

Ⓖ borrow more books

Ⓗ spend less on candy and CDs

Ⓙ imagine herself in a new skirt

27 Diana wants to buy a new skirt. Instead, she —

Ⓐ follows her new budget

Ⓑ changes her budget again

Ⓒ works hard to earn more money

Ⓓ asks her mother to buy the skirt for her

© Hampton-Brown

GO ON ➡

COMPREHENSION / CRITICAL THINKING

DIRECTIONS Read the selection. Then read each item. Choose the best answer. Mark your answer. *(4 points each)*

Things Money Can't Buy

I like money. I guess that's because I always want things, like games and fun stuff to eat. One day I decided I would look for money everywhere I went and collect as much as possible. That day I went to the store for some popcorn and found a dollar on the floor. I showed the bill to the clerk, and he said, "Finders keepers." In other words, "If you found it, you can keep it." That made me smile!

Later that day I found a quarter in the park and a ten-dollar bill on the sidewalk! The next morning, I saw a familiar paper beside a trash barrel and ran to pick it up. I hadn't really seen the man walking in front of me. As I pushed past the man, I bumped into him and almost made him fall.

GO ON ➡

Things Money Can't Buy, continued

"Sorry, Sir," I said. "I didn't see you."

He laughed kindly, "That's okay, I didn't see you either."

Then I noticed that the man held a white cane with a red tip, and I realized he was blind.

"Where is a boy like you going in such a hurry?" asked the man.

"I was trying to pick up a dollar from the ground!" I said.

"Is money that important?" The man lifted his face up toward the sky and continued, "A boy like you should be riding a bike or playing soccer on a day like this."

I looked around at the beautiful day. A cool breeze was blowing and the sun was warm and bright. Most of my friends were probably outside playing. At that moment I remembered that I had spent every minute of the last few days looking for money. I hadn't even noticed the perfect soccer weather.

Suddenly, I didn't care about the money anymore. "Thank you, Sir," I called. "You just helped me realize how important money is — and isn't! There are some things money can't buy, and a beautiful day is one of them."

© Hampton-Brown

GO ON ➡

COMPREHENSION / CRITICAL THINKING

28 **In the beginning of the selection, the boy's goal is to —**

Ⓕ collect money

Ⓖ get good grades

Ⓗ make some new friends

Ⓙ be a great soccer player

29 **What does the boy do first to reach his goal?**

Ⓐ He talks to a blind man.

Ⓑ He sells popcorn at the store.

Ⓒ He finds a dollar on the floor.

Ⓓ He buys games and fun things to eat.

30 **Which of these events does not help the boy reach his goal?**

Ⓕ The clerk says, "Finders keepers."

Ⓖ The boy finds a quarter in the park.

Ⓗ The boy finds a ten-dollar bill on the sidewalk.

Ⓙ The blind man says, "You should be playing soccer."

31 **What is the outcome of the selection?**

Ⓐ The boy gives the man his money.

Ⓑ The boy helps the man go back home.

Ⓒ The boy goes back to the store to find more money.

Ⓓ The boy stops looking for money and enjoys the day.

© Hampton-Brown

STOP

Unit 7 • Answer Key

B Beginning Progress Test

VOCABULARY
(4 points each)

1 C   5 A
2 F   6 G
3 B   7 D
4 J

GRAMMAR
(4 points each)

8 H   12 F
9 D   13 D
10 H   14 G
11 D   15 B

COMPREHENSION / CRITICAL THINKING
(5 points each)

16 G   20 G
17 A   21 C
18 J   22 J
19 C   23 A

I Intermediate Progress Test

VOCABULARY
(4 points each)

1 A   6 H
2 J   7 D
3 A   8 H
4 H   9 B
5 C   10 F

GRAMMAR
(2 points each)

11 C   17 C
12 G   18 J
13 B   19 D
14 J   20 G
15 B   21 A
16 G   22 J

COMPREHENSION / CRITICAL THINKING
(4 points each)

23 B   28 G
24 H   29 B
25 A   30 G
26 H   31 C
27 D

A Advanced Progress Test

VOCABULARY
(4 points each)

1 A   6 J
2 J   7 D
3 C   8 F
4 F   9 B
5 C   10 G

GRAMMAR
(2 points each)

11 C   17 C
12 G   18 J
13 B   19 A
14 J   20 F
15 B   21 C
16 G   22 G

COMPREHENSION / CRITICAL THINKING
(4 points each)

23 C   28 F
24 F   29 C
25 C   30 J
26 H   31 D
27 A

Unit 7 • Self-Assessment

I Can Speak English!

1. I can give reasons for my actions.

     🗨 I am glad I bought _____

     because _____ .

2. I can give information about something.

     🗨 I have a _____ . It is made of _____ .

My New Words

_____

_____

_____

_____

_____

_____

_____

_____

_____

I Can Read in English!

3. I can tell what a character wants and how a story ends.

     ☐ yes   ☐ not yet

4. I can tell how problems are solved.

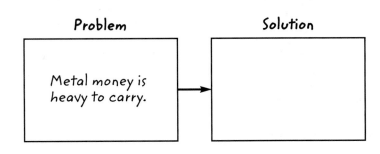

Problem	Solution
Metal money is heavy to carry. →	

What I've Read

☐ My Rows and Piles of Coins

☐ Money

☐ _____

☐ _____

Unit 8 • Directions for Ⓑ Progress Test

Distribute the test pages. Before students begin each subtest, read aloud the directions and use the script to work through each sample item.

Read aloud the directions on page 78. Then work through the sample item. Say:

Sample
Look at the pictures in the box. Which picture shows a jacket? Point to the picture. (Pause.) *The second bubble is filled in because the second picture shows a jacket.*

Items 1–6
Read each question aloud. Provide time for students to mark their answers.

GRAMMAR

Read aloud the directions on page 80. Then work through the sample item. Say:

Sample
Look at the picture in the box. Look at the sentence. There is a word missing. Let's try each word. Listen:

> *The boy moves* big.
> *The boy moves* quiet.
> *The boy moves* under.
> *The boy moves* quietly.

The fourth bubble is filled in because quietly *is the best answer.*

Items 7–13
Read aloud each sentence with its answer choices. Provide time for students to mark their answers.

COMPREHENSION / CRITICAL THINKING

Selection 1 and Items 14–17
Read aloud the directions on page 82. Say: *Now listen to the selection. The title is:*

Dinah at the Beach

Look at Picture 1. Dinah's sister and Dad like to swim. They race into the ocean. Dinah is afraid of the waves.

Look at Picture 2. Dinah sees a pretty black rock. She looks for another pretty rock. Soon she has many rocks.

Look at Picture 3. Mom calls. Dinah is surprised that it is time for lunch.

Look at Picture 4. "Look at the pretty rocks, Dad," Dinah says. "Can we come to the beach again tomorrow?"

Then read each question aloud. Provide time for students to mark their answers.

Selection 2 and Items 18–21
Read aloud the directions on page 84. Say: *Now listen to the selection. The title is:*

Gems of the World
Some people make jewelry out of rocks. We call these beautiful rocks "gems." Gems come in many different colors. Some gems are harder than others. Gems come from many places all over the world. The chart below tells about some common gems.

Point to the chart and say:

The chart is called "Gems Around the World." It tells the name of each gem, its color, its hardness, and where the gem comes from.

Then read through each row of the chart. For example:

An amethyst is purple. Its hardness is 7. This gem comes from Africa, Brazil, Canada, Mexico, Uruguay, and the United States.

Then read each question aloud. Provide time for students to mark their answers.

Unit 8 • Directions for ➊ and Ⓐ Progress Tests

Distribute the test pages. Before students begin each subtest, read aloud the directions and use the script to work through each sample item.

VOCABULARY

Read aloud the directions on page 78. Then work through the sample item. Say:

Sample

Read the sentence in the box. (Pause.) *Which word goes in the blank? Let's try each one:*

> Carlo wears his new car to school.
> Carlo wears his new book to school.
> Carlo wears his new jacket to school.
> Carlo wears his new building to school.

The third bubble is filled in because jacket *is the best answer.*

Items 1–10

Tell students to complete the remaining items in the same way. Provide time for students to mark their answers.

GRAMMAR

Read aloud the directions on page 80. Then work through the sample item. Say:

Sample

Read the sentences. (Pause.) *What is the best way to join the sentences into one, longer sentence? Let's try each choice:*

> Pilar comes from Spain, if *Maki comes from Japan.*
> Pilar comes from Spain, or *Maki comes from Japan.*
> Pilar comes from Spain, but *Maki comes from Japan.*
> Pilar comes from Spain, because *Maki comes from Japan.*

The third bubble is filled in because Pilar comes from Spain, but Maki comes from Japan *is the best way to join the two sentences into one sentence.*

Items 11–14

Tell students to complete the remaining items in the same way. Provide time for them to mark their answers.

GRAMMAR continued

Read aloud the directions on page 81. Then work through the sample item. Say:

Sample

Read the sentence. (Pause.) *Which word goes in the blank? Let's try each one:*

> Carla stores her rock collection safe in a special box.
> Carla stores her rock collection safer in a special box.
> Carla stores her rock collection safely in a special box.
> Carla stores her rock collection safest in a special box.

The third bubble is filled in because safely *is the best answer.*

Items 15–18

Tell students to complete the remaining items in the same way. Provide time for them to mark their answers.

COMPREHENSION / CRITICAL THINKING

Selections and Items 19–30

Read aloud the directions for each selection. Provide time for students to read the selection and mark their answers.

DIRECTIONS Record the student's name and test date. Use the **Answer Key** on page 87a to score the student's test. Then, in the Student Profile, circle the item number of each correct answer and circle the plus or minus sign to indicate mastery. Calculate the subtest scores and then the total test score. To help you group students for reteaching, transfer the minus sign for any unmastered skill to the **Class Profile** (page 78f).

Student Name _____ Date _____

| Subtest | Tested Skills | ITEM ANALYSIS | | TEST SCORES |
		Item Numbers	Mastery	No. Correct × Points = Score
VOCABULARY	Key Words	1 2 3 4 5 6	5 out of 6 + −	_____ × 4 = ⬜ /24
GRAMMAR	Adverbs	7 8 9 10 11 12 13	6 out of 7 + −	_____ × 4 = ⬜ /28
COMPREHENSION / CRITICAL THINKING	Analyze Story Elements (characters)	14 15 16 17	3 out of 4 + −	_____ × 6 = ⬜ /48
	Interpret Graphic Aids	18 19 20 21	3 out of 4 + −	

TOTAL UNIT 8 PROGRESS TEST ⬜ /100

© Hampton-Brown

DIRECTIONS Record the student's name and test date. Use the **Answer Key** on page 87a to score the student's test. Then, in the Student Profile, circle the item number of each correct answer and circle the plus or minus sign to indicate mastery. Calculate the subtest scores and then the total test score. To help you group students for reteaching, transfer the minus sign for any unmastered skill to the **Class Profile** (page 78f).

Student Name _____   Date _____

Subtest	Tested Skills	ITEM ANALYSIS		TEST SCORES
		Item Numbers	Mastery	No. Correct × Points = Score
VOCABULARY	Key Words	1 2 3 4 5 6 7 8 9 10	8 out of 10 + −	_____ × 4 = ⧄40
GRAMMAR	Adverbs	15 16 17 18	3 out of 4 + −	_____ × 3 = ⧄24
	Compound and Complex Sentences	11 12 13 14	3 out of 4 + −	
COMPREHENSION / CRITICAL THINKING	Analyze Story Elements (characters)	19 20 21 23	3 out of 4 + −	_____ × 3 = ⧄36
	Make Inferences and Predictions	22 24 29 30	3 out of 4 + −	
	Interpret Graphic Aids	25 26 27 28	3 out of 4 + −	
			TOTAL UNIT 8 PROGRESS TEST	⧄100

Unit 8 • Student Profile for Advanced Progress Test

DIRECTIONS Record the student's name and test date. Use the **Answer Key** on page 87a to score the student's test. Then, in the Student Profile, circle the item number of each correct answer and circle the plus or minus sign to indicate mastery. Calculate the subtest scores and then the total test score. To help you group students for reteaching, transfer the minus sign for any unmastered skill to the **Class Profile** (page 78f).

Student Name _____ Date _____

Subtest	Tested Skills	ITEM ANALYSIS		TEST SCORES
		Item Numbers	Mastery	No. Correct × Points = Score
VOCABULARY	Key Words	1 2 3 4 5 6 7 8 9 10	8 out of 10 + −	_____ × 4 = /40
GRAMMAR	Adverbs	15 16 17 18	3 out of 4 + −	_____ × 3 = /24
	Compound and Complex Sentences	11 12 13 14	3 out of 4 + −	
COMPREHENSION / CRITICAL THINKING	Analyze Story Elements (characters)	19 20 21 22	3 out of 4 + −	_____ × 3 = /36
	Make Inferences and Predictions	23 24 29 30	3 out of 4 + −	
	Interpret Graphic Aids	25 26 27 28	3 out of 4 + −	
			TOTAL UNIT 8 PROGRESS TEST	/100

© Hampton-Brown

Unit 8 • Class Profile
Date _____

DIRECTIONS Use the **Unit 8 Student Profiles** to complete this chart. In each row, write the student's name, fill in the bubble for the test form taken, and mark a minus sign (–) for any skill not yet mastered. Then group students and use the reteaching ideas and practice exercises to help students reach mastery.

Student Name	Test Form	Key Words	Adverbs	Compound and Complex Sentences	Analyze Story Elements (characters)	Make Inferences and Predictions	Interpret Graphic Aids
	Ⓑ Ⓘ Ⓐ						
	Ⓑ Ⓘ Ⓐ						
	Ⓑ Ⓘ Ⓐ						
	Ⓑ Ⓘ Ⓐ						
	Ⓑ Ⓘ Ⓐ						
	Ⓑ Ⓘ Ⓐ						
	Ⓑ Ⓘ Ⓐ						
	Ⓑ Ⓘ Ⓐ						
	Ⓑ Ⓘ Ⓐ						
	Ⓑ Ⓘ Ⓐ						
	Ⓑ Ⓘ Ⓐ						
	Ⓑ Ⓘ Ⓐ						
	Ⓑ Ⓘ Ⓐ						
	Ⓑ Ⓘ Ⓐ						
	Ⓑ Ⓘ Ⓐ						
	Ⓑ Ⓘ Ⓐ						
	Ⓑ Ⓘ Ⓐ						
	Ⓑ Ⓘ Ⓐ						
	Ⓑ Ⓘ Ⓐ						
	Ⓑ Ⓘ Ⓐ						
	Ⓑ Ⓘ Ⓐ						
	Ⓑ Ⓘ Ⓐ						
RETEACHING RESOURCES		Ⓑ Ⓘ Ⓐ AH T38	Ⓑ AH T40 Ⓘ Ⓐ EAYC 269–270	Ⓘ Ⓐ EAYC 182, 238	Ⓑ Ⓘ Ⓐ LB TG	Ⓘ Ⓐ LB TG	Ⓑ Ⓘ Ⓐ LB TG
PRACTICE EXERCISES		PB 120, 130	EAYC 398	EAYC 383 PB 135	PB 124	PB 126–127	PB 125, 128, 129

KEY: **AH:** Assessment Handbook **EAYC:** English at Your Command!
LB TG: Leveled Books Teacher's Guide **PB:** Practice Book

Unit 8 • Rocky Tales

VOCABULARY

DIRECTIONS Listen to each question. Then choose the correct picture.
Mark your answer. *(4 points each)*

⭐**Sample**

Which picture shows a <u>jacket</u>?

Ⓐ   Ⓑ   Ⓒ   Ⓓ

1 Which picture shows a <u>museum</u>?

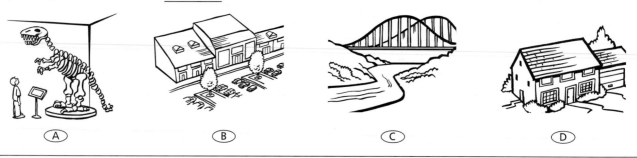

Ⓐ   Ⓑ   Ⓒ   Ⓓ

2 Which picture shows something <u>liquid</u>?

Ⓕ   Ⓖ   Ⓗ   Ⓙ

3 Which picture shows a <u>meteorite</u>?

Ⓐ   Ⓑ   Ⓒ   Ⓓ

GO ON ➡

4   Which picture shows <u>layers</u>?

   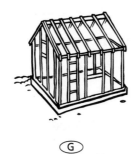      

Ⓕ   Ⓖ   Ⓗ   Ⓙ

5   The rock is <u>enormous</u>. Which picture shows this?

Ⓐ   Ⓑ   Ⓒ   Ⓓ

6   Find the arrow in each picture. Which arrow points to something <u>solid</u>?

Ⓕ   Ⓖ   Ⓗ   Ⓙ

STOP

GRAMMAR

DIRECTIONS Look at the picture. Listen to the sentence with each answer. Choose the word or words that complete the sentence correctly. Mark your answer. *(4 points each)*

Sample

The boy moves _____.

Ⓐ big

Ⓑ quiet

Ⓒ under

Ⓓ quietly

7 Layla reaches the ocean _____.

Ⓐ go

Ⓑ sun

Ⓒ bright

Ⓓ quickly

8 The girl _____ dances on Saturdays.

Ⓕ nice

Ⓖ clever

Ⓗ always

Ⓙ beautiful

9 He puts the rope _____ the box.

Ⓐ blue

Ⓑ near

Ⓒ good

Ⓓ around

10 The man looks _____ for his dog.

Ⓕ old

Ⓖ tall

Ⓗ sound

Ⓙ everywhere

© Hampton-Brown

GO ON ➡

GRAMMAR

11 Lupita eats _____.

Ⓐ fun

Ⓑ early

Ⓒ under

Ⓓ morning

12 The girl whispers _____.

Ⓕ friend

Ⓖ softly

Ⓗ secret

Ⓙ different

13 The turtle moves _____.

Ⓐ high

Ⓑ time

Ⓒ shell

Ⓓ slowly

STOP

COMPREHENSION / CRITICAL THINKING

DIRECTIONS Listen to the selection. Then listen to each question. Choose the best answer. Mark your answer. *(6 points each)*

Dinah at the Beach

1

Dinah's sister and Dad like to swim. They race into the ocean. Dinah is afraid of the waves.

2

Dinah sees a pretty black rock. She looks for another pretty rock. Soon she has many rocks.

3

Mom calls. Dinah is surprised that it is time for lunch.

4

"Look at the pretty rocks, Dad," Dinah says. "Can we come to the beach again tomorrow?"

GO ON ➡

COMPREHENSION / CRITICAL THINKING

14 How do Dinah's sister and Dad feel?

sad   proud   angry   excited

Ⓕ   Ⓖ   Ⓗ   Ⓙ

15 How does Dinah feel in the beginning of the selection?

sad   proud   afraid   excited

Ⓐ   Ⓑ   Ⓒ   Ⓓ

16 How does Dinah feel when she finds the rocks?

bored   interested   tired   hungry

Ⓕ   Ⓖ   Ⓗ   Ⓙ

17 How does Dinah feel at the end of the selection?

angry   worried   happy   surprised

Ⓐ   Ⓑ   Ⓒ   Ⓓ

GO ON

© Hampton-Brown

COMPREHENSION / CRITICAL THINKING

DIRECTIONS Listen to the selection. Then listen to each question.
Choose the best answer. Mark your answer. *(6 points each)*

Gems of the World

Some people make jewelry out of rocks. We call these beautiful rocks "gems." Gems come in many different colors. Some gems are harder than others. Gems come from many places all over the world. The chart below tells about some common gems.

Gems Around the World

Gem	Color	Hardness (1 = softest 10 = hardest)	Where the gem comes from
amethyst	purple	7	Africa, Brazil, Canada, Mexico, Uruguay, United States
diamond	white	10	Australia, Brazil, Russia, United States
emerald	green	7.5–8	Brazil, Colombia, East Africa
garnet	red	6.5–7.5	Australia, Brazil, India, Sri Lanka
ruby	red	9	Afghanistan, Australia, Brazil, Burma, Cambodia, Madagascar, Pakistan, Zimbabwe
topaz	yellow	8	Brazil, Mexico, Pakistan, Russia, United States

© Hampton-Brown

GO ON

COMPREHENSION / CRITICAL THINKING

18 Look at the chart. Which gem is green?

♡	🜄	□	◯
ruby	topaz	emerald	amethyst
F	G	H	J

19 Look at the chart. Which gem is the hardest?

◊	◇	□	◯
garnet	diamond	emerald	amethyst
A	B	C	D

20 Look at the chart. Which gem comes from Burma?

♡	◊	◇	◯
ruby	garnet	diamond	amethyst
F	G	H	J

21 Look at the chart. Which two gems come from Russia?

◊ ♡	◯ ♡	□ 🜄	◇ 🜄
garnet and ruby	amethyst and ruby	emerald and topaz	diamond and topaz
A	B	C	D

STOP

Unit 8 • Rocky Tales

DIRECTIONS Read each item. Choose the word that goes in the blank.
Mark your answer. *(4 points each)*

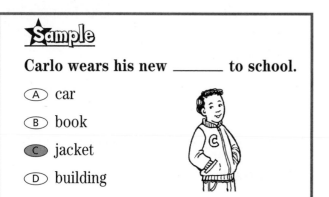

★ **Sample**

Carlo wears his new _____ to school.

- Ⓐ car
- Ⓑ book
- **Ⓒ jacket**
- Ⓓ building

1 The sailors _____ the ship when it began to sink.

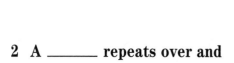

- Ⓐ kept
- Ⓑ bought
- Ⓒ surprised
- Ⓓ abandoned

2 A _____ repeats over and over again.

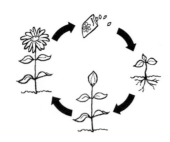

- Ⓕ load
- Ⓖ cycle
- Ⓗ pebble
- Ⓙ museum

3 Pete _____ as he moves the heavy box.

- Ⓐ flies
- Ⓑ waves
- Ⓒ sleeps
- Ⓓ strains

4 My glass fell over. All the _____ spilled on the table.

- Ⓕ hail
- Ⓖ light
- Ⓗ liquid
- Ⓙ culture

5 I feel _____ when I can't talk to my friends.

- Ⓐ tired
- Ⓑ lonely
- Ⓒ proud
- Ⓓ strong

GO ON ➡

VOCABULARY

6 Enzo made a long _____ from Italy to the United States.

Ⓕ canyon

Ⓖ contest

Ⓗ journey

Ⓙ summer

7 A huge _____ made a hole in the ground.

Ⓐ cloudy

Ⓑ volcano

Ⓒ weather

Ⓓ meteorite

8 Let's visit the _____ to learn about dinosaurs.

Ⓕ cellar

Ⓖ nation

Ⓗ market

Ⓙ museum

9 The boulder was so _____ it smashed the car.

Ⓐ dull

Ⓑ warm

Ⓒ silent

Ⓓ enormous

10 The _____ inside the Earth is very hot.

Ⓕ wind

Ⓖ plant

Ⓗ magma

Ⓙ waterfall

STOP

GRAMMAR

DIRECTIONS Read each item. Choose the best way to join each pair of sentences into one, longer sentence. Mark your answer. *(3 points each)*

Sample

Pilar comes from Spain.
Maki comes from Japan.

> Pilar comes from Spain, _____ Maki comes from Japan.

Ⓐ if

Ⓑ or

🔘 but

Ⓓ because

---

11 I can push the rock to the car.
I can carry it there.

> I can push the rock to the car, _____ I can carry it there.

Ⓐ or

Ⓑ but

Ⓒ when

Ⓓ because

---

12 Nhol felt sad. He began to cry.

> Nohl felt sad, _____ he began to cry.

Ⓕ or

Ⓖ but

Ⓗ and

Ⓙ because

---

13 It was warm. The sun came out.

> It was warm _____ the sun came out.

Ⓐ if

Ⓑ or

Ⓒ but

Ⓓ because

---

14 We smiled. We saw the blue rock.

> We smiled _____ we saw the blue rock.

Ⓕ if

Ⓖ or

Ⓗ but

Ⓙ when

STOP

© Hampton-Brown

Name _____ Date _____

DIRECTIONS Read the sentences. Choose the word or words that go in each blank. Mark your answer. *(3 points each)*

⭐**Sample**

Carla stores her rock collection _____ in a special box.

Ⓐ safe

Ⓑ safer

Ⓒ safely

Ⓓ safest

---

15 Carla cares about the rocks. She handles them very _____ .

Ⓐ careful

Ⓑ carefully

Ⓒ carefuller

Ⓓ more careful

16 When Carla finds a new rock, she _____ shows it to me.

Ⓕ large

Ⓖ there

Ⓗ looks

Ⓙ always

17 I look _____ to see if the rock has a lot of colors.

Ⓐ closest

Ⓑ most close

Ⓒ more closer

Ⓓ more closely

18 _____ Carla adds the rock to her collection.

Ⓕ She

Ⓖ With

Ⓗ Then

Ⓙ Finds

STOP

© Hampton-Brown

COMPREHENSION / CRITICAL THINKING

DIRECTIONS Read the selection. Then read each item. Choose the best answer. **Mark your answer.** *(3 points each)*

Kali's Dream

One night, Kali dreamed she saw a rock fall from the sky. Kali couldn't believe what she saw! Then she heard a strange voice and jumped away from the rock. It might be dangerous!

"Is anybody there?" asked the voice.

Suddenly, a tiny, green creature came out of the rock.

"Oh, hello!" said the creature. "I am the Emperor of Mars! Where are Earth's beautiful red deserts and enormous canyons?"

Kali smiled. She never thought she would meet an emperor! "Those places are far from here," she replied.

"I must go and find them," said the emperor. Kali watched sadly as the emperor climbed back into his rock and flew away.

When Kali woke up, she smiled about her silly dream.

© Hampton-Brown

GO ON ➡

COMPREHENSION / CRITICAL THINKING

19 Look at the chart. What goes on the line for number 19?

  (A) sad

  (B) proud

  (C) surprised

  (D) disappointed

Character Chart

How Kali feels	Why Kali feels that way
_____19_____	A rock falls from the sky.
scared	_____20_____

20 Look at the chart. What goes on the line for number 20?

  (F) The rock flies into her house.

  (G) A big creature moves the rock.

  (H) Hot lava comes out of the rock.

  (J) She hears a voice from the rock.

21 When she meets the emperor, Kali feels —

  (A) tired

  (B) angry

  (C) afraid

  (D) happy

22 What do you think the emperor will do next?

  (F) He will go back to Mars.

  (G) He will visit Kali's neighbor.

  (H) He will walk into Kali's house.

  (J) He will look for deserts and canyons.

23 Kali feels silly when —

  (A) she goes to sleep

  (B) the emperor is lost

  (C) she remembers her dream

  (D) the emperor and his rock fly away

24 From this selection, you can tell that Kali —

  (F) likes rocks

  (G) is afraid of the dark

  (H) lives far from the desert

  (J) knows a lot about space

GO ON

© Hampton-Brown

COMPREHENSION / CRITICAL THINKING

DIRECTIONS Read the selection. Then read each item. Choose the best answer. Mark your answer. *(3 points each)*

A Rocky Park

Arches National Park is in the Utah desert. It is very hot and dry in the park, but you can see many beautiful rocks there. Wind, rain, and heat have changed the rocks into interesting shapes.

Visitors to Arches National Park start at the Visitor Center. They can get a map there and then explore the park.

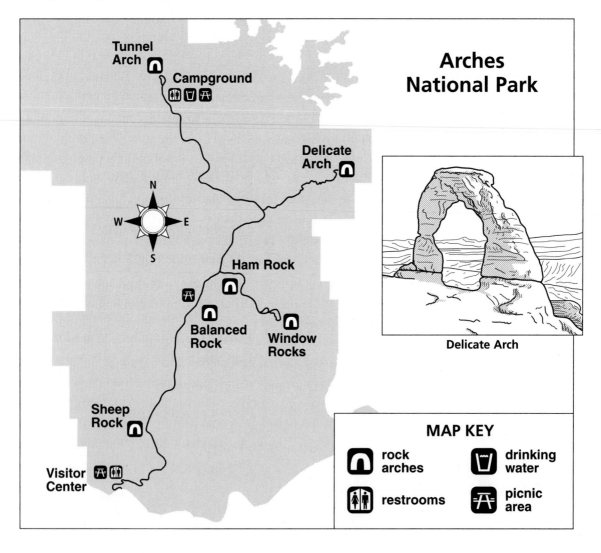

Arches National Park

Delicate Arch

MAP KEY

🔲 rock arches   🔲 drinking water

🔲 restrooms   🔲 picnic area

© Hampton-Brown

GO ON ➡

COMPREHENSION / CRITICAL THINKING

25 **Look at the map. Where can visitors find drinking water?**

- Ⓐ Ham Rock
- Ⓑ Sheep Rock
- Ⓒ Campground
- Ⓓ Delicate Arch

26 **Look at the map. Near Balanced Rock, visitors can find —**

- Ⓕ Tunnel Arch
- Ⓖ a picnic area
- Ⓗ Delicate Arch
- Ⓙ some restrooms

27 **Look at the map. Where is Window Rocks?**

- Ⓐ north of Ham Rock
- Ⓑ west of Sheep Rock
- Ⓒ east of Balanced Rock
- Ⓓ south of the Visitor Center

28 **Look at the map. To go from Balanced Rock to the Campground, visitors must go —**

- Ⓕ east
- Ⓖ west
- Ⓗ north
- Ⓙ south

29 **When people hike from the Visitor Center to Window Rocks, they probably take —**

- Ⓐ fresh water
- Ⓑ heavy rocks
- Ⓒ fancy shoes
- Ⓓ deep tunnels

30 **Most people visit Arches National Park to —**

- Ⓕ hear music
- Ⓖ learn about sheep
- Ⓗ see interesting rocks
- Ⓙ get away from wind and rain

STOP

Unit 8 • Rocky Tales

VOCABULARY

DIRECTIONS Read each item. Choose the word that goes in the blank.
Mark your answer. *(4 points each)*

⭐**Sample**

Carlo wears his new _____ to school.

- Ⓐ car
- Ⓑ book
- Ⓒ jacket
- Ⓓ building

---

1 Pete _____ as he moves the heavy box.

- Ⓐ sleeps
- Ⓑ blends
- Ⓒ strains
- Ⓓ breaks

2 The rock _____ repeats over and over again.

- Ⓕ load
- Ⓖ cycle
- Ⓗ pebble
- Ⓙ boundary

3 When I don't see my friends, I feel _____.

- Ⓐ tired
- Ⓑ lonely
- Ⓒ proud
- Ⓓ clever

4 My glass of juice fell over. All the _____ spilled on the floor!

- Ⓕ hail
- Ⓖ light
- Ⓗ liquid
- Ⓙ culture

5 The sailors _____ the ship when it began to sink.

- Ⓐ kept
- Ⓑ bought
- Ⓒ surprised
- Ⓓ abandoned

© Hampton-Brown

GO ON ➡

VOCABULARY

6 Enzo made a long _____ from Italy to the United States.

Ⓕ shelter

Ⓖ journey

Ⓗ contest

Ⓙ reward

7 Did you see the huge _____ that landed on the field?

Ⓐ cloud

Ⓑ magma

Ⓒ volcano

Ⓓ meteorite

8 Heat and _____ squeezed the sand together into rocks.

Ⓕ light

Ⓖ erosion

Ⓗ pressure

Ⓙ weather

9 The boulder was so _____ it smashed the car.

Ⓐ dull

Ⓑ warm

Ⓒ beautiful

Ⓓ enormous

10 Let's visit the _____ to learn more about outer space.

Ⓕ cellar

Ⓖ nation

Ⓗ market

Ⓙ museum

© Hampton-Brown

STOP

GRAMMAR

DIRECTIONS Read each item. Choose the best way to join each pair of sentences into one, longer sentence. Mark your answer. *(3 points each)*

★ **Sample**

Pilar comes from Spain.
Maki comes from Japan.

Ⓐ Pilar comes from Spain, if Maki comes from Japan.

Ⓑ Pilar comes from Spain, or Maki comes from Japan.

Ⓒ Pilar comes from Spain, but Maki comes from Japan.

Ⓓ Pilar comes from Spain, because Maki comes from Japan.

---

11 I can climb the rock. I can walk around it.

Ⓐ I can climb the rock when walk around it.

Ⓑ I can climb the rock because walk around it.

Ⓒ I can climb the rock, or I can walk around it.

Ⓓ I can climb the rock, but I can walk around it.

12 Nhol felt sad. He lost his special crystal.

Ⓕ Felt sad Nhol lost his special crystal.

Ⓖ Nhol felt sad, or he lost his special crystal.

Ⓗ Nhol felt sad, and he lost his special crystal.

Ⓙ Nhol felt sad because he lost his special crystal.

13 A rock sinks in water. Wood floats.

Ⓐ A rock sinks in water floats wood.

Ⓑ A rock sinks in water, but wood floats.

Ⓒ When wood floats, a rock sinks in water.

Ⓓ A rock sinks in water because wood floats.

14 The children smile. They see the moon rock.

Ⓕ Smile the children see the moon rock.

Ⓖ Smile and see the children the moon rock.

Ⓗ The children smile but they see the moon rock.

Ⓙ The children smile when they see the moon rock.

STOP

© Hampton-Brown

Ⓐ 80

GRAMMAR

DIRECTIONS Read the sentences. Choose the word or words that go in each blank. Mark your answer. *(3 points each)*

Carla stores her rock collection __Sample__ in a special box. You can tell she cares about the rocks because she handles them so ___15___.

Sometimes Carla takes me rock hunting. When she discovers a new rock, she ___16___ shows it to me. Then she says, "If you look ___17___, you can see many colors in the rock."

___18___ she found a very unusual rock. I knew she wanted to keep it, but she handed it to me instead.

"Here," she said kindly, "I have a lot of rocks. You can have this one."

Sample

Ⓐ safe

Ⓑ safer

Ⓒ safely

Ⓓ safest

15 Ⓐ careful

Ⓑ carefully

Ⓒ carefuller

Ⓓ more careful

16 Ⓕ large

Ⓖ always

Ⓗ around

Ⓙ happiness

17 Ⓐ closest

Ⓑ most close

Ⓒ more closer

Ⓓ more closely

18 Ⓕ Carla

Ⓖ Large

Ⓗ Surprise

Ⓙ Yesterday

STOP

COMPREHENSION / CRITICAL THINKING

DIRECTIONS Read the selection. Then read each item. Choose the best answer. **Mark your answer.** *(3 points each)*

Only a Rock . . . Or Is It?

What a day! Luisa didn't know any answers during history class, and her science experiment was all wrong. She was feeling unhappy, so Dad took her on a hike after school. They followed an interesting bird into the woods. Suddenly, they were lost and the bird had disappeared. Everything seemed to be going wrong again!

Luisa kicked a pile of leaves angrily, and her toe hit something hard. She reached down and picked up a bumpy, silver rock. Instantly, Luisa knew where the trail was! As she and Dad walked home, Luisa began to feel better. At least something was going right!

At home, Luisa had a whole page of math problems to do, but she couldn't solve even the first one! She picked up the rock to remind her of a good part of the day. Suddenly, she knew the answer to the problem! She tried the next problem and knew its answer, too.

"Wow! How did I know that? Was there something special about this rock?" Luisa wondered.

GO ON ➡

COMPREHENSION / CRITICAL THINKING

Only a Rock . . . Or Is It?, continued

Luisa held the rock as she worked on the rest of her math homework and studied for a science test. She kept it in her pocket while she ate her dinner. She even held it as she fell asleep.

The next day, Luisa took the rock to school. She held it during her science test, and again she knew every answer! This rock was amazing! Luisa felt like the smartest, most talented person in the universe. The rock made everything easy!

The next weekend Luisa went to visit her uncle. He knew all about rocks, so Luisa brought hers to show him. When Uncle Andrés saw it, he said, "What a beautiful piece of hematite. There are a lot of those around here." He opened a drawer full of them.

Luisa's eyes opened wide. If her rock wasn't special, why did she seem so clever when she held it? Maybe she was smart without the rock. Maybe all she had to do was study and try harder. Would she get the right answers if she didn't have the rock with her? She would try an experiment to find out.

GO ON ▶

COMPREHENSION / CRITICAL THINKING

19 **Look at the chart. What goes on the line for number 19?**

Ⓐ The bird is interesting.

Ⓑ The leaves are too dry.

Ⓒ Dad takes her on a hike.

Ⓓ She doesn't do well at school.

20 **Look at the chart. What goes on the line for number 20?**

Ⓕ tired

Ⓖ proud

Ⓗ curious

Ⓙ disappointed

Character Chart

How Luisa feels	Why Luisa feels that way
unhappy	_____19_____
_____20_____	When she holds the rock, she can do math problems.

21 **Why does Luisa start to feel smart and talented?**

Ⓐ Her dad helps her study.

Ⓑ She knows the word "hematite."

Ⓒ Her uncle takes her to a museum.

Ⓓ She knows the answers on the science test.

22 **When Uncle Andrés shows Luisa his hematite collection, she is —**

Ⓕ disappointed in her uncle

Ⓖ unsure that her rock is special

Ⓗ afraid that she'll lose her rock

Ⓙ angry that he has so many rocks

23 **The next day, Luisa will probably —**

Ⓐ leave the rock at home

Ⓑ give the rock to her uncle

Ⓒ send the rock to a museum

Ⓓ take the rock to school again

24 **From the selection, you can tell that Luisa —**

Ⓕ enjoys collecting coins

Ⓖ knows a lot about history

Ⓗ wants to do well in school

Ⓙ likes science more than math

© Hampton-Brown

GO ON ➡

DIRECTIONS Read the selection. Then read each item. Choose the best answer. Mark your answer. *(3 points each)*

Fossils and Dinosaurs

What Are Fossils?

Fossils are very special rocks because they tell us a lot about what Earth was like in the past. When a plant or animal dies, its soft parts rot and become part of the soil. The hard parts sometimes turn into rocks. These rocks are called fossils.

fossil of a dinosaur tooth

What Do Fossils Tell About Dinosaurs?

Scientists search for fossils all the time. They study them to learn about animals that lived on Earth in the past. Dinosaur fossils are particularly interesting because dinosaurs lived so long ago. Fossils of dinosaur parts, such as teeth and bones, tell a lot about dinosaurs and how they lived.

A dinosaur with sharp, pointed teeth probably used them to tear up chunks of meat. What a dinosaur ate can tell us about the dinosaur's habitat, or where it lived. For example, if it ate water plants, it probably lived near a river.

The number of bones in a dinosaur's backbone shows how long the dinosaur was. The number of neck bones tells how long its neck was. The size of a dinosaur's skull might even tell how smart it was!

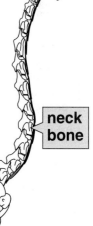

dinosaur

skull

neck bone

© Hampton-Brown

GO ON

Fossils and Dinosaurs, continued

Scientists have found that some dinosaurs were bigger than most animals living today. One kind of dinosaur called tyrannosaurus rex, or T. rex, weighed as much as the biggest elephant! Here is how T. rex compares to some other large animals.

Large Animals

Animals	Length	Weight	Food	Habitat
African elephant	18–24 feet	8,000 to 15,000 pounds	grass bark fruit roots leaves	forests river valleys
blue whale	78–80 feet	200,000 to 300,000 pounds	tiny ocean animals that are like shrimp	oceans
green anaconda	16–33 feet	150 to 400 pounds	turtles deer birds fish	rivers trees
ostrich	5–7 feet	198 to 286 pounds	seeds flowers leaves insects	deserts
T. rex	40–50 feet	14,000 to 16,000 pounds	other dinosaurs	forests near rivers

© Hampton-Brown

GO ON ➡

COMPREHENSION / CRITICAL THINKING

25 **Look at the chart. Which of these animals is the shortest?**

   Ⓐ T. rex

   Ⓑ ostrich

   Ⓒ blue whale

   Ⓓ green anaconda

26 **Look at the chart. Which of these animals weighs the most?**

   Ⓕ T. rex

   Ⓖ blue whale

   Ⓗ green anaconda

   Ⓙ African elephant

27 **Look at the chart. Which of these animals eats only plants?**

   Ⓐ T. rex

   Ⓑ blue whale

   Ⓒ green anaconda

   Ⓓ African elephant

28 **Look at the chart. Which of these animals would not be found near a river?**

   Ⓕ T. rex

   Ⓖ ostrich

   Ⓗ green anaconda

   Ⓙ African elephant

29 **You can tell from the selection that —**

   Ⓐ dinosaurs were not very smart

   Ⓑ most people are not interested in dinosaurs

   Ⓒ scientists have learned a lot about dinosaurs

   Ⓓ dinosaurs now live in many parts of the world

30 **From the selection, you can predict that in the future —**

   Ⓕ scientists will find more dinosaur fossils

   Ⓖ dinosaurs will live in deserts and valleys

   Ⓗ fossils will rot and become part of the soil

   Ⓙ elephants will weigh more than they do now

© Hampton-Brown

STOP

Unit 8 • Answer Key

B Beginning Progress Test

VOCABULARY
(4 points each)

1 (A)   4 (H)
2 (F)   5 (B)
3 (D)   6 (F)

GRAMMAR
(4 points each)

7 (D)   11 (B)
8 (H)   12 (G)
9 (D)   13 (D)
10 (J)

**COMPREHENSION /
CRITICAL THINKING**
(6 points each)

14 (J)   18 (H)
15 (C)   19 (B)
16 (G)   20 (F)
17 (C)   21 (D)

I Intermediate Progress Test

VOCABULARY
(4 points each)

1 (D)   6 (H)
2 (G)   7 (D)
3 (D)   8 (J)
4 (H)   9 (D)
5 (B)   10 (H)

GRAMMAR
(3 points each)

11 (A)   15 (B)
12 (H)   16 (J)
13 (D)   17 (D)
14 (J)   18 (H)

**COMPREHENSION /
CRITICAL THINKING**
(3 points each)

19 (C)   25 (C)
20 (J)   26 (G)
21 (D)   27 (C)
22 (J)   28 (H)
23 (C)   29 (A)
24 (H)   30 (H)

A Advanced Progress Test

VOCABULARY
(4 points each)

1 (C)   6 (G)
2 (G)   7 (D)
3 (B)   8 (H)
4 (H)   9 (D)
5 (D)   10 (J)

GRAMMAR
(3 points each)

11 (C)   15 (B)
12 (J)   16 (G)
13 (B)   17 (D)
14 (J)   18 (J)

**COMPREHENSION /
CRITICAL THINKING**
(3 points each)

19 (D)   25 (B)
20 (H)   26 (G)
21 (D)   27 (D)
22 (G)   28 (G)
23 (A)   29 (C)
24 (H)   30 (F)

Unit 8 • Self-Assessment

I Can Speak English!

1. I can make up a story.

Once, _____.

2. I can define and explain things.

A museum is _____.

In a museum, you

can find _____.

My New Words

_____

_____

_____

_____

_____

_____

_____

_____

I Can Read in English!

3. I can tell how a character feels and why.

☐ yes   ☐ not yet

4. I can tell the main ideas and details.

The Life Story of a Rock

II. Rocks change and move.

A. _____

B. _____

What I've Read

☐ Call Me Ahnighito

☐ The Life Story of a
Rock

☐ _____

☐ _____

Peer-Assessment

Partner's Work
☐ Speaking 💬
☐ Writing ✏️
☐ Drawing 🎨
☐ Role-Play 🎭
☐ Other

1. What did you like best about your partner's work?

_____

_____

_____

_____

2. What else did your partner do well?

_____

_____

_____

_____

3. What can your partner do to improve?

_____

_____

_____

_____

4. Tell your partner one thing to try next time.

_____

_____

_____

© Hampton-Brown

Language Assessments

▶ **Performance-Assessment Opportunities and Scoring Rubrics**

Unit 1 • Language Assessment

IF THE SHOE FITS

Date _____

PERFORMANCE ASSESSMENT 1

Testing Point: Role-Play a Conversation, page T43b

- **Language Function: Express Needs and Feelings**
- **DIRECTIONS** Listen as the student role-plays. Check the box in the Rubric that most closely matches your observation.

Rubric

- ☐ **BEGINNING** Uses fragments or simple sentences with errors *(I scared. I need you help.)*
- ☐ **INTERMEDIATE** Uses simple sentences *(I feel scared. I need help.)* or more detailed sentences with errors *(I feel scared when Angel here. I need you help.)*
- ☐ **ADVANCED** Uses complete sentences with details *(I feel scared when Angel talks to me. I need your help. Please come with me.)*

IN GARY SOTO'S SHOES

Date _____

PERFORMANCE ASSESSMENT 2

Testing Point: Ask and Answer Questions, page T53

- **Language Function: Ask and Answer Questions**
- **DIRECTIONS** Listen as groups use the question words to ask and answer questions. Check the box in the Rubric that most closely matches your observation of each student.

Rubric

- ☐ **BEGINNING** Forms questions and simple statements with errors *(Who like this story? I like.)*
- ☐ **INTERMEDIATE** Forms questions and short sentences *(Who is this? This is Gary Soto.)* or more detailed questions and statements with errors *(When is this picture of Gary Soto? This picture is in high school.)*
- ☐ **ADVANCED** Asks detailed questions and gives detailed answers. *(Why did Gary Soto decide to finish high school? He knew he wanted a better job than working in a tire factory.)*

UNIT WRAP-UP

Date _____

PERFORMANCE ASSESSMENT 3

Testing Point: End of Unit

- **Grammar: Complete Sentences, Sentence Types**
- **Visual Prompt:** Student Book page 21
- **DIRECTIONS** Say: *In this picture Rigo has a strong feeling. Imagine you are Rigo. Tell me what you need. Now imagine you are his mother. Ask Rigo a question. Imagine you are Rigo again and answer her question. Use a complete sentence.*

The student correctly uses:

☐ exclamations   ☐ questions

☐ complete sentences

Unit 2 • Language Assessment

Date _____

PERFORMANCE ASSESSMENT 1
Testing Point: Make a Totem Pole, page T93b

- **Language Function:
  Express Ideas and Opinions**
- **DIRECTIONS** Listen as the student reacts to the different totem poles by sharing ideas and opinions. Check the box in the Rubric that most closely matches your observation.

Rubric

☐ **BEGINNING** Uses simple sentences with errors (*My pole show my brother born.*) or completes the frame with errors (*I like Quan's totem pole because good story.*)

☐ **INTERMEDIATE** Uses simple sentences or more detailed sentences with errors (*My totem pole shows when my brother was born. I think Quan's pole is best because pictures show his whole family history.*)

☐ **ADVANCED** Uses complete sentences with details (*My totem pole shows when my brother was born. I think that Quan's totem pole is the best because the pictures are clear. I can tell his family is very important to him.*)

NATIVE HOMES

Date _____

PERFORMANCE ASSESSMENT 2
Testing Point: Build a Scale Model, page T122b

- **Language Function: Make Comparisons**
- **DIRECTIONS** Listen as the student compares two models. If necessary, prompt the student with questions to elicit comparisons of the type, size, and materials used. Check the box in the Rubric that most closely matches your observation.

Rubric

☐ **BEGINNING** Uses fragments (*wood, grass*) or simple sentences with errors (*This house is wood. This house is grass.*)

☐ **INTERMEDIATE** Forms short sentences (*This house is made of wood. This house is made of grass.*) or more detailed sentences with errors (*This house is from wood, but this house is from grass.*)

☐ **ADVANCED** Gives detailed answers (*This longhouse is made of wood, but the woven grass home is made of grass. The longhouse is longer than the woven grass home, too.*)

UNIT WRAP-UP

Date _____

PERFORMANCE ASSESSMENT 3
Testing Point: End of Unit

- **Grammar: Plural Nouns**
- **Visual Prompt:** Student Book pages 74–75
- **DIRECTIONS** Point to the bird on page 74 and ask: *How many birds do you see? Tell me in a complete sentence.* Then point to page 75. Ask: *Do you see one boat or more than one? Do you see one man or more than one? Tell me how many you see.* As you point to the sand and the sea, ask: *What is this? Can you count it?*

| The student uses plural nouns correctly. |
| ☐ yes   ☐ not yet |

- **Grammar: Possessive Nouns**
- **Visual Prompt:** Student Book page 76
- **DIRECTIONS** Point to the illustration and name the characters with the student. Point to the man and ask: *Whose hat is this?* Point to one of the girl's feet and ask: *Whose foot is this?* Point to the bear's stick and ask: *Whose stick is this?*

| The student uses possessive nouns correctly. |
| ☐ yes   ☐ not yet |

Unit 3 • Language Assessment

Date _____

PERFORMANCE ASSESSMENT 1
Testing Point: Research a Tornado, page T170b

- **Language Function: Describe Events**
- **DIRECTIONS** Listen as the student tells about the tornado, including where it was and what happened. Check the box in the Rubric that most closely matches your observation.

Rubric

☐ **BEGINNING** Uses fragments (*in Kansas*) or simple sentences with errors (*In Kansas have the tornado.*)

☐ **INTERMEDIATE** Uses simple sentences (*The tornado was in Kansas.*) or more detailed sentences with errors (*During the tornado in Kansas, the wind blowed many houses down.*)

☐ **ADVANCED** Uses complete sentences with details (*A huge tornado went through Kansas in April, 1991. The winds blew over 100 miles per hour.*)

THE BIG STORM   Date _____

PERFORMANCE ASSESSMENT 2
Testing Point: Give a Weather Forecast, page T196a

- **Language Function: Give Information**
- **DIRECTIONS** Listen as the student gives the weather forecast. Check the box in the Rubric that most closely matches your observation.

Rubric

☐ **BEGINNING** Uses fragments (*warm here*) or simple sentences with errors (*Tomorrow is warm.*)

☐ **INTERMEDIATE** Forms short sentences (*It will be warm tomorrow.*) or more detailed sentences with errors (*The temperature of tomorrow will be 88 degree.*)

☐ **ADVANCED** Uses detailed sentences (*The temperature will be up to 88 degrees tomorrow. It will be cooler at the ocean!*)

UNIT WRAP-UP   Date _____

PERFORMANCE ASSESSMENT 3
Testing Point: End of Unit

- **Grammar: Subject-Verb Agreement**
- **Visual Prompt:** Student Book page 136
- **DIRECTIONS** Point to the mother and ask: *What does she do? Is she busy? Tell me in a complete sentence.* Then point to the children and ask: *What do they do? How do you think they feel: happy or sad?* If this prompt does not elicit the verb *are*, ask: *Are they brother and sister?* Finally, ask: *Are you happy or sad today?*

The student correctly uses subject-verb agreement with:

☐ action verbs   ☐ am

☐ is   ☐ are

© Hampton-Brown

Unit 4 • Language Assessment

THE SECRET FOOTPRINTS

PERFORMANCE ASSESSMENT 1
Testing Point: Research Legends, page T234a

- **Language Function: Describe**
- **DIRECTIONS** Listen as the student uses color, size, and shape words to describe the water creature. Check the box in the Rubric that most closely matches your observation.

Rubric

☐ **BEGINNING** Uses fragments *(big, green)* or simple sentences with errors *(It live in dark lake.)*

☐ **INTERMEDIATE** Uses simple sentences *(It is big. It lives in a dark lake.)* or more detailed sentences with errors *(It is big and have shiny scales.)*

☐ **ADVANCED** Uses complete sentences with details *(The creature is big and lives at the bottom of a dark lake. Its powerful tail can crush boats.)*

HELLO, FISH!

PERFORMANCE ASSESSMENT 2
Testing Point: Play a Fishy Game, page T260a

- **Language Function: Elaborate**
- **DIRECTIONS** Listen as the student gives clues about the fish. Check the box in the Rubric that most closely matches your observation.

Rubric

☐ **BEGINNING** Uses simple sentences with errors *(I am yellow fish.)*

☐ **INTERMEDIATE** Uses short sentences *(I am a yellow fish. I have a long tail.)* or more detailed sentences with errors *(I am a yellow fish, long tail, and sharp teeth.)*

☐ **ADVANCED** Uses detailed sentences *(I am a yellow fish with a long tail and sharp teeth.)*

UNIT WRAP-UP

PERFORMANCE ASSESSMENT 3
Testing Point: End of Unit

- **Grammar: Descriptive Adjectives**
- **Visual Prompt:** Student Book pages 238–239
- **DIRECTIONS** Say: *Imagine you are swimming in the ocean with these fish. How many fish do you see? What colors and shapes are they? Are they big or small? Now tell me how the water feels and what you hear.*

The student uses descriptive adjectives correctly.
☐ yes
☐ not yet

- **Grammar: Comparative and Superlative Adjectives**
- **Visual Prompt:** Student Book pages 238–239
- **DIRECTIONS** Point to the shark and the eel. Say: *Compare the shark and the eel. Use a complete sentence.* Then point to one of the small orange fish below the shark and say: *Now compare this fish to the shark and the eel. Tell me in a complete sentence.*

The student correctly uses:
☐ comparative adjectives
☐ superlative adjectives

Unit 5 • Language Assessment

THE LOTUS SEED

Date _____

PERFORMANCE ASSESSMENT 1
Testing Point: Role-Play the Future, page T286a

- **Language Function:**
  Express Ideas and Feelings
- **DIRECTIONS** Listen as the student plays the role of grandparent or grandchild. Then listen again as the student gives ideas about culture. Check the box in the Rubric that most closely matches your observations.

Rubric

☐ **BEGINNING** Uses simple sentences with errors (*That is toy from grandfather. Is special.*)

☐ **INTERMEDIATE** Uses simple sentences (*I love this Russian toy. My grandfather made it.*) or more detailed sentences with errors (*My grandfather give this toy to me when I was baby. Gifts helps you remember people.*)

☐ **ADVANCED** Uses complete sentences with details (*I love this Russian toy my grandfather gave me. Some gifts are special because someone you love made them.*)

WHERE WE COME FROM

Date _____

PERFORMANCE ASSESSMENT 2
Testing Point: Make an Immigration Graph, page T304a

- **Language Function: Make Comparisons**
- **DIRECTIONS** Listen as the student makes comparisons about the information in the graph. Check the box in the Rubric that most closely matches your observation.

Rubric

☐ **BEGINNING** Uses fragments (*many in 1980, few in 1960*) or simple sentences with errors (*There is more Chinese people in 1980.*)

☐ **INTERMEDIATE** Forms short sentences (*More people came in 1980.*) or more detailed sentences with errors (*The biggest change is in 1980 when many Chinese people come.*)

☐ **ADVANCED** Uses detailed sentences (*The biggest change was in 1980 when the most people immigrated from China to the U.S.*)

UNIT WRAP-UP

Date _____

PERFORMANCE ASSESSMENT 3
Testing Point: End of Unit

- **Grammar: Possessive Pronouns**
- **Visual Prompt:** Student Book pages 290–291
- **DIRECTIONS** Point to the photo of the girl on page 290 and the boys at the bottom of page 291 as you say: *This girl wears a scarf. These boys wear robes. Whose scarf is red and white? Whose robes are red? Answer in a complete sentence. Use a word like* her, his, *or* their. *Then point to a pumpkin and ask:* Whose pumpkin is this?

| The student uses possessive pronouns correctly. |
| ☐ yes   ☐ not yet |

- **Grammar: Subject and Object Pronouns**
- **Visual Prompt:** Student Book page 268
- **DIRECTIONS** Point to the photo of the family and say: *Imagine you are the dad in the middle of this picture. This is your family.* Ask questions to prompt pronoun usage such as: *Who are you? Who is the other man?* and so on until students have used a variety of subject and object pronouns.

| The student correctly uses: |
| ☐ subject pronouns   ☐ object pronouns |

Unit 6 • Language Assessment

A QUARTER'S WORTH OF FAME

PERFORMANCE ASSESSMENT 1

Testing Point: Conduct an Interview, page T329

- **Language Function:**
  Ask for and Give Information
- **DIRECTIONS** Listen as the student asks and answers questions during the role-play. Check the box in the Rubric that most closely matches your observation.

Rubric

☐ **BEGINNING** Uses simple questions and statements with errors *(Like other quarter? I like quarter of Indiana.)*

☐ **INTERMEDIATE** Forms simple questions and statements *(What other quarter do you like? I like the Indiana quarter.)* or more detailed questions and statements with errors *(Besides you quarter, which quarter do you like? I like the quarter of Indiana because race car.)*

☐ **ADVANCED** Forms more complex questions and statements with details *(Besides yours, which quarter do you like best? I like the Indiana quarter because it has a race car and I really like race cars.)*

THE TREE THAT WOULD NOT DIE

PERFORMANCE ASSESSMENT 2

Testing Point: Make a Video, page T369b

- **Language Function: Persuade**
- **DIRECTIONS** Listen to the student's persuasive video. Check the box in the Rubric that most closely matches your observation.

Rubric

☐ **BEGINNING** Uses gestures, props, and fragments *(need a home, animals on street)* or simple sentences with errors *(You must to give money. Animals need people help.)*

☐ **INTERMEDIATE** Forms short sentences *(Animals need homes. We must help them.)* or more detailed sentences with errors *(If we care about it, we give money to help animals.)*

☐ **ADVANCED** Uses detailed sentences *(If we care about animals, we must adopt homeless animals and give money to shelters.)*

UNIT WRAP-UP

PERFORMANCE ASSESSMENT 3

Testing Point: End of Unit

- **Grammar: Verb Tense**
- **Visual Prompt:** Student Book page 312
- **DIRECTIONS** Point to the landforms and say: *Imagine you are on a trip around the U.S. Tell me where you go and what you do. First tell me what you do today. Then tell me about what you did yesterday. Then tell me about what you will do tomorrow. Use complete sentences.*

The student correctly uses:

☐ present tense ☐ past tense

☐ future tense

Unit 7 • Language Assessment

MY ROWS AND PILES OF COINS

PERFORMANCE ASSESSMENT 1
Testing Point: Justify, page T397

- **Language Function: Justify**
- **DIRECTIONS** Listen as the student role-plays other characters and justifies his or her actions. Check the box in the Rubric that most closely matches your observation.

Rubric

☐ **BEGINNING** Uses fragments *(no sell no money)* or simple sentences with errors *(I will not sell bicycle. You not have money.)*

☐ **INTERMEDIATE** Forms simple sentences *(I will not sell this bicycle. You do not have enough money.)* or more detailed sentences with errors *(I do not sell this bicycle because you need more money.)*

☐ **ADVANCED** Forms sentences with details *(I will not sell you this bicycle because you do not have enough money to buy it.)*

MONEY

PERFORMANCE ASSESSMENT 2
Testing Point: Shop at a Class Store, page T427b

- **Language Function: Give Information**
- **DIRECTIONS** Listen as the student tells which product has the best value. Check the box in the Rubric that most closely matches your observation.

Rubric

☐ **BEGINNING** Uses fragments *(this rice, 1 pound, $2)* or simple sentences with errors *(The rice bag is 1 pound $2.)*

☐ **INTERMEDIATE** Forms short sentences *(This rice is $2 per pound.)* or more detailed sentences with errors *(The rice of Ivan is $2 per pound and is the more cheap.)*

☐ **ADVANCED** Uses detailed sentences *(Ivan's rice is $2 per pound and is the least expensive rice.)*

UNIT WRAP-UP

PERFORMANCE ASSESSMENT 3
Testing Point: End of Unit

- **Grammar: Helping Verbs**
- **Visual Prompt:** Student Book pages 406–407
- **DIRECTIONS** Point to page 406 and ask: *What is this woman doing today? What was she doing yesterday? What has this man done? What have the chicks done?* Then point to page 407 and ask: *What are these people doing? What were they doing an hour ago?*

The student correctly uses helping verbs:		
☐ is	☐ has	☐ was
☐ are	☐ have	☐ were

- **Grammar: Complete Sentences**
- **Visual Prompt:** Student Book pages 406–407
- **DIRECTIONS** Point to the woman on page 406 and say: *Tell me two things this woman does at the same time. Use a complete sentence.* Point to the people on page 407 and ask: *What do the butcher and baker do? Use a complete sentence.*

The student uses complete sentences correctly.	
☐ yes	☐ not yet

Unit 8 • Language Assessment

CALL ME AHNIGHITO

PERFORMANCE ASSESSMENT 1
Testing Point: Tell a Story, page T440–441

- **Language Function: Tell an Original Story**
- **DIRECTIONS** Listen as the student tells a story. Check the box in the Rubric that most closely matches your observation.

Rubric

☐ **BEGINNING** Uses the pattern to create sentences with errors (*I remember I am 4 years.*)

☐ **INTERMEDIATE** Uses the pattern to form more detailed sentences with errors (*I remember when I had four years, and I wanted that I read books.*)

☐ **ADVANCED** Forms complex sentences with details (*I remember when I was four and wanted to read a book. I sat and waited and wished that someone would teach me.*)

THE LIFE STORY OF A ROCK

PERFORMANCE ASSESSMENT 2
Testing Point: Research Rocks Around the World, page T478b

- **Language Function: Define and Explain**
- **DIRECTIONS** Listen as the student defines the mineral on the country's stamp and explains why it is important. Check the box in the Rubric that most closely matches your observation.

Rubric

☐ **BEGINNING** Uses fragments (*emerald green stone, many in Brazil*) or simple sentences with errors (*In Brazil are many emeralds.*)

☐ **INTERMEDIATE** Forms short sentences (*There are many emeralds in Brazil.*) or more detailed sentences with errors (*A stamp of Brazil shows the emerald. It is green gems.*)

☐ **ADVANCED** Uses detailed sentences (*One stamp from Brazil shows an emerald which is a green gem they mine there.*)

UNIT WRAP-UP

PERFORMANCE ASSESSMENT 3
Testing Point: End of Unit

- **Grammar: Adverbs, Comparative Adverbs**
- **Visual Prompt:** Student Book page 436
- **DIRECTIONS** Point to the boy holding the wagon and say: *He put the the big rock in the wagon and brought it to the museum. How did he lift the rock? How did the wagon move?* Then point to the woman with the magnifying glass and say: *This woman is looking at the rock. Compare how she and the children are looking at it. Who is looking at the rock the most carefully?*

The student correctly uses:

☐ adverbs   ☐ comparative adverbs

Writing Assessments

▶ **Good Writing Traits Rubric**

▶ **Class Writing Profile**

▶ **Writing Progress Form**

▶ **Writing Self-Assessment**

▶ **Writing Conference Form**

▶ **Writing Checklists**

▶ **Unit Writing Tests**

Good Writing Traits Rubric

Overall Scale Score: _____

Scale	Focus and Coherence	Organization	Development of Ideas	Voice	Written Conventions
4	**Related Ideas** ☐ Paragraphs and the writing as a whole are focused. **Completeness** ☐ The writing feels complete. It has a beginning, relevant details, and a conclusion.	**Structure** ☐ The organizing strategy is well-suited to the writer's purpose. **Progression of Ideas** ☐ Ideas flow logically and smoothly, with meaningful transitions.	**Content Quality** ☐ The writer takes a risk and treats the topic in an interesting way, with insight and thoughtfulness. **Elaboration** ☐ Ideas are developed in depth.	**Individuality** ☐ The writing sounds genuine and unique. **Word Choice** ☐ Words and phrases are interesting and appropriate to the writer's purpose and audience.	**Grammar, Usage, Mechanics, and Spelling** ☐ There are only a few errors. **Sentence Fluency** ☐ Sentences are varied and effective.
3	**Related Ideas** ☐ Paragraphs and the writing as a whole are mostly focused, but there are a few sudden shifts. **Completeness** ☐ The writing feels complete. It has a beginning, mostly relevant details, and a conclusion.	**Structure** ☐ The organizing strategy is generally suited to the writer's purpose. **Progression of Ideas** ☐ Most ideas flow logically and smoothly, but there are a few gaps.	**Content Quality** ☐ The writer does not take much of a risk, but does treat the topic in a thoughtful way. **Elaboration** ☐ Ideas are somewhat developed.	**Individuality** ☐ For the most part, the writing sounds genuine and unique. **Word Choice** ☐ Words and phrases are mostly interesting and appropriate to the writer's purpose and audience.	**Grammar, Usage, Mechanics, and Spelling** ☐ Errors are minor and/or infrequent. **Sentence Fluency** ☐ There is some sentence variety. Sentences are generally effective.
2	**Related Ideas** ☐ There are a number of sudden shifts between ideas. **Completeness** ☐ The writing feels somewhat incomplete. It is missing a beginning and/or an ending. Important details seem to be missing.	**Structure** ☐ There is an organizing strategy, but it does not suit the writer's purpose. **Progression of Ideas** ☐ There are breaks in logic and very few transitions.	**Content Quality** ☐ The topic is covered, but in an uninteresting way. **Elaboration** ☐ Ideas are listed or mentioned superficially.	**Individuality** ☐ A few passages sound genuine and unique. **Word Choice** ☐ Words and phrases are somewhat interesting and appropriate to the writer's purpose and audience.	**Grammar, Usage, Mechanics, and Spelling** ☐ Errors are frequent, but the meaning is clear. **Sentence Fluency** ☐ Sentences are somewhat awkward and have missing words.
1	**Related Ideas** ☐ The writing is not focused. **Completeness** ☐ There is no sense of completeness.	**Structure** ☐ No organizing strategy is evident. **Progression of Ideas** ☐ Writing is illogical, wordy, and/or repetitious.	**Content Quality** ☐ The writing is uninteresting. **Elaboration** ☐ There is little or no development of ideas.	**Individuality** ☐ There is little or no sense of the writer. **Word Choice** ☐ Words and phrases are not appropriate to the writer's purpose or audience.	**Grammar, Usage, Mechanics, and Spelling** ☐ Errors are severe and/or frequent and are a barrier to understanding. **Sentence Fluency** ☐ Sentences are awkward and have missing words.

Good Writing Traits Class Profile

Assignment _____ Date _____

DIRECTIONS Use the **Good Writing Traits Rubric** on page 97 to score students' work. Then plot the scores on the Rubric below by writing each student's initials in the appropriate cell. Identify the trait(s) with which the most students need practice. Then use the practice activities in this Handbook to strengthen students' abilities in that trait(s).

Scale	Focus and Coherence	Organization	Development of Ideas	Voice	Written Conventions
4					
3					
2					
1					
Practice Activities	Assessment Handbook page T42	Assessment Handbook page T42	Assessment Handbook page T42	Assessment Handbook page T42	Assessment Handbook page T42

Writing Progress Form

DIRECTIONS Review the completed Rubric for each writing sample. Record the score for each trait in the chart to see the student's strengths as well as the traits that need development. Then highlight the writing samples that exemplify the student's best work by trait and collect them in the student's writing portfolio.

	Focus and Coherence	Organization	Development of Ideas	Voice	Written Conventions
Writing Form: _____ **Purpose:** _____ **Date:** _____					
Writing Form: _____ **Purpose:** _____ **Date:** _____					
Writing Form: _____ **Purpose:** _____ **Date:** _____					
Writing Form: _____ **Purpose:** _____ **Date:** _____					
Writing Form: _____ **Purpose:** _____ **Date:** _____					
Writing Form: _____ **Purpose:** _____ **Date:** _____					

Writing Self-Assessment

1. I wrote a _____.

2. I used a computer.
☐ yes   ☐ no

3. I made a list of ideas.
☐ yes   ☐ no

4. In my draft, the ideas were clear.
☐ all   ☐ most   ☐ not many

5. When I revised, I'm glad that I changed this: _____

_____

_____

6. When I edited and proofread my work, I caught this mistake: _____

_____

_____

7. This is my favorite part of my writing: _____

_____

_____

8. This is the one thing I want to work on: _____

_____

Name _____

Writing Conference Form

DIRECTIONS Meet with the student to discuss several examples of his or her written work. First, review each sample together. Ask: *What do you like best about your writing? What did you learn from writing this?* Record the student's responses and your own ideas.

Then use the questions at the bottom of the page to help the student reflect on his or her progress as a writer and to set new learning goals.

Writing Sample: _____ Date Written: _____

Teacher's Ideas: _____

_____

Writer's Ideas: _____

_____

Writing Sample: _____ Date Written: _____

Teacher's Ideas: _____

_____

Writer's Ideas: _____

_____

Writing Sample: _____ Date Written: _____

Teacher's Ideas: _____

_____

Writer's Ideas: _____

_____

© Hampton-Brown

How do you feel about the writing you have done? _____

Which writing sample are you most proud of? _____

What can you do to make your writing better? _____

Writing Checklist

Biography

Look for:	Does your biography have this?
a title that names the person	☐
facts about the person's life	☐
dates of important events	☐
order words	☐

Writing Checklist

Dialogue for a Play

Look for:	Does your dialogue have this?
characters' names	☐
a colon after each character's name	☐
the exact words of each character	☐

Writing
Checklist

Message

Look for:	Does your message have this?
a date	☐
the name of the person the message is for	☐
important information	☐

Unit 2 | Native Land

- ✂

Writing
Checklist

Cinquain

Look for:	Does your poem have this?
a title	☐
line 1: 2 syllables line 2: 4 syllables line 3: 6 syllables line 4: 8 syllables line 5: 2 syllables	☐ ☐ ☐ ☐ ☐
words that tell how things look, sound, feel, or smell	☐

© Hampton-Brown

Friendly Letter

Look for:	Does your letter have this?
a heading with a date	☐
a greeting	☐
a body with news and information	☐
a closing with a signature	☐

Unit 4 | Watery World

Name _____ Date _____

Recipe

Look for:	Does your recipe have this?
a title that tells what you are doing or making	☐
ingredients and how much of each	☐
numbered steps	☐

Unit 5 | Cultural Ties

Personal Narrative

Look for:	Does your narrative have this?
a title	☐
a beginning, a middle, and an end	☐
words that tell how you felt	☐
I, *me*, and *my*	☐
order words	☐

Unit 6 | This State of Mine

- ✂ - - -

Letter to an Advice Column

Look for:	Does your letter have this?
a date	☐
a greeting	☐
description of a problem	☐
a closing with a made-up name	☐

Story

Look for:	Does your story have this?
a title	☐
characters	☐
a setting	☐
a good beginning, middle, and end	☐

Unit 8 | Rocky Tales

- ✂ - - - - - -

Report

Look for:	Does your report have this?
a title that tells what your report is about	☐
an interesting introduction	☐
a paragraph for each main idea	☐
a topic sentence and facts for each paragraph	☐
a conclusion that sums up the report	☐

© Hampton-Brown

Unit 1 • Writing Test Student Profile

DIRECTIONS Record the student's name and test date. Use the **Answer Key** on page 136 to score the Revising and Editing section. Then, in the Student Profile, circle the item number of each correct answer and circle the plus or minus sign to indicate mastery. To score the written composition, use the **Good Writing Traits Rubric** on page 97. Look at scores on the individual traits and award a holistic score for the composition. Then calculate the total score for the Unit Writing Test.

Student Name _____   **Date** _____

| Subtest | Tested Skills | ITEM ANALYSIS | | TEST SCORES |
		Item Numbers	Mastery	No. Correct × Points = Score
REVISING / EDITING	**Written Conventions: Sentence Fluency** (complete sentences)	1 2 3 6	3 out of 4 + −	_____ × 5 = ☐ /20
	Written Conventions: Spelling	4 5 7 8	3 out of 4 + −	_____ × 5 = ☐ /20
WRITTEN COMPOSITION	**Write to Express**	Overall Score from Rubric: _____ × 15 = ☐ /60		
		TOTAL UNIT 1 WRITING TEST ☐ /100		

DIRECTIONS Rosa wrote this story about shopping. She wants you to help her revise and edit the story. Read her draft. Then read each question. Choose the best answer. Mark your answer.

Shopping with Caroline

1 I like to shop with my older sister Caroline. **2** One day I wanted to buy a jacket and a scarf. **3** My sister said to my mom, "I will take Rosa shopping!" **4** Knows a lot of good stores.

5 We rode the bus to our favorite store. **6** It is called Perfectly Worn. **7** Go there? **8** That store sells great used clothes! **9** Our friend Pam owns the store. **10** We always notice how helpfull she is.

11 Pam waved when my sister and I walked in. **12** She helped me find a cute green jacket with orange buttons. **13** It looked almost brand-new, so I couldn't reffuse. **14** Then Pam picked out a scarf from a basket. **15** Was soft and fuzzy.

16 Caroline paid for the clothes. **17** Then she said, "Now we can have some fun!"

18 We played dress-up at Perfectly Worn. **19** Pam didn't mined us trying different styles. **20** We wore big floppy hats and sunglasses. **21** We smiled proudly at the way we looked!

GO ON

REVISING AND EDITING

1 **What is the correct way to write Sentence 4?**

   Ⓐ Caroline a lot of good stores.

   Ⓑ Caroline knows a lot of good stores.

   Ⓒ Caroline she knows a lot of good stores.

   Ⓓ Correct as it is

2 **What is the correct way to write Sentence 7?**

   Ⓕ You go there?

   Ⓖ Do you go there?

   Ⓗ Does you go there?

   Ⓙ Correct as it is

3 **What is the correct way to write Sentence 9?**

   Ⓐ Owns the store.

   Ⓑ Our friend Pam.

   Ⓒ Our friend she owns the store.

   Ⓓ Correct as it is

4 **What change should be made in Sentence 10?**

   Ⓕ Change *notice* to *notis*.

   Ⓖ Change *notice* to *notise*.

   Ⓗ Change *helpfull* to *helpful*.

   Ⓙ Make no change.

5 **What change should be made in Sentence 13?**

   Ⓐ Change *reffuse* to *refuse*.

   Ⓑ Change *almost* to *all most*.

   Ⓒ Change *brand-new* to *brand knew*.

   Ⓓ Make no change.

6 **What is the correct way to write Sentence 15?**

   Ⓕ The scarf soft and fuzzy.

   Ⓖ The scarf was soft and fuzzy.

   Ⓗ Was a soft, fuzzy, warm scarf.

   Ⓙ Correct as it is

7 **What change should be made in Sentence 19?**

   Ⓐ Change *mined* to *mind*.

   Ⓑ Change *styles* to *stylles*.

   Ⓒ Change *mined* to *minde*.

   Ⓓ Make no change.

8 **What is the correct way to write Sentence 21?**

   Ⓕ We smiled proudle at the way we looked!

   Ⓖ We smiled proudlly at the way we looked!

   Ⓗ We smiled proudley at the way we looked!

   Ⓙ Correct as it is

STOP

WRITTEN COMPOSITION

> Write a composition to tell how you feel when you wear your favorite clothes.

The information in the box below will help you remember what you should think about when you write your composition.

REMEMBER—YOU SHOULD

☐ write to tell how you feel when you wear your favorite clothes

☐ make sure that each sentence you write helps the reader understand your composition

☐ write about your ideas in detail so that the reader really understands what you are saying

☐ try to use correct spelling, capitalization, punctuation, grammar, and sentences

---

Use the back of this page to plan your writing. Use a separate sheet of paper to write your composition.

Unit 2 • Writing Test Student Profile

DIRECTIONS Record the student's name and test date. Use the **Answer Key** on page 136 to score the Revising and Editing section. Then, in the Student Profile, circle the item number of each correct answer and circle the plus or minus sign to indicate mastery. To score the written composition, use the **Good Writing Traits Rubric** on page 97. Look at scores on the individual traits and award a holistic score for the composition. Then calculate the total score for the Unit Writing Test.

Student Name _____   Date _____

Subtest	Tested Skills	ITEM ANALYSIS		TEST SCORES
		Item Numbers	Mastery	No. Correct × Points = Score
REVISING / EDITING	Written Conventions: Mechanics (capitalization and punctuation)	1 2 5 6	3 out of 4 + −	_____ × 5 = ⬚/20
	Organization: Progression of Ideas	3 4 7 8	3 out of 4 + −	_____ × 5 = ⬚/20
WRITTEN COMPOSITION	Write to Express	Overall Score from Rubric: _____ × 15 =		⬚/60
			TOTAL UNIT 2 WRITING TEST	⬚/100

DIRECTIONS Jamil wrote this biography. He wants you to help him revise and edit the biography. Read his draft. Then read each question. Choose the best answer. Mark your answer.

Nampeyo

1 Nampeyo was born in 1860 in First Mesa, arizona.
2 She learned to make pottery from her grandmother.
3 Her grandmother was a member of a tribe called the hopi. **4** Nampeyo was a famous Native American potter.

5 When Nampeyo was young, everyone in her village knew her pottery. **6** Then, in 1875, a man named thomas keam opened a store near the village. **7** He sold Nampeyo's pots in his store. **8** More people were now able to see Nampeyo's work. **9** Later, Mr Keam asked Hopi potters to make pottery in a special style. **10** It was a very old Native American style called Sikyatki. **11** Her Sikyatki designs became famous all over the world. **12** Nampeyo made beautiful yellow pots with Sikyatki designs.

13 Nampeyo also taught other people how to make Sikyatki pots. **14** When Nampeyo was about 65 years old, she started to lose her sight. **15** Her husband Lesso painted the pots for her. **16** She could still make pots by feeling the clay. **17** Her daughters and granddaughters helped continue the work.

© Hampton-Brown

GO ON ➡

Name _____ Date _____

1 **What is the correct way to write Sentence 1?**

Ⓐ Nampeyo was born in 1860 in First mesa, arizona.

Ⓑ Nampeyo was born in 1860 in First Mesa, Arizona.

Ⓒ Nampeyo was born in 1860 in first Mesa, arizona.

Ⓓ Correct as it is

2 **What is the correct way to write Sentence 3?**

Ⓕ Her grandmother was a member of a Tribe called the hopi.

Ⓖ Her grandmother was a member of a tribe called the Hopi.

Ⓗ Her Grandmother was a member of a tribe called the Hopi.

Ⓙ Correct as it is

3 **Where is the best place for Sentence 4?**

Ⓐ Before Sentence 1

Ⓑ Before Sentence 3

Ⓒ Before Sentence 6

Ⓓ Best where it is

4 **Does Sentence 5 help ideas flow smoothly? Choose the best way to write it.**

Ⓕ Nampeyo was a young girl.

Ⓖ Nampeyo knew everyone in the village.

Ⓗ When Nampeyo was young, she loved her grandmother.

Ⓙ Best as it is

5 **What change should be made in Sentence 6?**

Ⓐ Change *thomas keam* to *thomas Keam*.

Ⓑ Change *thomas keam* to *Thomas keam*.

Ⓒ Change *thomas keam* to *Thomas Keam*.

Ⓓ Make no change.

6 **What change should be made in Sentence 9?**

Ⓕ Change *Mr* to *mr*.

Ⓖ Change *Mr* to *Mr.*

Ⓗ Change *Mr* to *MR*.

Ⓙ Make no change.

7 **Where is the best place for Sentence 11?**

Ⓐ After Sentence 8

Ⓑ After Sentence 9

Ⓒ After Sentence 12

Ⓓ Best where it is

8 **What is the best thing to do with Sentence 16?**

Ⓕ Take it out.

Ⓖ Put it after Sentence 13.

Ⓗ Put it after Sentence 14.

Ⓙ Best where it is

STOP

WRITTEN COMPOSITION

> Write a composition to tell how you feel about a place in nature.

The information in the box below will help you remember what you should think about when you write your composition.

REMEMBER—YOU SHOULD

☐   write to tell how you feel about a place in nature

☐   make sure that each sentence you write helps the reader understand your composition

☐   write about your ideas in detail so that the reader really understands what you are saying

☐   try to use correct spelling, capitalization, punctuation, grammar, and sentences

Use the back of this page to plan your writing. Use a separate sheet of paper to write your composition.

Unit 3 • Writing Test Student Profile

DIRECTIONS Record the student's name and test date. Use the **Answer Key** on page 136 to score the Revising and Editing section. Then, in the Student Profile, circle the item number of each correct answer and circle the plus or minus sign to indicate mastery. To score the written composition, use the **Good Writing Traits Rubric** on page 97. Look at scores on the individual traits and award a holistic score for the composition. Then calculate the total score for the Unit Writing Test.

Student Name _____   Date _____

Subtest	Tested Skills	ITEM ANALYSIS		TEST SCORES
		Item Numbers	Mastery	No. Correct × Points = Score
REVISING / EDITING	Development of Ideas	1 3 5 8	3 out of 4 + −	_____ × 5 = ⬚/20
	Written Conventions: Usage (subject-verb agreement)	2 4 6 7	3 out of 4 + −	_____ × 5 = ⬚/20
WRITTEN COMPOSITION	Write to Inform	Overall Score from Rubric: _____ × 15 =		⬚/60
		TOTAL UNIT 3 WRITING TEST		⬚/100

© Hampton-Brown

REVISING AND EDITING

DIRECTIONS Fay wrote this report about her vacation. She wants you to help her revise and edit the article. Read her draft. Then read each question. Choose the best answer. Mark your answer.

An Exciting Vacation

1 We went on a trip to Cape Hatteras. **2** Cape Hatteras is famous for beautiful beaches. **3** It are famous for hurricanes, too.

4 It was a long drive to Cape Hatteras. **5** On the way, we played a game. **6** The game is called Counting Cows. **7** We try to count all the cows in the fields. **8** My brother always win the game!

9 After arriving at Cape Hatteras, we went straight to the beach. **10** The weather was clear and sunny. **11** We swam in the warm water. **12** You should always wear sunscreen at the beach.

13 On the second day, the weather became cool and breezy. **14** The water was rough. **15** At night we watched the news. **16** The TV reporter said, "We has important information about the weather. **17** A hurricane is coming toward us!"

18 Many people decided to leave the coast. **19** They were scared because hurricanes is dangerous. **20** Then the storm changed directions. **21** It went out to sea and never hit land.

22 I will not forget this exciting vacation!

© Hampton-Brown

GO ON

Name _____   Date _____

1 **Does Sentence 1 need more details? Choose the best way to write it.**

   (A) Last month we went on a trip.

   (B) Last month we went to Cape Hatteras.

   (C) Last month we went on a trip to Cape Hatteras, North Carolina.

   (D) Best as it is

2 **What change should be made in Sentence 3?**

   (F) Change *are* to *is*.

   (G) Change *It* to *They*.

   (H) Change *are* to *am*.

   (J) Make no change.

3 **Should Sentences 5 and 6 be combined? Choose the best way to write them.**

   (A) On the way, the game is called Counting Cows.

   (B) On the way, we played a game called Counting Cows.

   (C) On the way, we played a game it is called Counting Cows.

   (D) Best not to combine them

4 **What is the correct way to write Sentence 8?**

   (F) My brother always win the games!

   (G) My brother always wins the game!

   (H) My brothers always wins the game!

   (J) Correct as it is

5 **What is the best thing to do with Sentence 12?**

   (A) Take it out.

   (B) Put it before Sentence 9.

   (C) Put it before Sentence 11.

   (D) Best as it is

6 **What change should be made in Sentence 16?**

   (F) Change *We* to *I*.

   (G) Change *has* to *is*.

   (H) Change *has* to *have*.

   (J) Make no change.

7 **What is the correct way to write Sentence 19?**

   (A) They was scared because hurricanes is dangerous.

   (B) They were scared because hurricane are dangerous.

   (C) They were scared because hurricanes are dangerous.

   (D) Correct as it is

8 **What is the best thing to do with Sentence 21?**

   (F) Take it out.

   (G) Put it after Sentence 17.

   (H) Put it after Sentence 18.

   (J) Best as it is

© Hampton-Brown

STOP

WRITTEN COMPOSITION

Write a composition to describe a storm.

The information in the box below will help you remember what you should
think about when you write your composition.

REMEMBER—YOU SHOULD

☐   write to describe a storm

☐   make sure that each sentence you write helps
the reader understand your composition

☐   write about your ideas in detail so that the
reader really understands what you are saying

☐   try to use correct spelling, capitalization,
punctuation, grammar, and sentences

Use the back of this page to plan your writing. Use a separate sheet of paper
to write your composition.

© Hampton-Brown

Unit 4 • Writing Test Student Profile

DIRECTIONS Record the student's name and test date. Use the **Answer Key** on page 136 to score the Revising and Editing section. Then, in the Student Profile, circle the item number of each correct answer and circle the plus or minus sign to indicate mastery. To score the written composition, use the **Good Writing Traits Rubric** on page 97. Look at scores on the individual traits and award a holistic score for the composition. Then calculate the total score for the Unit Writing Test.

Student Name _____   Date _____

| Subtest | Tested Skills | ITEM ANALYSIS | | TEST SCORES |
		Item Numbers	Mastery	No. Correct × Points = Score
REVISING / EDITING	**Development of Ideas: Elaboration**	1 4 5 8	3 out of 4 + −	_____ × 5 = ⬚/20
	Written Conventions: Grammar (comparative adjectives)	2 3 6 7	3 out of 4 + −	_____ × 5 = ⬚/20
WRITTEN COMPOSITION	**Write to Inform**	Overall Score from Rubric: _____ × 15 = ⬚/60		
		TOTAL UNIT 4 WRITING TEST		⬚/100

REVISING AND EDITING

DIRECTIONS Rodney wrote this description about a beach. He wants you to help him revise and edit the description. Read his draft. Then read each question. Choose the best answer. Mark your answer.

On the Beach

1 I am sitting on a beautiful, sandy beach. **2** Everywhere I look, I see sparkling white sand and blue water. **3** Seagulls make circles. **4** The birds cry loudly. **5** Foamy waves roar and crash against the sand. **6** They are loud than the birds. **7** The warm sun shines brightly on my face. **8** Today is the warmest day of the summer.

9 I lie quietly on my back. **10** Puffy clouds float across the blue sky. **11** One cloud looks like an elephant. **12** Another cloud looks like a fuzzy mouse. **13** The mouse is large than the elephant. **14** I watch them drift slowly in the breeze.

15 Next to my blanket are some white seashells with brown and black spots. **16** Biggest shell is shaped like a bowl. **17** I put the smaller shells in it.

18 Then I stand up and run across the hot, grainy sand. **19** I jump. **20** The water cools me off as I splash through the refreshing waves.

GO ON ➡

REVISING AND EDITING

1 **Does Sentence 3 need more details? Choose the best way to write it.**

    (A) Seagulls fly in the air.

    (B) Seagulls are in the air.

    (C) Seagulls make circles in the air.

    (D) Best as it is

2 **What is the correct way to write Sentence 6?**

    (F) They are louder than the birds.

    (G) They are loudest than the birds.

    (H) They are more loud than the birds.

    (J) Correct as it is

3 **What is the correct way to write Sentence 8?**

    (A) Today is the warm day of the summer.

    (B) Today is the warmer day of the summer.

    (C) Today is the most warmest day of the summer.

    (D) Correct as it is

4 **Does Sentence 9 need more details? Choose the best way to write it.**

    (F) I lie quietly there.

    (G) I lie down quietly.

    (H) I lie quietly at the beach.

    (J) Best as it is

5 **Does Sentence 11 need more details? Choose the best way to write it.**

    (A) One puffy cloud looks like an elephant.

    (B) One cloud looks like an elephant in the sky.

    (C) One cloud looks like an elephant with a long trunk.

    (D) Best as it is

6 **What is the correct way to write Sentence 13?**

    (F) The mouse is larger the elephant.

    (G) The mouse is larger than the elephant.

    (H) The mouse is more larger than the elephant.

    (J) Correct as it is

7 **What is the correct way to write Sentence 16?**

    (A) A biggest shell is shaped like a bowl.

    (B) The biggest shell is shaped like a bowl.

    (C) The most biggest shell is shaped like a bowl.

    (D) Correct as it is

8 **Does Sentence 19 need more details? Choose the best way to write it.**

    (F) I jump into the icy water.

    (G) I jump around the beach.

    (H) I jump into the air at the beach.

    (J) Best as it is

STOP

WRITTEN COMPOSITION

> Write a composition to describe something that
> lives underwater.

The information in the box below will help you remember what you should
think about when you write your composition.

REMEMBER—YOU SHOULD

☐   write to describe something that lives
    underwater

☐   make sure that each sentence you write helps
    the reader understand your composition

☐   write about your ideas in detail so that the
    reader really understands what you are saying

☐   try to use correct spelling, capitalization,
    punctuation, grammar, and sentences

Use the back of this page to plan your writing. Use a separate sheet of paper
to write your composition.

Unit 5 • Writing Test Student Profile

DIRECTIONS Record the student's name and test date. Use the **Answer Key** on page 136 to score the Revising and Editing section. Then, in the Student Profile, circle the item number of each correct answer and circle the plus or minus sign to indicate mastery. To score the written composition, use the **Good Writing Traits Rubric** on page 97. Look at scores on the individual traits and award a holistic score for the composition. Then calculate the total score for the Unit Writing Test.

Student Name _____ **Date** _____

| Subtest | Tested Skills | ITEM ANALYSIS | | TEST SCORES |
		Item Numbers	Mastery	No. Correct × Points = Score
REVISING / EDITING	Written Conventions: Spelling	1 3 4 6	3 out of 4 + −	_____ × 5 = /20
	Written Conventions: Grammar (pronouns)	2 5 7 8	3 out of 4 + −	_____ × 5 = /20
WRITTEN COMPOSITION	Write to Inform	Overall Score from Rubric: _____ × 15 =		/60
		TOTAL UNIT 5 WRITING TEST		/100

REVISING AND EDITING

DIRECTIONS José wrote this letter to his friend Luis. José wants you to help him revise and edit the letter. Read his draft. Then read each question. Choose the best answer. Mark your answer.

---

355 Washington Street

Orange, CA 92866

September 25, 2003

Dear Luis,

1 How are you? **2** I am fine! **3** Thank you for sending the photograph of us at the science museum. **4** I will never forget that spesial day!

5 Here is a picture of me at my new school. **6** My teacher, Mr. Sanchez, took the picture. **7** She is a good teacher. **8** We call him the emperer because his chair looks like a throne! **9** Mr. Sanchez speaks both English and Spanish. **10** Yesterday he taught me some new English words. **11** I promised to remember their meanings.

12 I have two new friends. **13** Their names are Miguel and Inés, and both of them are fantastic soccer players. **14** Them live in my neighborhood. **15** You will meet them when you come here next month. **16** I can't wait for you to arive!

17 When you visit, you can see my new apartment. **18** You will like her. **19** Please write to me soon!

Your friend,

José

REVISING AND EDITING

1 **What change should be made in Sentence 4?**

    (A) Change *spesial* to *special*.

    (B) Change *spesial* to *speshal*.

    (C) Change *spesial* to *speshial*.

    (D) Make no change.

2 **What is the correct way to write Sentence 7?**

    (F) It is a good teacher.

    (G) He is a good teacher.

    (H) Him is a good teacher.

    (J) Correct as it is

3 **What change should be made in Sentence 8?**

    (A) Change *because* to *becuz*.

    (B) Change *throne* to *thrown*.

    (C) Change *emperer* to *emperor*.

    (D) Make no change.

4 **What change should be made in Sentence 11?**

    (F) Change *their* to *there*.

    (G) Change *remember* to *ramember*.

    (H) Change *remember* to *rimmember*.

    (J) Make no change.

5 **What is the correct way to write Sentence 14?**

    (A) He live in my neighborhood.

    (B) They live in my neighborhood.

    (C) Their live in my neighborhood.

    (D) Correct as it is

6 **What change should be made in Sentence 16?**

    (F) Change *for* to *four*.

    (G) Change *you* to *your*.

    (H) Change *arive* to *arrive*.

    (J) Make no change.

7 **What is the correct way to write Sentence 18?**

    (A) You will like it.

    (B) You will like him.

    (C) You will like them.

    (D) Correct as it is

8 **What is the correct way to write Sentence 19?**

    (F) Please write my soon!

    (G) Please write to my soon!

    (H) Please write to mine soon!

    (J) Correct as it is

STOP

Name _____ **Date** _____

Write a true story about a tradition you have in your family.

The information in the box below will help you remember what you should think about when you write your composition.

REMEMBER—YOU SHOULD

☐ write a true story about a tradition you have in your family

☐ make sure that each sentence you write helps the reader understand your composition

☐ write about your ideas in detail so that the reader really understands what you are saying

☐ try to use correct spelling, capitalization, punctuation, grammar, and sentences

---

Use the back of this page to plan your writing. Use a separate sheet of paper to write your composition.

Unit 6 • Writing Test Student Profile

DIRECTIONS Record the student's name and test date. Use the **Answer Key** on page 136 to score the Revising and Editing section. Then, in the Student Profile, circle the item number of each correct answer and circle the plus or minus sign to indicate mastery. To score the written composition, use the **Good Writing Traits Rubric** on page 97. Look at scores on the individual traits and award a holistic score for the composition. Then calculate the total score for the Unit Writing Test.

Student Name _____   Date _____

| Subtest | Tested Skills | ITEM ANALYSIS | | TEST SCORES |
		Item Numbers	Mastery	No. Correct × Points = Score
REVISING / EDITING	**Written Conventions: Usage** (verb tense)	1 3 5 8	3 out of 4 + −	_____ × 5 = ⬚ /20
	Written Conventions: Mechanics (capitalization and punctuation)	2 4 6 7	3 out of 4 + −	_____ × 5 = ⬚ /20
WRITTEN COMPOSITION	**Write to Entertain**	Overall Score from Rubric: _____ × 15 = ⬚ /60		
		TOTAL UNIT 6 WRITING TEST		⬚ /100

REVISING AND EDITING

DIRECTIONS Hiroshi wrote this personal narrative about his family trip. He wants you to help him revise and edit the narrative. Read his draft. Then read each question. Choose the best answer. Mark your answer.

Our Family Trip

1 My family went on a long trip last summer. **2** We visited several places in the United States. **3** We have an amazing time.

4 Our vacation began in New Orleans, Louisiana. **5** We took a steamboat ride on the Mississippi River? **6** We also went to a museum. **7** We ate spicy food at a different restaurant each day. **8** I learned a lot about the history of New Orleans.

9 After New Orleans, we went to see Mount Rushmore. **10** It is in South Dakota. **11** Mount Rushmore has the heads of four presidents carved in the rock. **12** they are Presidents Washington, Jefferson, Lincoln, and Roosevelt.

13 After Mount Rushmore, we flew west to Sequoia National Park in California. **14** There we see the world's largest trees. **15** These trees are called sequoias. **16** Giant sequoias live for 3,000 years and grow as tall as 300 feet. **17** Did you know that **18** Those trees are huge **19** I visit Sequoia National Park again someday.

GO ON ➡

REVISING AND EDITING

1 **What is the correct way to write Sentence 3?**

   Ⓐ We has an amazing time.

   Ⓑ We had an amazing time.

   Ⓒ We will have an amazing time.

   Ⓓ Correct as it is

2 **What is the correct way to write Sentence 5?**

   Ⓕ we took a steamboat ride on the Mississippi River?

   Ⓖ we took a steamboat ride on the Mississippi River.

   Ⓗ We took a steamboat ride on the Mississippi River.

   Ⓙ Correct as it is

3 **What is the correct way to write Sentence 10?**

   Ⓐ It be in South Dakota.

   Ⓑ It are in South Dakota.

   Ⓒ It will be in South Dakota.

   Ⓓ Correct as it is

4 **What is the correct way to write Sentence 12?**

   Ⓕ they are Presidents Washington, Jefferson, Lincoln, and Roosevelt

   Ⓖ They are Presidents Washington, Jefferson, Lincoln, and Roosevelt.

   Ⓗ They are Presidents Washington, Jefferson, Lincoln, and Roosevelt?

   Ⓙ Correct as it is

5 **What change should be made in Sentence 14?**

   Ⓐ Change *see* to *saw*.

   Ⓑ Change *see* to *seen*.

   Ⓒ Change *see* to *will see*.

   Ⓓ Make no change.

6 **What is the correct way to write Sentence 17?**

   Ⓕ Did you know that.

   Ⓖ did you know that?

   Ⓗ Did you know that?

   Ⓙ Correct as it is

7 **What is the best way to write Sentence 18?**

   Ⓐ those trees are huge!

   Ⓑ Those trees are huge!

   Ⓒ Those trees are huge?

   Ⓓ Best as it is

8 **What is the correct way to write Sentence 19?**

   Ⓕ I visited Sequoia National Park again someday.

   Ⓖ I will visit Sequoia National Park again someday.

   Ⓗ I was to visit Sequoia National Park again someday.

   Ⓙ Correct as it is

STOP

WRITTEN COMPOSITION

Write a story about something important in
your state.

The information in the box below will help you remember what you should
think about when you write your composition.

REMEMBER—YOU SHOULD

☐ write a story about something important in
   your state

☐ make sure that each sentence you write helps
   the reader understand your composition

☐ write about your ideas in detail so that the
   reader really understands what you are saying

☐ try to use correct spelling, capitalization,
   punctuation, grammar, and sentences

Use the back of this page to plan your writing. Use a separate sheet of paper
to write your composition.

© Hampton-Brown

Unit 7 • Writing Test Student Profile

DIRECTIONS Record the student's name and test date. Use the **Answer Key** on page 136 to score the Revising and Editing section. Then, in the Student Profile, circle the item number of each correct answer and circle the plus or minus sign to indicate mastery. To score the written composition, use the **Good Writing Traits Rubric** on page 97. Look at scores on the individual traits and award a holistic score for the composition. Then calculate the total score for the Unit Writing Test.

Student Name _____   **Date** _____

Subtest	Tested Skills	ITEM ANALYSIS		TEST SCORES
		Item Numbers	**Mastery**	**No. Correct × Points = Score**
REVISING / EDITING	**Written Conventions: Mechanics** (apostrophes)	1 5 6 8	3 out of 4 + −	_____ × 5 = ⬚ /20
	Focus and Coherence	2 3 4 7	3 out of 4 + −	_____ × 5 = ⬚ /20
WRITTEN COMPOSITION	Write to Inform	Overall Score from Rubric: _____ × 15 =		⬚ /60
		TOTAL UNIT 7 WRITING TEST		⬚ /100

© Hampton-Brown

REVISING AND EDITING

DIRECTIONS Tami wrote this persuasive letter to her neighbor. She wants you to help her revise and edit the letter. Read her draft. Then read each question. Choose the best answer. Mark your answer.

123 Elm Avenue
Chicago, IL 60660
June 15, 2004

Dear Neighbors,

1 My name is Tami Liu, and I am in fourth grade. **2** I want to buy a bicycle this summer. **3** The only problem is that I dont have enough money. **4** I need to earn $50. **5** My friend Carla already has a new bike.

6 Please hire me! **7** I can do all kinds of jobs. **8** For example, I can wash your car every week. **9** I can walk your dog and feed your cat. **10** Your animals will love the extra attention! **11** I can even water all of your plants when you go on a trip. **12** I can help you, and you can help me. **13** Doesn't that sound like a good idea?

14 It isnt' too late to call me. **15** I have a telephone in my room. **16** Are'nt you ready for some help? **17** I am ready to work!

Sincerely,
Tami Liu

REVISING AND EDITING

1 **What change should be made in Sentence 3?**

Ⓐ Change *dont* to *dont'*.

Ⓑ Change *dont* to *do'nt*.

Ⓒ Change *dont* to *don't*.

Ⓓ Make no change.

2 **What is the best thing to do with Sentence 5?**

Ⓕ Take it out.

Ⓖ Change *new* to *yellow*.

Ⓗ Put it before Sentence 1.

Ⓙ Best as it is

3 **What is the best thing to do with Sentence 8?**

Ⓐ Take it out.

Ⓑ Take out *For example,*.

Ⓒ Put it after Sentence 9.

Ⓓ Best as it is

4 **Does Sentence 12 need more details? Choose the best way to write it.**

Ⓕ I can help around the house, and you can help me.

Ⓖ I can help you do your stuff, and you can help me a lot.

Ⓗ I can help you with your chores, and you can help me earn money.

Ⓙ Best as it is

5 **What is the correct way to write Sentence 13?**

Ⓐ Doesnt that sound like a good idea?

Ⓑ Doesnt' that sound like a good idea?

Ⓒ Does'nt that sound like a good idea?

Ⓓ Correct as it is

6 **What is the correct way to write Sentence 14?**

Ⓕ It isnt too late to call me.

Ⓖ It isn't too late to call me.

Ⓗ It is'nt too late to call me.

Ⓙ Correct as it is

7 **Does Sentence 15 give enough information? Choose the best way to write it.**

Ⓐ I have a telephone number.

Ⓑ My telephone number is 555-6789.

Ⓒ I have a blue telephone in my room.

Ⓓ Best as it is

8 **What change should be made in Sentence 16?**

Ⓕ Change *Are'nt* to *Arent*.

Ⓖ Change *Are'nt* to *Arent'*.

Ⓗ Change *Are'nt* to *Aren't*.

Ⓙ Make no change.

STOP

WRITTEN COMPOSITION

> Write a composition to tell about ways to
> earn money.

The information in the box below will help you remember what you should
think about when you write your composition.

REMEMBER—YOU SHOULD

☐ write to tell about ways to earn money

☐ make sure that each sentence you write helps the
reader understand your composition

☐ write about your ideas in detail so that the reader
really understands what you are saying

☐ try to use correct spelling, capitalization,
punctuation, grammar, and sentences

Use the back of this page to plan your writing. Use a separate sheet of paper
to write your composition.

Unit 8 • Writing Test Student Profile

DIRECTIONS Record the student's name and test date. Use the **Answer Key** on page 136 to score the Revising and Editing section. Then, in the Student Profile, circle the item number of each correct answer and circle the plus or minus sign to indicate mastery. To score the written composition, use the **Good Writing Traits Rubric** on page 97. Look at scores on the individual traits and award a holistic score for the composition. Then calculate the total score for the Unit Writing Test.

Student Name _____   Date _____

Subtest	Tested Skills	ITEM ANALYSIS		TEST SCORES
		Item Numbers	Mastery	No. Correct × Points = Score
REVISING / EDITING	Written Conventions: Grammar (adverbs)	1 3 5 6	3 out of 4 + —	_____ × 5 = ☐/20
	Written Conventions: Sentence Combining	2 4 7 8	3 out of 4 + —	_____ × 5 = ☐/20
WRITTEN COMPOSITION	Write to Entertain	Overall Score from Rubric: _____ × 15 = ☐/60		
		TOTAL UNIT 8 WRITING TEST		☐/100

DIRECTIONS Lydia wrote this story about a birthday gift. She wants you to help her revise and edit the story. Read her draft. Then read each question. Choose the best answer. Mark your answer.

Is This a Gift?

1 On Saturday at noon, Hakim remembered something. **2** It was Leon's birthday! **3** There was going to be a party at Leon's house in an hour. **4** Hakim needed to think of a gift!

5 Then Hakim got an idea. **6** He wrapped his gift and went to the party.

7 At Leon's house, everyone played games and ate ice cream. **8** Leon began to open his gifts. **9** Leon grinned. **10** He unwrapped a new video game. **11** Then he opened the gift from Hakim. **12** Leon looked confused.

13 "Is this a gift?" Leon asked. **14** "It is just a rock!"

15 "It is a special rock," said Hakim. **16** "It is very, very old. **17** Look careful at the rock. **18** Can you see the shape of the insect? **19** Long ago, the insect was in some soil. **20** Pressure made the soil into a rock."

21 "Oh, it's a fossil!" Leon said happy. **22** Leon knew about fossils. **23** He often read about dinosaurs.

24 Hakim felt very proud. **25** His gift was different, it was good.

GO ON

REVISING AND EDITING

1 What is the best way to write Sentence 4?

Ⓐ Hakim needed to think of a gift later!

Ⓑ Hakim needed to think of a gift today!

Ⓒ Hakim needed to think of a gift quickly!

Ⓓ Best as it is

2 Should Sentences 5 and 6 be combined? Choose the best way to write them.

Ⓕ Hakim got an idea and wrapped his gift and went to the party.

Ⓖ Then Hakim got an idea he wrapped his gift, and went to the party.

Ⓗ Then Hakim got an idea, but he wrapped his gift and went to the party.

Ⓙ Best not to combine them

3 What is the best way to write Sentence 8?

Ⓐ Leon began to open his gifts slowly.

Ⓑ Leon then began to open his gifts slow.

Ⓒ Leon began to very slow open his gifts.

Ⓓ Best as it is

4 Should Sentences 9 and 10 be combined? Choose the best way to write them.

Ⓕ Leon grinned, he unwrapped a new video game.

Ⓖ Leon grinned when he unwrapped a new video game.

Ⓗ Leon grinned, but he unwrapped a new video game.

Ⓙ Best not to combine them

5 What is the best way to write Sentence 17?

Ⓐ Look at the rock.

Ⓑ Careful look at the rock.

Ⓒ Look carefully at the rock.

Ⓓ Best as it is

6 What is the best way to write Sentence 21?

Ⓕ "Oh, it's a fossil!" Leon said.

Ⓖ "Oh, it's a fossil!" Leon said happly.

Ⓗ "Oh, it's a fossil!" Leon said happily.

Ⓙ Best as it is

7 Should Sentences 22 and 23 be combined? Choose the best way to write them.

Ⓐ Leon knew about fossils, he often read about dinosaurs.

Ⓑ Leon knew about fossils because he often read about dinosaurs.

Ⓒ Leon knew about fossils, and because he often read about dinosaurs.

Ⓓ Best not to combine them

8 What is the correct way to write Sentence 25?

Ⓕ His gift was different, or it was good.

Ⓖ His gift was different, but it was good.

Ⓗ His gift was different when it was good.

Ⓙ Correct as it is

STOP

Name _____ Date _____

WRITTEN COMPOSITION

> Write a story about a special rock.

The information in the box below will help you remember what you should
think about when you write your composition.

REMEMBER—YOU SHOULD

☐   write to tell a story about a special rock

☐   make sure that each sentence you write helps
the reader understand your composition

☐   write about your ideas in detail so that the
reader really understands what you are saying

☐   try to use correct spelling, capitalization,
punctuation, grammar, and sentences

Use the back of this page to plan your writing. Use a separate sheet of paper
to write your composition.

Writing Test Answer Keys

Unit 1
1 B
2 G
3 D
4 H
5 A
6 G
7 A
8 J

Unit 2
1 B
2 G
3 A
4 J
5 C
6 G
7 C
8 H

Unit 3
1 C
2 F
3 B
4 G
5 A
6 H
7 C
8 J

Unit 4
1 C
2 F
3 D
4 J
5 C
6 G
7 B
8 F

Unit 5
1 A
2 G
3 C
4 J
5 B
6 H
7 A
8 J

Unit 6
1 B
2 H
3 D
4 G
5 A
6 H
7 B
8 G

Unit 7
1 C
2 F
3 D
4 H
5 D
6 G
7 B
8 H

Unit 8
1 C
2 J
3 A
4 G
5 C
6 H
7 B
8 G

Reading Fluency Measures

▶ **Benchmark Passages**

▶ **Fluency Progress Report**

As soon as the temperature drops, people start getting excited up in Nome, Alaska. They never go to bed at night without peeking out their windows first. They want to see what the weather is doing. If a light snow is falling, they know that by morning the roads will be dangerous. That's where the sled dogs come into play.

Sled dogs are fun, peppy, medium-sized dogs. Their colors are different, but they all have thick, downy coats of fur. The dogs' tails curl up when they are excited.

There's nothing a sled dog loves more than the cold, fierce winds of winter. Even though most owners build shelters for their sled dogs, the dogs prefer to sleep outside. They tuck their noses into their tails. They snuggle their bodies deep in the snow.

Sled dogs are playful, intelligent, and very vocal. They do not bark. Instead, they howl likes wolves. It's not uncommon for a pack of sled dogs to have a group howl at sunset and sunrise.

A person who owns sled dogs can be sure that their sleep will be disturbed on the mornings after a deep snow has fallen. The dogs will be up on the roofs of their doghouses, welcoming the snow with their long yowls of anticipation. "Wake up, wake up, WAKE UP!" They seem to be howling. "We want to play in the snow!"

The two most important things in a sled dog's life are running and pulling. Quite simply, that is what they are born to do.

A sled dog will like nothing better than to trot in front of a person on skis or a sled filled with supplies. They've been known to race with their owners on bikes or rollerblades. Pulling is a good way for them to get exercise and stay in shape all summer long. It's also great for the dogs' owners.

Together the dog and person team can romp and play in many ways during the snowless months. Nothing beats the thrill, however, of winter's return and a dog sled run through the snow.

As soon as the temperature drops, people start getting excited	10
up in Nome, Alaska. They never go to bed at night without peeking	23
out their windows first. They want to see what the weather is doing.	36
If a light snow is falling, they know that by morning the roads will be	51
dangerous. That's where the sled dogs come into play.	60
Sled dogs are fun, peppy, medium-sized dogs. Their colors are	71
different, but they all have thick, downy coats of fur. The dogs' tails	84
curl up when they are excited.	90
There's nothing a sled dog loves more than the cold, fierce winds	102
of winter. Even though most owners build shelters for their sled dogs,	114
the dogs prefer to sleep outside. They tuck their noses into their tails.	127
They snuggle their bodies deep in the snow.	135
Sled dogs are playful, intelligent, and very vocal. They do not	146
bark. Instead, they howl likes wolves. It's not uncommon for a pack	158
of sled dogs to have a group howl at sunset and sunrise.	170
A person who owns sled dogs can be sure that their sleep will be	184
disturbed on the mornings after a deep snow has fallen. The dogs	196
will be up on the roofs of their doghouses, welcoming the snow with	209
their long yowls of anticipation. "Wake up, wake up, WAKE UP!"	220
They seem to be howling. "We want to play in the snow!"	232
The two most important things in a sled dog's life are running	244
and pulling. Quite simply, that is what they are born to do.	256
A sled dog will like nothing better than to trot in front of a	270
person on skis or a sled filled with supplies. They've been known to	283
race with their owners on bikes or rollerblades. Pulling is a good way	296
for them to get exercise and stay in shape all summer long. It's also	310
great for the dogs' owners.	315
Together the dog and person team can romp and play in many	327
ways during the snowless months. Nothing beats the thrill, however,	337
of winter's return and a dog sled run through the snow.	348

© Hampton-Brown

SCORE   _____ − _____ = _____
words attempted   number of errors   words correct per
in one minute   minute (wcpm)

Charlie Clark had been a mailman for thirty years. He was used to delivering mail in all types of weather. He'd delivered letters on delightful days, and he'd delivered letters on dreadful days.

Charlie was proud of his work and happy with his job. Never, in all his years as a mailman, had Charlie ever had a problem with a mailbox. Other mailmen complained about mailboxes on their routes, but not Charlie.

He didn't have any worries until one day when he noticed there was a new box on his route. The mailbox was nailed to a branch of a dead tree. It was battered, dented, and badly rusted. The flag at its side was crooked and bent.

Charlie felt bad about it. "People should treat their mailboxes with more respect," he muttered as he dug through his bag.

He had letters addressed to the box, so he pulled it open and set them inside. He was about to pull his hand out when the box bit him. It had a grip on his hand and wouldn't let go.

Charlie looked up and down the street for someone to help him, but there was no one in sight. He wrestled with the box for an hour, until the box spit out his hand.

The next day he had more letters addressed to that box. With the letters in his hand, he stopped in front of it. He waited for something to happen, but the box was quiet today.

Charlie quickly slipped the letters inside and almost got his hand out before the box latched onto him again.

This time Charlie and the mailbox had a fierce battle. Charlie hit and kicked the box, but still the box wouldn't let go. Finally, Charlie was out of breath, and he had to stop. He rested his head on the mailbox.

Suddenly, he had an idea. "There, there," he told the mailbox, patting it gently. "Why don't you let me go so I can deliver the rest of my mail?"

The mailbox began to purr and let him go nicely.

Charlie Clark had been a mailman for thirty years. He was used   12

to delivering mail in all types of weather. He'd delivered letters on   24

delightful days, and he'd delivered letters on dreadful days.   33

Charlie was proud of his work and happy with his job. Never, in   46

all his years as a mailman, had Charlie ever had a problem with a   60

mailbox. Other mailmen complained about mailboxes on their routes,   69

but not Charlie.   72

He didn't have any worries until one day when he noticed there   84

was a new box on his route. The mailbox was nailed to a branch of a   100

dead tree. It was battered, dented, and badly rusted. The flag at its   113

side was crooked and bent.   118

Charlie felt bad about it. "People should treat their mailboxes   128

with more respect," he muttered as he dug through his bag.   139

He had letters addressed to the box, so he pulled it open and set   153

them inside. He was about to pull his hand out when the box bit   167

him. It had a grip on his hand and wouldn't let go.   179

Charlie looked up and down the street for someone to help him,   191

but there was no one in sight. He wrestled with the box for an hour,   206

until the box spit out his hand.   213

The next day he had more letters addressed to that box. With   225

the letters in his hand, he stopped in front of it. He waited for   239

something to happen, but the box was quiet today.   248

Charlie quickly slipped the letters inside and almost got his hand   259

out before the box latched onto him again.   267

This time Charlie and the mailbox had a fierce battle. Charlie hit and   280

kicked the box, but still the box wouldn't let go. Finally, Charlie   292

was out of breath, and he had to stop. He rested his head on the mailbox.   308

Suddenly, he had an idea. "There, there," he told the mailbox,   319

patting it gently. "Why don't you let me go so I can deliver the rest   334

of my mail?"   337

The mailbox began to purr and let him go nicely.   347

SCORE	_____ words attempted in one minute	−	_____ number of errors	=	_____ words correct per minute (wcpm)

It was difficult moving to a new house. When I was eight, we left our old neighborhood and moved to a new one. We packed my dresser, my bunk bed, my computer, and my scooter. In every room of the house, boxes were piled high like building blocks.

The house felt still. I walked from room to room trying to remember what each one used to be like. As I walked through the living room, I noticed orange scribble marks on the wallpaper. My younger brother made those marks when we used to play art museum. Entering my bedroom, I noticed a large scratch on the hardwood floor. That was where my puppy, Clyde, and I used to play fetch with his toy kitten. Wandering down the hallway, I noticed pencil marks near the bathroom door. That was where my father used to measure me to see how tall I had grown each birthday. I already began to miss the wallpaper on the walls and the light fixtures on the ceilings.

"This has always been my house," I thought. "I don't want to leave." There had to be some way I could keep my house.

Looking out my bedroom window, I noticed the tree house Dad and I constructed years before. I hurried to the backyard, climbed up to my tree house, and decided not to go unless my tree house went too. I would keep the tree house to myself, and then I would be happy.

Just then my neighbor Logan arrived to say goodbye. "I wish you could stay, but I know you'll have even more fun at your new house," he said sadly.

Suddenly, I began to think of someone beside myself. I thought about my house, my yard, and my neighbors. I would miss everything, but I was going to get a new house, a new yard, and new neighbors. Logan, though, was just losing a friend. I realized then that Logan needed the tree house more than I did.

It was difficult moving to a new house. When I was eight, we   13

left our old neighborhood and moved to a new one. We packed my   26

dresser, my bunk bed, my computer, and my scooter. In every room   38

of the house, boxes were piled high like building blocks.   48

The house felt still. I walked from room to room trying to   60

remember what each one used to be like. As I walked through the   73

living room, I noticed orange scribble marks on the wallpaper. My   84

younger brother made those marks when we used to play art   95

museum. Entering my bedroom, I noticed a large scratch on the   106

hardwood floor. That was where my puppy, Clyde, and I used to play   119

fetch with his toy kitten. Wandering down the hallway, I noticed   130

pencil marks near the bathroom door. That was where my father   141

used to measure me to see how tall I had grown each birthday.   154

I already began to miss the wallpaper on the walls and the light   167

fixtures on the ceilings.   171

"This has always been my house," I thought. "I don't want to   183

leave." There had to be some way I could keep my house.   195

Looking out my bedroom window, I noticed the tree house Dad and   208

I constructed years before. I hurried to the backyard, climbed up to my   220

tree house, and decided not to go unless my tree house went too.   233

I would keep the tree house to myself, and then I would be happy.   247

Just then my neighbor Logan arrived to say goodbye. "I wish you   259

could stay, but I know you'll have even more fun at your new   272

house," he said sadly.   276

Suddenly, I began to think of someone beside myself. I thought   287

about my house, my yard, and my neighbors. I would miss   298

everything, but I was going to get a new house, a new yard, and   312

new neighbors. Logan, though, was just losing a friend. I realized   323

then that Logan needed the tree house more than I did.   334

SCORE	_____	−	_____	=	_____
	words attempted in one minute		number of errors		words correct per minute (wcpm)

Name _____

Fluency Progress Report

DIRECTIONS Administer the three benchmark fluency assessments three times during the school year: fall, winter, and spring. Place a dot to indicate the words read correctly per minute (wcpm). Connect the dots to show student progress over the year. Then record the median (middle) score for each administration and whether the student has achieved the grade-level norm.

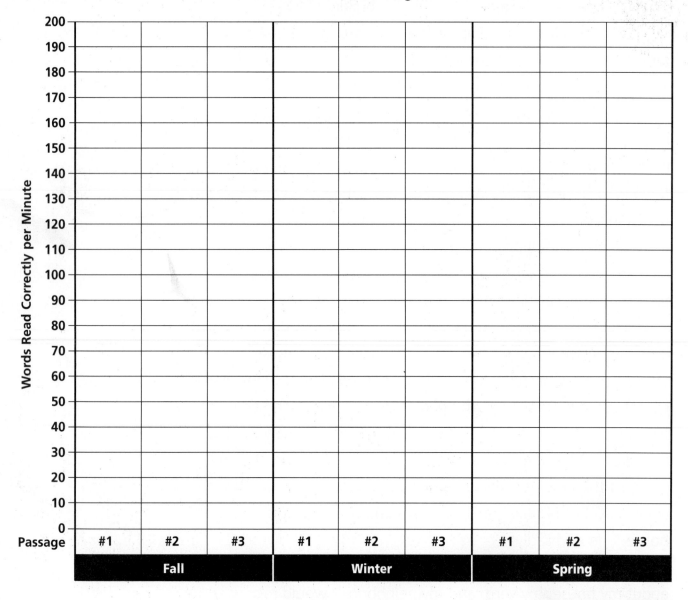

Grade 4 Norm for Fall: 95 wcpm
☐ meets   ☐ does not meet

Grade 4 Norm for Winter: 110 wcpm
☐ meets   ☐ does not meet

Grade 4 Norm for Spring: 122 wcpm
☐ meets   ☐ does not meet

	Median Score
Fall	_____ wcpm
Winter	_____ wcpm
Spring	_____ wcpm

© Hampton-Brown